BICYCLE VACATION

MINNESOTA and WISCONSIN

GUIDE

D1455514

BICYCLE VACATION GUIDE

MINNESOTA and WISCONSIN

The Everything Guide to Planning Your Bicycle Vacation

DOUG SHIDELL

Photos by Doug Shidell
Cover design by Jay Monroe
Interior production and design by Mori Studio, Inc.
Trail information by Doug Shidell
Vacation information by April Baum
Maps by Doug Shidell

4401 Grand Ave.
Minneapolis, MN 55419
www. bikeverywhere.com

13 12 11 10 09 08   1 2 3 4 5 6

ISBN 13: 978-0-9746625-6-5

Disclaimer: No road can be guaranteed safe. No trail is without hazards. Road and trail conditions can change without notice and traffic conditions can change unexpectedly. The maps and descriptions are intended to aid in the selection of routes, but do not guarantee safety while riding. Use your best judgement. Ride at your own risk.

Printed in the United States.

DEDICATION

To my Mother,
who has patiently listened as I've rambled on about book and map publishing.

ACKNOWLEDGEMENTS

Special thanks to April Baum for her research on the tourist information for this edition of Bicycle Vacation Guide and to Brent Campbell for copyediting the manuscript.

PREFACE

New bicycle trails don't just happen. They are the result of strong citizen support, a well organized campaign and money. We at Bikeverywhere are pleased to introduce you to the non-profit group most responsible for growing and protecting hundreds of miles of state trails in Minnesota. The Parks & Trails Council of Minnesota, in coordination with local advocacy groups, has played an essential role in creating the Gateway Trail, the Cannon Valley Trail, the Paul Bunyan Trail and many more trails in Minnesota.

Since 1954, the Parks & Trails Council has been in the business of saving special places across Minnesota. In the early days, with a small membership, the group was responsible for creating Afton, Fort Snelling and Grand Portage State Parks. In more recent years, they have added almost a mile of spectacular rocky shoreline to Split Rock Lighthouse State Park and helped fund the extension of the Root River Trail in southeastern Minnesota.

The Parks & Trails Council has made this fourth edition of Bicycle Vacation Guide possible, and essential. Because of their efforts and those of local trail advocacy groups, Minnesota has one of the highest number of trail miles in the country and more miles are being added each year. We don't mind. It gives us another excuse to get out and ride.

We support the Parks & Trails Council because we see their impact each time we update our guide. We urge you to join us in supporting the Parks & Trails Council of Minnesota. To learn more, visit their website at www.parksandtrails.org or call 651-726-2457. With your help, the Parks & Trails Council of Minnesota will be able to preserve more trails and parkland for our generation and that of many generations to come.

Sincerely,
Doug Shidell
Bikeverywhere

CONTENTS

 **MINNESOTA**

 **WISCONSIN**

About The Trail

This trail offers some of the best bicycling views available of the North Shore of Lake Superior. It is being built piecemeal as part of the overall reconstruction of Highway 61. The longest section, 14.3 miles, currently runs from just east of Gooseberry Falls to Beaver Bay. Shorter segments have been finished near Tofte and Grand Marais. Check the website for expected completion dates for new sections.

Trail Highlights

The most scenic section is a one mile segment that skirts the lakeside of the Silver Creek Tunnel. Stunning views of Lake Superior and the distraction of watching rock climbers make this short stretch better suited to walking than biking. The trail segment through Split Rock Lighthouse State Park dips into the park on a long descent, then climbs back to the highway right away. It's a challenge, but a great way to see the park and excellent views of Lake Superior from the high bluffs between the park and Beaver Bay.

About The Roads

See Road Highlights for information about Scenic Drive. Highway 61 north of Two Harbors has high traffic, including trucks. It is not recommended as a bicycle route.

Road Highlights

Scenic Drive, between Duluth and Two Harbors, has low traffic, wide shoulders, great views of Lake Superior, numerous waysides and rest stops and frequent Restaurantss for lunch breaks.

How To Get There

From Duluth, take Scenic North Shore Drive (Highway 61). Scenic Drive begins near the east side of Duluth where the highway splits. Split Rock Lighthouse State Park is approximately fifty miles east of Duluth on Highway 61.

Vital Trail Information:

Trail Distance: 14

Trail Surface: Asphalt

Access Points: Silver Creek Tunnel, Gooseberry Falls, Split Rock Lighthouse State Park, Beaver Bay

Fees and Passes: None

Trail Website:
www.GitchiGamiTrail.com

Split Rock River to Beaver Bay: 8.4 miles

Gooseberry Falls: 1.2 miles

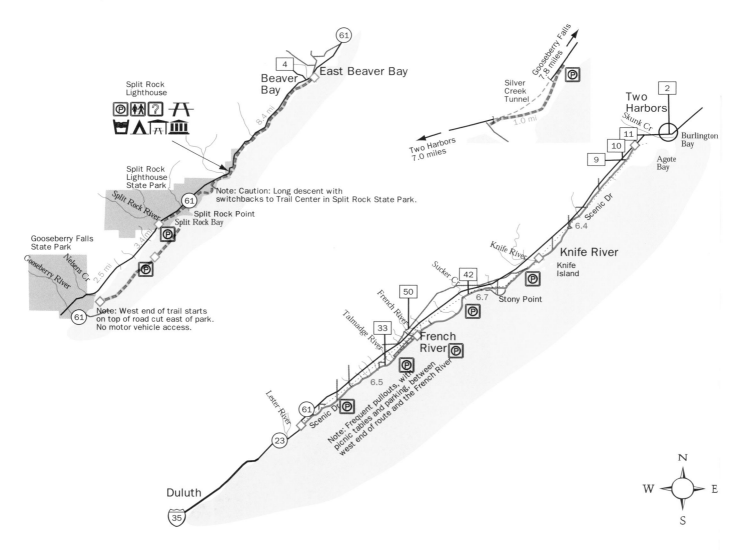

Split Rock
Lighthouse

Split Rock
Lighthouse
State Park

Gooseberry Falls
State Park

Gooseberry River

Nelsens Cr.

Split Rock River

Beaver
Bay

East Beaver Bay

Split Rock Point
Split Rock Bay

Note: Caution: Long descent with switchbacks to Trail Center in Split Rock State Park.

Note: West end of trail starts on top of road cut east of park. No motor vehicle access.

8.4 mi

3.4 mi

2.5 mi

Silver Creek
Tunnel

Two Harbors
7.0 miles

Gooseberry Falls
7.8 miles

Two
Harbors

Burlington
Bay

Skunk Cr.

Agote
Bay

Scenic Dr

6.4

Knife River

Knife River
Knife Island

Stony Point

Sucker Cr.

6.7

French River

Talmadge River

French
River

6.5

Note: Frequent pullouts, with picnic tables and parking, between west end of route and the French River.

Lester River

Scenic Dr

Duluth

1.0 mi

N
W — E
S

Tourist Information

Gitchi-Gami Trail Association
Web: www.ggta.org

Lutsen/Tofte Tourism Association
Toll Free: (888) 616-6784
Phone: (218) 663-7804
Web: www.americasnorthcoast.org

North Shore Visitor
Web: www.northshorevisitor.com

Silver Bay Information Center
Phone: (218) 226-3143

Lodging

Motels/Resorts

Beaver Bay
Cove Point Lodge
4614 Hwy 61
Toll Free: (800) 598-3221
Phone: (218) 226-3221
Fax: (218) 226-4445
Email reservations@covepointlodge.com
Web: www.covepointlodge.com

Schroeder
Lamb's Resort Cabins & Campground
P.O. Box 415
Phone: (218) 663-7292
Fax: (218) 663-7057
Web: www.boreal.org/lambsresort

Superior Ridge Resort-Motel
8041 W Hwy 61
Toll Free: (800) 782-1776
Phone: (218) 663-7189
Email: supridge@boreal.org
Web: www.superiorridge.com

Temperance Traders Cabins
P.O. Box 58
Phone: (218) 663-0111
Email: info@northshorecabins.com
Web: www.northshorecabins.com

Silver Bay
Lax Lake Resort & Campground
5736 Lax Lake Rd
Phone: (218) 353-7424
Web: www.laxlakeresort.com

Tettegouche State Park
5702 Hwy 61
Toll Free: (888) 646-6367
Phone: (218) 226-6365
Fax: (218) 226-6366
Web: www.stayatmnparks.com

Tofte
Americinn
P.O. Box 2296
Toll Free: (800) 625-7042
Phone: (218) 663-7899
Fax: (218) 663-7387
Email: info@americinntofte.com
Web: www.AmericInnTofte.com

Bluefin Bay on Lake Superior
P.O. Box 2125
Toll Free: (800) 258-3346
Phone: (218) 663-7296
Email: emailus@bluefinbay.com
Web: www.bluefinbay.com

Chateau LeVeaux
6626 Hwy 61
Toll Free: (800) 445-5773
Phone: (218) 663-7223
Email: info@chateauleveaux.com
Web: www.chateauleveaux.com

Cobblestone Cabins
6660 W Hwy 61
Phone: (218) 663-7957
Web: www.cobblestonecabins.biz/

Sugar Beach Resort
P.O. Box 2236
Phone: (218) 663-7595
Web: www.toftesugarbeach.com

Two Harbors
Castle Haven Cabins
3067 E Castle Danger Rd
Phone: (218) 834-4303
Web: www.castlehaven.net/

Erickson's Gooseberry Cabins
3044 E Castle Danger Rd
Phone: (218) 834-3873
Email: info@gooseberrycabins.net
Web: www.gooseberrycabins.net/

Gooseberry Park Motel/Cabins
2778 Hwy 61
Toll Free: (800) 950-0283
Phone: (218) 834-3751
Web: www.gooseberryparkcabins.com

Lodging cont'd

Two Harbors

Gooseberry Trailside Suites
3317 Hwy 61
Toll Free: (800) 715-1110
Phone: (218) 226-3905
Email: savoy@gooseberry.com
Web: www.gooseberry.com

Grand Superior Lodge
2826 Hwy 61
Toll Free: (800) 627-9565
Phone: (218) 834-3796
Email: info@grandsuperior.com
Web: www.grandsuperior.com

Bed and Breakfast

Beaver Bay

Northland Trails Guest House
Hwy 61
Box 521
Phone: (218) 226-4199
Email: northland@lakenet.com
Web: www.northlandtrails.com

Two Harbors

J. Gregers Country Inn
3320 Hwy 61
Toll Free: (888) 226-4614
Phone: (218) 226-4614
Email: judyandbryce@jgregersinn.com
Web: www.jgregersinn.com

NorthernRail Traincar Suites
1730 Hwy 3
Toll Free: (877) 834-0955
Phone: (218) 834-0955
Web: www.northernrail.net/

Camping

Beaver Bay

Split Rock Lighthouse State Park
3755 Split Rock Lighthouse Rd
Toll Free: (888) 646-6367
Phone: (218) 226-6377
Web: www.stayatmnparks.com

Schroeder

Lamb's Resort Cabins & Campground
P.O. Box 415
Phone: (218) 663-7292
Fax: (218) 663-7057
Web: www.boreal.org/lambsresort

Temperance River State Park
7620 W Hwy 61
Toll Free: (888) 646-6367
Phone: (218) 663-7476
Web: www.stayatmnparks.com

Silver Bay

Lax Lake Resort & Campground
5736 Lax Lake Rd
Phone: (218) 353-7424
Web: www.laxlakeresort.com

Tettegouche State Park
5702 Hwy 61
Toll Free: (888) 646-6367
Phone: (218) 226-6365
Fax: (218) 226-6366
Web: www.stayatmnparks.com

Two Harbors

Gooseberry State Park
3206 Hwy 61
Toll Free: (866) 857-2757
Phone: (218) 834-3855
Fax: (218) 834-3787
Web: www.stayatmnparks.com

Bike Rental

Lutsen

Lutsen Mountains
Box 129 County Rd 36
Phone: (218) 663-7281
Email: ski@lutsen.com
Web: www.lutsen.com

Tofte

Bluefin Bay Resort
P.O. Box 2125
Toll Free: (800) 258-3346
Phone: (218) 663-7860
Email: emailus@bluefinbay.com
Web: www.bluefinbay.com

Sawtooth Outfitters
P.O. Box 2214
Phone: (218) 663-7643
Email: info@sawtoothoutfitters.com
Web: www.sawtoothoutfitters.com

Festivals and Events

Schroeder

September

John Schroeder Day
Festivities commemorate Schroeder history. Downtown near Cross River Bridge find food vendors, craftsmen, artists, kids' games, musical entertainment and spaghetti dinner. See world famous minnow races daily plus raffle drawings.
Phone: (218) 663-7706

Tofte

July

Independence Day Celebration
In Tofte Town Park, experience Tofte Trek, a parade, food, music and fireworks at dusk. Fourth of July.
Toll Free: (888) 616-6784
Phone: (218) 663-7804
Web: www.61north.com

Alternate Activities

Naturalist Programs
The U.S. Forest Service Resort Naturalist Program offers a wide variety of family-oriented nature activities featuring bears, moose, voyageurs and wildflowers. The programs are hosted by many of the resorts and hotels, and all programs are free and available to everyone regardless of where you may be staying on the shore. There are morning and evening programs daily, Tuesday through Saturday. For times, locations and topics see posted schedules at participating locations.
Phone: (218) 663-8060

Beaver Bay

Kayaking - Lake Superior Water Trail
The State of Minnesota has set up a water trail for sea kayakers along the shores of Lake Superior. It will eventually extend the entire way around Lake Superior.
Web: www.lswta.org

East Beaver Bay

Lake Superior Excursions aboard the Grandpa Woo
Board the forty passenger Grandpa Woo at the public launch in East Beaver Bay or Agate Bay in Two Harbors and tour Superior's coastline. Highlights include the craggy shoreline, river mouths, Silver Cliff, Encampment Island, Split Rock Lighthouse and Palisade Head.
Phone: (218) 226-4100
Web: www.grandpawoo.com

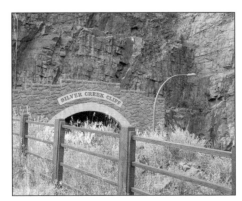

Silver Bay's Bayside Park

Located on the shore of Lake Superior off Highway 61 just east of Beaver Bay and west of Silver Bay, the park features a boat landing, picnic tables, fire pits, and a beach. Pick agates on the beach or hike a short trail to a scenic lookout. Web: www.silverbay.com/bayside.htm

Tettegouche State Park

Hike to rocky, wind-swept Shovel Point or back into one of the four quiet inland lakes. Don't miss the beautiful High Falls on the Baptism River, the highest waterfall inside Minnesota's borders. Explore sixteen miles of hiking trails. Tettegouche Camp is on the National Register of Historic Places. Cabins of the old hunting camp are now rented as walk, bike, or ski-in lodging. Phone: (218) 226-6365

Tofte

Lake Superior Sport Fishing

Take a relaxing and scenic fishing trip with Tofte Charters. Toll Free: (866) 663-9932 Phone: (218) 663-9932 Web: www.toftecharters.com

North Shore Commercial Fishing Museum

Exhibits take you across the cultural landscape of North Shore commercial fishermen and their families. Partake in galleries, lectures, presentations and ongoing programs. Phone: (218) 663-7804 Web: www.commercialfishingmuseum.org

Alternate Activities cont'd

Schroeder

Sugarloaf Interpretive Center

Visit interpretive displays about geology, ecology and culture of the North Shore. Specially arranged hikes, programs and rental of the Interpretive Center are available. Open May through September on Saturday and Sunday. Phone: (218) 525-0001 Web: www.sugarloafnorthshore.org/

Temperance River State Park

The Temperance River, which drops 162 feet in a half mile, is a series of cascades, the last of which occurs about 100 feet from its mouth at Lake Superior. View large potholes and cauldrons in the gorge. The park has a fishing stream and six miles of foot trails. Phone: (218) 663-7476

Silver Bay

Palisade Head

See incredible views of Lake Superior, Shovel Point and 200 foot cliffs. Off Highway 61 about four miles northeast of Silver Bay, watch for signs. Follow the gravel road to the top. Open seasonally.

Alternate Activities cont'd

Tofte

Carlton Peak

This is the highest peak on the Minnesota North Shore at 927 feet above lake level, or 1,529 feet above sea level. Scenic hiking trails stretch 3.4 miles round-trip to the peak or 5.2 miles round-trip to the overlook. From Highway 61 in Tofte, go north on the Sawbill Trail (County Road 2) for two miles to the parking area on the east/right. Walk across the Sawbill Trail and follow the snowmobile trail.
Phone: (218) 663-7476

Two Harbors

Split Rock Lighthouse

Split Rock Lighthouse was built on top of a 130 foot cliff in 1910. Tour the lighthouse, fog signal building and keeper's home. See exhibits and film in the history center adjacent to Split Rock Lighthouse State Park.
Phone: (218) 226-6377

Gooseberry Falls State Park

Don't miss this stop on the Lake Superior shoreline with five waterfalls, historic log and stone buildings, a wayside rest and picnic grounds. The visitor center has exhibits, a nature store, trail center and naturalist programs. Hike eighteen miles of trails and ride twelve miles of mountain bike trails. Also check out river and Lake Superior fishing.
Phone: (218) 834-3855
Web: www.stayatmnparks.com

Superior Hiking Trail

Beginning just north of Two Harbors, MN, and ending just before the Canadian border, the 235 mile trail connects seven state parks and features waterfalls, rivers, lakes and diverse forests. Foot travel only.
Phone: (218) 834-2700
Web: www.shta.org

Restaurants

Beaver Bay

Lemon Wolf Café

Phone: (218) 226-7225
Web: www.lemonwolfbears.com

Cove Point Lodge Dining Room

Menu: Fine Dining
Toll Free:(800) 598-3221
Phone: (218) 226-3221
Web: www.covepointlodge.com

Northern Lights Restaurants

Phone: (218) 226-3012

Schroeder

Satellite's Country Inn

Phone: (218) 663-7574

Silver Bay

Northwoods Café

Menu: Home Cooking
Phone: (218) 226-3699

Tofte

Coho Cafe Bakery & Deli

Phone: (218) 663-8032

Bluefin Grille

Menu: Seafood
Phone: (218) 663-7296

Two Harbors

Rustic Inn Café

Phone: (218) 834-2488
Web: www.rusticinncafe.com

About The Trail

From Grand Rapids to Gilbert, the trail dips, rolls and twists its way from mining town to open pit. It skirts the edge of active mines and 300 foot deep pit lakes. It wanders down the back streets of small towns, hooks up with abandoned roads and runs next to old rail lines with aspens sprouting between the rail ties. The Iron Range is full of history and everything from museums and mine views to the long hills of mine tailings reflects its active industrial past. The Mesabi Trail never wanders far from that history. The seventy-nine mile stretch from Grand Rapids to McKinley is finished in all but one four mile segment. This is an ideal trail for anyone who likes a few hills, a lot of history and unexpected scenery.

Trail Highlights

The fifteen mile stretch from Mt. Iron to Eveleth is the most charming, with the prettiest stretch between Gilbert and Virginia. In Virginia, follow Veteran's Drive through Olcott Park. Allow some time in the park to explore the greenhouse and enjoy the flower gardens. The Hibbing section is the richest in Iron Range history. The Greyhound Bus Origin Museum and Hull Rust Mahoning Mine View are both within blocks of the Hibbing Trailhead. The Trailhead in Grand Rapids starts from the north end of the fairgrounds, then skirts the edge of a pit lake. Later it crosses the Prairie River and works its way to the sleepy town of Taconite. If you have time, take the spur trail to Gunn Park, a donation from the Blandin Foundation.

About The Roads

Paved roads are limited in the central part of the trail and the through-routes usually carry a lot of traffic. The ends of the trail have better connecting road loops.

Road Highlights

County Roads 4 and 97 offer a pleasant alternate to Highway 135 between Biwabik and the McKinley Trailhead.

How To Get There

Highway 169 goes straight north from the Twin Cities to Grand Rapids, then connects the Range cities along the trail. Turn south on Highways 53/135 near Virginia, and follow Highway 135 to the Gilbert trailhead. Highway 53 from Duluth runs due north to Eveleth and Virginia near the eastern end of the trail. Travel distance from the Twin Cities to the Range cities is approximately 200 miles, depending on your destination.

Vital Trail Information:

Trail Distance: 88

Trail Surface: Asphalt

Access Points: Grand Rapids, Coleraine, Bovey, Taconite, Hibbing, Chisholm, Buhl, Kinney, Mt. Iron, Virginia, Gilbert, Eveleth, Biwabik, Giants Ridge

Fees and Passes: The Mesabi Trail Wheel Pass costs $12.80 for an annual and $3.50 for a 2 day special pass

Trail Website: www.mesabitrail.com

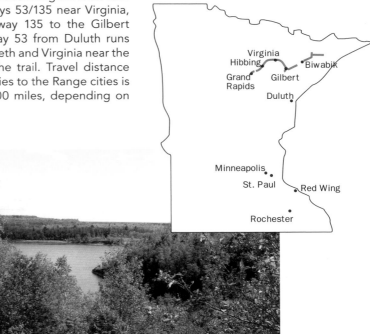

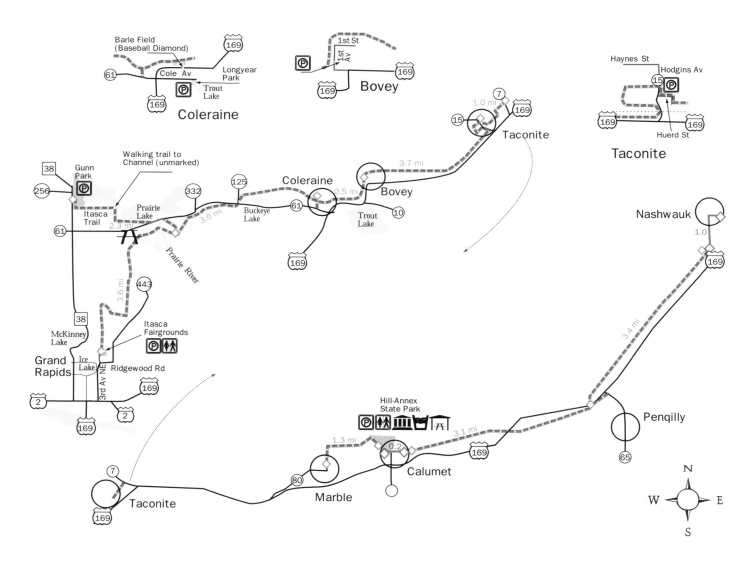
Grand Rapids to Nashwauk: 20.2 miles

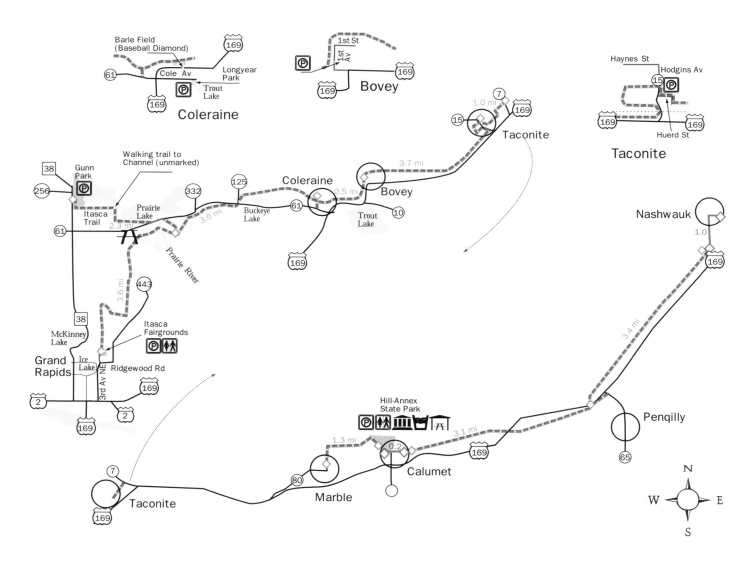

Barle Field
(Baseball Diamond)
169
61
Cole Av
Longyear Park
169
Trout Lake
Coleraine

1st St
1st Av
169
Bovey
169

Haynes St
Hodgins Av
15
Taconite
169
Huerd St
169
Taconite

7
15
169
Taconite
1.0 mi

3.7 mi

Walking trail to Channel (unmarked)
38
Gunn Park
256
Itasca Trail
61
2.3 mi
Prairie Lake
332
125
Coleraine
61
Bovey
0.5 mi
10
Trout Lake
3.6 mi
Buckeye Lake
169

Nashwauk
1.0
169

Prairie River
443
3.6 mi
Itasca Fairgrounds
38
McKinney Lake
Grand Rapids
Ice Lake
3rd Av NE
Ridgewood Rd
2
169
169
2

3.4 mi

Hill-Annex State Park
Penqilly
65

1.3 mi
0.2
3.1 mi
80
Calumet
Marble
169
7
Taconite
169

N
W   E
S

Nashwauk to Eveleth: 54.6 miles

Note: See City Maps for detail of towns along trail.

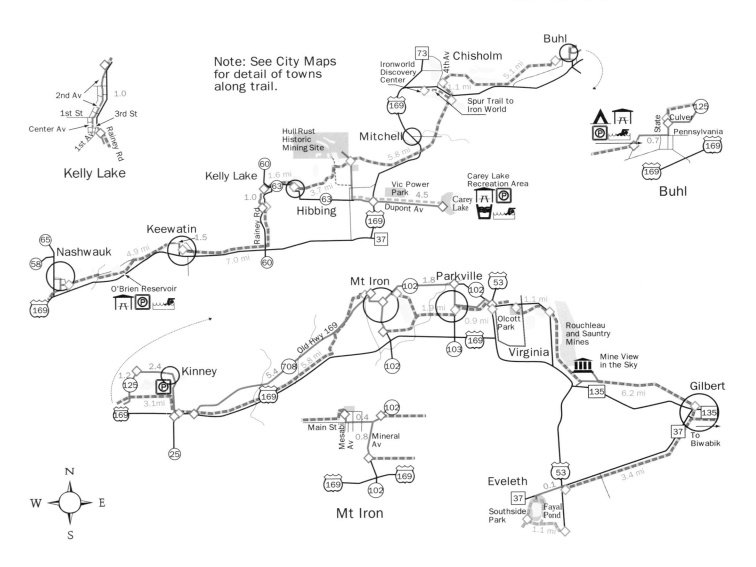

Kelly Lake

2nd Av — 1.0
1st St — 3rd St
Center Av
1st Av — Rainey Rd

Chisholm
73
4th Av
Ironworld Discovery Center
169
Spur Trail to Iron World
5.1 mi
1.1 mi

Buhl

Hull Rust Historic Mining Site

Mitchell
5.8 mi

Kelly Lake
60 — 1.6 mi
63 — 1.0
3.7 mi
63
Hibbing

Vic Power Park — 4.5
Dupont Av
169
37
Carey Lake
Carey Lake Recreation Area

State
Culver — 125
Pennsylvania
0.7
169
169

Buhl

65
58
Nashwauk
169
O'Brien Reservoir
4.9 mi
1.5
Keewatin
Rainey Rd
7.0 mi
60

Mt Iron
Parkville — 53
102 — 1.8
102
1.1 mi
1.9 mi
Olcott Park
0.9 mi
169
103
102

Rouchleau and Sauntry Mines
Virginia
Mine View in the Sky
135 — 6.2 mi

Gilbert
135

Kinney
1.2 — 2.4
125
169
3.1mi
5.4 — 708 — 5.8 mi
Old Hwy 169
169
25

Mt Iron
102
Main St — 0.4
Mesabi Av — 0.8 Mineral Av
102
169 — 102 — 169

37
To Biwabik
53
3.4 mi

Eveleth
37 — 0.1
Southside Park
Fayal Pond
1.1 mi

N
W — E
S

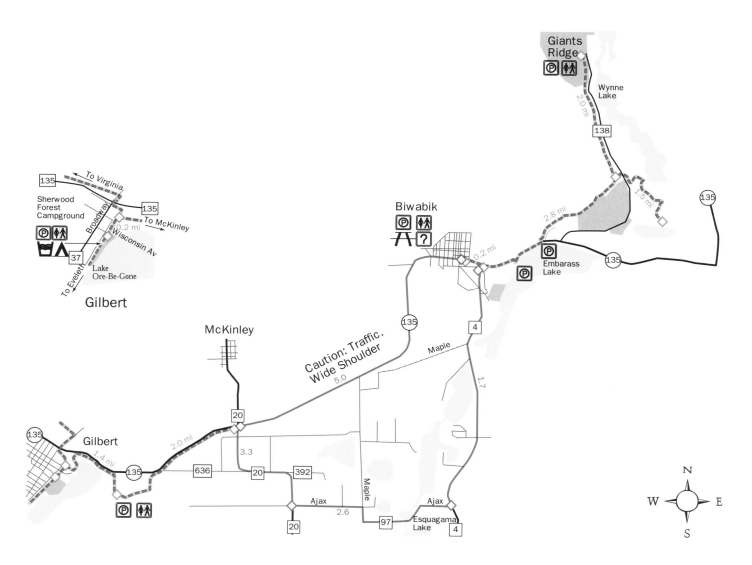

Gilbert to Giant's Ridge: 13.1 miles

Giants
Ridge

Wynne
Lake

2.0 mi

138

1.5 mi

135

135

2.8 mi

Biwabik

?

0.2 mi

Embarass
Lake

135

135

4

Maple

Caution: Traffic.
Wide Shoulder
5.0

1.7

McKinley

135

Sherwood
Forest
Campground

To Virginia

To McKinley

0.2 mi

Wisconsin Av

37

Lake
Ore-Be-Gone

To Evelett

Gilbert

135

135

Broadway

135

Gilbert

2.0 mi

1.4 mi

135

636

20

392

3.3

20

Maple

Ajax

20

2.6

97

Ajax

Esquagama
Lake

4

N

W   E

S

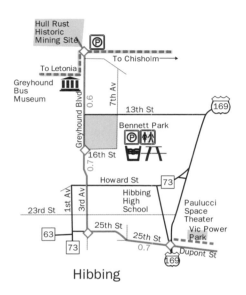

Hibbing

Hull Rust Historic Mining Site

To Chisholm→

To Letonia

Greyhound Bus Museum

Greyhound Blvd

7th Av

13th St — 169

Bennett Park

16th St

Howard St — 73

Hibbing High School

Paulucci Space Theater

23rd St — 1st Av / 3rd Av

63 — 25th St — 73

25th St 0.7

Dupont St — 169

Vic Power Park

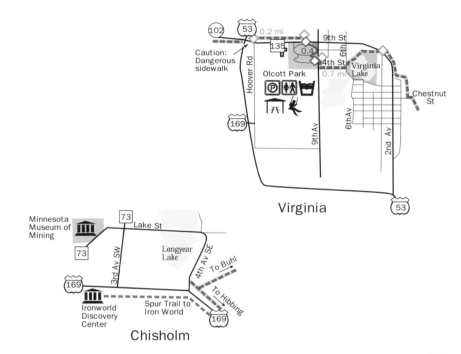

Virginia

102 — 53 — 0.2 mi — 9th St

Caution: Dangerous sidewalk

Hoover Rd

135 — 0.4 — 4th St — 6th

Olcott Park

0.7 mi

Virginia Lake

169

9th Av — 6th Av

Chestnut St

2nd Av — 53

Chisholm

Minnesota Museum of Mining — 73 — Lake St

73

3rd Av SW

Longyear Lake

4th Av SE — To Buhl

169

Ironworld Discovery Center

Spur Trail to Iron World

To Hibbing

169

Nashwauk

City Park

65

Central Av — 1.0

2nd St

86

169

169

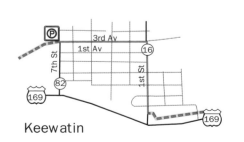

Keewatin

3rd Av

1st Av — 16

7th St

1st St

82

169

169

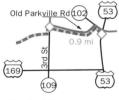

Parkville

Old Parkville Rd — 102 — 53

0.9 mi

3rd St

169 — 109 — 53

Tourist Information

Chisholm Area Chamber of Commerce
Toll Free: (800) 422-0806
Phone: (218) 254-7930
Email: info@chisholmchamber.com
Web: www.chisholmchamber.com

City of Biwabik
Phone: (218) 865-4183
Fax: (218) 865-4580
Email: info@cityOfBiwabik.com
Web: www.cityofbiwabik.com

City of Gilbert City Hall
Phone: (218) 748-2232
Fax: (218) 748-2234
Email: clerk@gilbertmn.org
Web: www.gilbertmn.org

City of Mountain Iron
Phone: (218) 748-7570
Email: cityadmn@mtniron.com
Web: www.mtniron.com

Hibbing Area Chamber of Commerce
Toll Free: (800) 444-2246
Phone: (218) 262-3895
Fax: (218) 262-3897
Email: hibbcofc@hibbing.org
Web: www.hibbing.org

Iron Range Tourism Bureau
Toll Free: (800) 777-8497
Phone: (218) 749-8161
Fax: (218) 749-8055
Email: info@ironrange.org
Web: www.irontrail.org

Laurentian Chamber of Commerce
Phone: (218) 741-2717
Fax: (218) 749-4913
Email: phubbard@laurentianchamber.org
Web: www.laurentianchamber.org

Mesabi Trail
Toll Free: (877) 637-2241
Phone: (218) 254-0086
Email: birdie.oddo@ironworld.com
Web: www.mesabitrail.com

Visit Grand Rapids
Toll Free: (800) 355-9740
Phone: (218) 326-9607
Email: answers@visitgrandrapids.com
Web: www.visitgrandrapids.com

Lodging

Motels/Resorts

Chisholm
Chisholm Suites
501 Iron Dr
Toll Free: (877) 255-3156
Phone: (218) 254-2000
Web: www.chisholminn.com

Eveleth
Super 8 Motel
1080 Industrial Park Dr
Hwy 53
Toll Free: (800) 800-8000
Phone: (218) 744-1661
Fax: (218) 744-4343
Email: resinf@cdhotel.com

Grand Rapids
AmericInn
1812 S Pokegama Ave
P.O. Box 435
Toll Free: (800) 396-5007
Phone: (218) 326-8999
Fax: (218) 326-9190
Email: grandrapids.mn@americinn.com

Country Inn
2601 S Hwy 169
Toll Free: (888) 201-1746
Phone: (218) 327-4960
Fax: (218) 327-4964
Email: cx_grap@countryinns.com

Forest Lake Motel
1215 NW 4th St
Toll Free: (800) 622-3590
Phone: (218) 326-6609
Email: info@forestlakemotel.biz
Web: www.forestlakemotel.biz

Itascan Motel
610 S Pokegama Ave
Toll Free: (800) 842-7733
Phone: (218) 326-3489
Email: info@itascan.com
Web: www.itascan.com

Rainbow Inn
1300 E Hwy 169
Toll Free: (888) 248-8050
Phone: (218) 326-9655
Fax: (218) 326-9651
Email: info@rainbowinn-gr.com
Web: www.rainbowinn-gr.com

Sawmill Inn
Hwy 169 S
2301 S Pokegama Ave
Toll Free: (800) 667-7508
Phone: (218) 326-8501
Email: sawmill@uslink.net
Web: www.sawmillinn.com

Super 8 Motel
1702 S Pokogama Ave
Toll Free: (800) 800-8000
Phone: (218) 327-1108
Fax: (218) 327-2155

Hibbing
Arrowhead Motel
3701 W 2nd Ave
Toll Free: (800) 890-3477
Phone: (218) 262-3477

Lodging cont'd

Motels/Resorts

Hibbing

Hibbing Park Hotel and Suites
1402 E Howard St
Hwy 169
Toll Free: (800) 262-3481
Phone: (218) 262-3481
Fax: (218) 262-1906
Email: hibbpark@rangebroadband.com
Web: www.hibbingparkhotel.com

Star Motel
3901 1st Ave
Toll Free
Phone: (218) 262-5728

Super 8 Motel
1411 E 40th St
Toll Free: (800) 800-8000
Phone: (218) 263-8982
Fax: (218) 263-8982

Virginia

AmericInn Lodge & Suites
5480 Mountain Iron Dr
Toll Free: (866) 778-2536
Phone: (218) 741-7839
Fax: (218) 741-9050
Email: Virginia.mn@americinn.com

Coates Plaza Hotel
502 Chestnut St
Phone: (218) 749-1000
Fax: (218) 749-6934
Web: www.coatesplazahotel.com

Lakeshor Motor Inn
404 N 6th Ave
Toll Free: (800) 569-8131
Phone: (218) 741-3360
Fax: (218) 741-3363
Email: info@lakeshor.com
Web: www.lakeshor.com

Ski View Motel
903 N 17th St
Phone: (218) 741-8918

Bed and Breakfast

Grand Rapids

Morning Glory Bed & Breakfast
726 NW 2nd Ave
Toll Free: (866) 926-3978
Phone: (218) 326-3978
Email: karen@morningglorybandb.com
Web: www.morningglorybandb.com

Hibbing

Mitchell-Tappan House
2125 4th Ave E
Toll Free: (888) 662-3862
Web: www.mitchell-tappanhouse.com

Camping

Biwabik

Vermilion Trail Park Campground
P.O. Box 529
Phone: (218) 865-4183
Email: camping@vermiliontrailgournd.com
Web: www.cityofbiwabik.com/
biw-campground.html

Buhl

Stubler Beach Campground
320 Jones St
P.O. Box 704
Phone: (218) 258-3226
Fax: (218) 258-3796

Gilbert

Sherwood Forest Campground
P.O. Box 548
Toll Free: (800) 403-1803
Phone: (218) 748-2221
Email: campgroundgilbertmn@yahoo.com
Web: www.gilbertmn.org/
sherwood%20forest.htm

Grand Rapids

Itasca County Fairgrounds
1336 NE 3rd Ave
Phone: (218) 326-6470

Prairie Lake Campground & RV Park
30730 Wabana Rd
Phone: (218) 326-8486
Email: prlkcamp@msn.com
Web: www.prairielakecamp.com

Hibbing

Forest Heights Campground
2240 25th St E
Phone: (218) 263-5782

Mountain Iron
West Two Rivers Campground
4988 Campground Rd
Phone: (218) 735-8831
Fax: (218) 748-7573
Email: parks@mountainiron.com

Side Lake

Bear Lake Campground
McCarthy Beach State Park
7622 McCarthy Beach Rd
Phone: (218) 254-7979

Bike Rental

Biwabik
Giant's Ridge Resort
County Rd 138
Toll Free: (800) 688-7669
Phone: (218) 865-3000
Email: info@giantsridge.com
Web: www.giantsridge.com

Grand Rapids
Itasca Trail Sports
Hwy 2
Phone: (218) 326-1716
Email: david@itascatrailsports.com
Web: www.itascatrailsports.com

Hibbing
Bikes on Howard
Phone: (218) 262-0899
Email: calvinandjill@bikesonhoward.com
Web: www.bikesonhoward.com

Bike Repair

Biwabik
Giants Ridge Resort
County Rd 138
Toll Free: (800) 688-7669
Phone: (218) 865-3000
Email: info@giantsridge.com
Web: www.giantsridge.com

Grand Rapids
Itasca Bike Ski and Fitness
Hwy 2
Phone: (218) 326-1716
Email: david@itascatrailsports.com
Web: www.itascatrailsports.com

Hibbing
Bikes on Howard
407 E Howard St
Phone: (218) 262-0899
Email: calvinandjill@bikesonhoward.com
Web: www.bikesonhoward.com

Virginia
Mesabi Recreation
720 9th St N
Phone: (218) 749-6719
Web: www.mesabirecreation.com

Bike Shuttle

Chisholm
Mesabi Trail Shuttle Service
Toll Free: (800) 688-7669
Phone: (218) 865-3002
Email: Craig.Johnson@giantsridge.com
Web: www.mesabitrail.com

Festivals and Events

Chisholm
June
International Polka Fest
At Ironworld, see non-stop polka music by thirty-five polka bands performing on four stages, a daily dance contest, Polka Hall of Fame inductions, polka mass and ethnic food. Fourth Weekend.
Toll Free: (800) 372-6437
Phone: (218) 254-7959
Web: www.ironworld.com

August
St. Louis County Fair
At Ironworld, check out exhibits, food, entertainment and the midway. First Weekend.
Toll Free: (800) 422-0806
Phone: (218) 254-7930

September
Chisholm Fire Days
Enjoy the kiddy parade, softball tourney, city-wide garage sales, food vendors and street dance. Second Weekend.
Toll Free: (800) 422-0806
Phone: (218) 254-7930
Web: www.chisholmchamber.com

Gilbert
July
4th of July Celebration
See the huge parade, street dance and fireworks July 3rd and kiddy parade and games July 4th.
Phone: (218) 748-2232
Web: www.gilbertmn.org

Grand Rapids
June
Judy Garland Festival
Mingle with the original Munchkins, who appeared in the Wizard of Oz, and other guest celebrities. Also enjoy the Taste of Grand Rapids, a film festival, collector's exchange and seminars. Fourth Weekend.
Toll Free: (800) 664-5839
Phone: (218) 327-9276
Web: www.judygarlandmuseum.com

Festivals and Events cont'd

Grand Rapids

July

Wood Craft Festival

At the Forest History Center, browse traditional wood crafts that are hand-crafted without power tools. Second Weekend.
Toll Free: (800) 355-9740
Phone: (218) 326-9607
Web: www.visitgrandrapids.com

August

Itasca County Fair

Itasca County Fairgrounds. Third Weekend.
Toll Free: (800) 355-9740
Phone: (218) 326-9607
Web: www.visitgrandrapids.com

Tall Timber Days

Downtown at the Old Central School, see logging displays, events and the street fair. First Full Weekend.
Toll Free: (800) 355-9740
Phone: (218) 326-9607
Web: www.visitgrandrapids.com

White Oak Rendezvous

Colorful reenactment of French Voyager rendezvous. First Full Weekend
Toll Free: (800) 355-9740
Phone: (218) 326-9607
Web: www.visitgrandrapids.com

Hibbing

Unknown

Dylan Days

Celebrate the life and music of Bob Dylan. Refer to website for dates.
Toll Free: (866) 305-3849
Phone: (218) 262-6145
Web: www.dylandays.com

July

Mines and Pines Jubilee

This ten day celebration boasts a parade, street dance, arts and crafts displays and sales, a fly-in breakfast, golf tourney, radio flyer show, flea market, fireworks, an ice-cream social and childrens' day events. Second Weekend.
Toll Free: (800) 444-2246
Phone: (218) 262-3895

Mountain Iron

July

4th of July Celebration

This is an old-fashioned celebration with sports tourneys, polka bands, a watermelon eating contest and a five minute parade. First Weekend.
Phone: (218) 748-7570

August

Merritt Days

The festival commemorates the discovery of iron ore in the area with a street dance, parade, pet show, live music and food vendors. Second Weekend.
Phone: (218) 748-7570
Web: www.mtniron.com

Virginia

June

Land of the Loon Festival

At Olcott Park and downtown, see the parade, jugglers, food vendors, arts and crafts and music. Third Weekend.
Phone: (218) 749-5555
Web: www.landoftheloonfestival.com

Alternate Activities

Biwabik

Giants Ridge

Don't miss over seventy-five miles of mountain biking trails, hiking trails, disc golf and an 18-hole championship golf course.
Toll Free: (800) 688-7669
Phone: (218) 865-3000
Web: www.giantsridge.com

Chisholm

Ironworld Discovery Center

Tours, exhibits and climb-on equipment displays, electric trolley, concerts, living history exhibits and ethnic Restaurantss are accessible via spur trail from the Mesabi Trail.
Toll Free: (800) 372-6437
Phone: (218) 254-7959
Web: www.ironworld.com

Alternate Activities cont'd

Chisholm

Minnesota Museum of Mining
See mining trucks, a steam locomotive, 1910 Atlantic steam shovel, early diamond drills, a replica underground mine and mining town. Open daily from the end of May to mid-September.
Toll Free: (800) 422-0806
Phone: (218) 254-5543
Web: www.fnbchisholm.com/mining

Eveleth

Veteran's Lake Park
Take advantage of the swimming beach, picnic area and camping.
Phone: (218) 744-7491

US Hockey Hall of Fame
Enjoy displays of enshrined players, the exhibit and film library, a shooting rink, Zamboni display, theater and gift shop. Open year 'round.
Toll Free: (800) 443-7825
Phone: (218) 744-5167

Gilbert

Iron Range Historical Society and Museum
Housed in Gilbert's old City Hall /Police Station/Jail building, the museum includes sleds used by the Will Steger North Pole Expedition, a mining exhibit, an old time jail and a research library. Open Monday and Tuesday 9:00am–7:00pm, other days by appointment.
Phone: (218) 749-3150
Web: www.gilbertmn.org

Grand Rapids

Old Central School
The turn of the century schoolhouse was converted into a marketplace, specialty shops and Restaurants. Itasca County.
Toll Free: (800) 355-9740
Phone: (218) 327-1834
Web: www.visitgrandrapids.com

Forest History Center
This open air living history center is operated by the Minnesota Historical Society and has a full-sized 1900 logging camp and costumed interpreters. Open seven days a week, June 1 through August 31.
Phone: (218) 327-4482
Web: www.mnhs.org/places/sites/fhc

Mississippi Melodie Showboat
See the outdoor theater on the banks of the Mississippi. Last three weekends of July.
Toll Free: (866) 336-3426
Phone: (218) 326-6619
Web: www.mississippimelodie.com

Judy Garland Birthplace
Visit her restored childhood home, including Judy Garland memorabilia and the carriage from the Wizard of Oz, and partake in educational hands-on exhibits in the museum.
Toll Free: (800) 664-5839
Phone: (218) 327-9276
Web: www.judygarlandmuseum.com

Children's Discovery Museum
A blend of permanent and changing educational exhibits. Open Monday through Saturday, 10:00am–5:00pm, Sunday 12:00pm–5:00pm.
Toll Free: (866) 236-5437
Phone: (218) 326-1900
Web: www.cdmkids.org

Hibbing

Hibbing High School
Mentioned in the National Register of Historic Places, this school has hand-painted murals, cut glass chandeliers, an 1800 seat auditorium and more. Open Monday through Saturday (summers) and by appointment during school year.
Phone: (218) 263-3675

Hull Rust Mahoning Mine
This is a National Historic Place. See the world's largest open pit mine, mine exhibits, scenic views and a walking trail at the Hibbing Trailhead. Open daily from Memorial Day to Labor Day.
Phone: (218) 262-4900
Web: www.hibbing.org

Greyhound Bus Origin Museum
Among the sights are vintage buses, models and artifacts from the 1900s. Open Monday through Saturday 9am–5pm, mid-May to September. Located at the Hibbing Trailhead.
Phone: (218) 263-5814
Web: www.greyhoundbusmuseum.org

Alternate Activities cont'd

Hibbing

Palucci Space Theater
Take in 70mm widescreen movies on various topics, watch multimedia presentations and visit the gift shop. Open year 'round. Call for times.
Phone: (218) 262-6720
Web: www.spacetheatre.mnscu.edu

Orr

Vince Shute Wildlife Sanctuary
About twenty miles north of Virginia, view wildlife black bears in a natural setting from an elevated observation deck. Open 5:00pm until dusk on summer evenings.
Phone: (218) 757-0172
Web: www.americanbear.org

Virginia

Olcott Park Greenhouse
Snap photos of a profusion of flowers and plants, some exotic, some common household plants. Located in Olcott Park near the heart of Virginia. Open daily June to Labor Day and weekdays rest of the year.
Phone: (218) 748-7509

Mineview in the Sky
Overlooks the Rouchleau Mine Group, the area's deepest mine, accessible directly from the Trail via a steep driveway. Open daily May to September, 9:00am–6:00pm.
Phone: (218) 741-2717

Heritage Museum
Maintained by the Virginia Area Historical Society, the permanent exhibits are housed in historical cabins and former park superintendent's residence.
Phone: (218) 741-1136
Web: homepage.virginiamn.com/ ~historicalsociety

Restaurants

Chisholm

Valentini's Supper Club
31 W Lake St
Phone: (218) 254-2607

Tom & Jerry's Bar
201 W Lake St
Phone: (218) 254-9980

Grand Rapids

Silver Spoon Café
18 NW 4th
Menu: Home Cooking
Phone: (218) 326-8646

Forest Lake Restaurants & Lounge
1201 NW 4th St
Menu: American Dishes
Phone: (218) 326-3423

Bridgeside Restaurants & Sports Bar
32946 Crystal Srings Rd
Menu: American Classics
Phone: (218) 326-0235

New China Restaurants
214 NW 1st Ave
Phone: (218) 327-1455

Mad Dog's Pizza
702 NW 4th St
Phone: (218) 326-1774

La Rosa Mexican American Restaurants & Lounge
1300 E Hwy 169
Phone: (218) 327-4000

Hong Kong Garden Restaurants
1300 E Hwy 169
Phone: (218) 327-1131

Hibbing

Grandma's in the Park Bar & Grill
1402 E Howard
Menu: Pasta, Steaks, Sandwiches and Salads
Toll Free: (800) 262-3481
Phone: (218) 262-3481
Web: www.hibbingparkhotel.com

Zimmy's Bar & Restaurants
531 E Howard
Toll Free: (866) 305-3849
Phone: (218) 262-6145
Web: www.zimmys.com

Virginia

Coates Plaza Hotel
502 Chestnut St
Phone: (218) 749-1000

Italian Bakery
205 1st St S
Toll Free: (800) 238-8830
Phone: (218) 741-3464
Web: www.potica.com

Four Seasons Restaurants & Lounge
Hwy 53 & 169
Phone: (218) 741-4200

About The Trail

This is a narrow, gently rolling trail that runs parallel to Park Drive. Frequent spurs give cyclists access to all of the highlights of the park, including scenic overlooks, a Pioneer Cemetery, campgrounds and the headwaters of the Mississippi River.

Trail Highlights

The 0.4 mile long boardwalk north of the campground is unique and fun to ride. Check out the tombstones at the Pioneer Cemetery and take time to relax on the large shaded picnic grounds along the trail.

About The Roads

Bikes are discouraged from using Park Road from the visitor center to the headwaters. Traffic is heavy and the road is narrow. Use the trail instead of the road. Wilderness Drive is a beautiful, one way rollercoaster of a ride through deep forests and past remote lakes in the western part of the park. The road is designated a bike route by the Department of Natural Resources. Traffic is low and slow moving.

Road Highlights

Wilderness Drive is the highlight of the park, but the lesser known Park Drive south of the Visitor Center is quite attractive and generally draws very little traffic. Make a loop by going out the south entrance of the park, then going north on Highway 71 and Highway 200 North until you get to the north entrance to the park. Finish the loop either on the bike path or wilderness Drive. Highways 71 and 200 may have heavy traffic during summer months. Both roads have good shoulders.

How To Get There

From the Twin Cities take Interstate 94 west to Sauk Centre. Go north on Highway 71 to Itasca State Park. The East entrance to the park is the most frequently used entrance. Travel time is about five hours.

Vital Trail Information:

Trail Distance: 6

Trail Surface: Asphalt

Access Points: Many points in Itasca State Park

Fees and Passes: State Park sticker for motor vehicles

Trail Website: www.dnr.state.mn.us

ITASCA STATE PARK ⚑ Northern Minnesota

Trail: 5.8 miles

Wilderness Drive: 9.6 miles

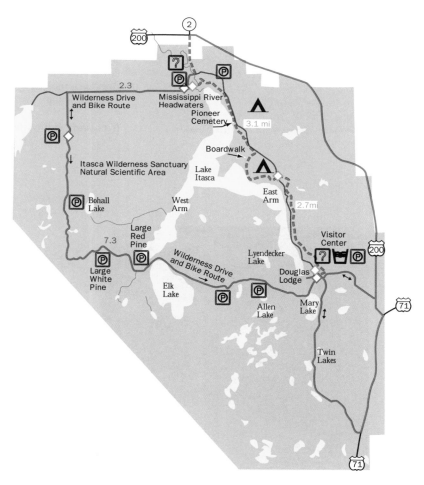

Tourist Information

Itasca Area Lakes
Toll Free: (888) 292-7118
Phone: (218) 732-8816
Email: info@itascaarea.com
Web: www.itascaarea.com

Itasca State Park
Phone: (218) 266-2100
Email: itasca.park@dnr.state.mn.us
Web: www.dnr.state.mn.us

Lodging

Motels/Resorts

Itasca State Park

Bert's Cabins
15782 Wilderness Dr
Phone: (218) 266-3312
Web: www.bertscabins.com

Mississippi Headwaters Hostel
Itasca State Park
36750 Main Park Dr
Phone: (218) 266-3415
Email: mhhostel@himinnesota.org

Lake George
Lake George Pines Motel
37197 US 71
Phone: (218) 266-3914

Melahn All Season Resort
Hc 70 Box 2206
Phone: (218) 266-3354

Park Rapids
Itasca State Park
36750 Main Park Dr
Phone: (218) 266-2100
Email: itasca.park@dnr.state.mn.us
Web: www.stayatmnparks.com

Little Norway Resort
32016 Little Mantrap Dr
Phone: (218) 732-5480
Fax:(218) 732-0963
Email: lnorway@wcta.net
Web: www.littlenorwayresort.com

Weigelwood Resort
56698 310th St
Toll Free: (800) 943-3357
Phone: (218) 732-4775
Email: weigelwood@hotmail.com
Web: www.weigelwood.20m.com

Wilderness Bay Resort & Campground
36701 Wilderness Bay Dr
Phone: (218) 732-5608
Email: vacation@wildernessbay.com
Web: www.wildernessbay.com

Bed and Breakfast

Park Rapids
LoonSong B&B
17248 Loonsong Ln
Toll Free: (888) 825-8135
Phone: (218) 266-3333
Fax:(218) 266-3383
Email: loonsong@arvig.net
Web: www.bbhost.com/loonsongbnb

Camping

Bagley
Long Lake Park & Campground
213 Main Ave N
Phone: (218) 657-2275
Web: www.longlakepark.com

Park Rapids
Camp Itasca
#19 Lake Itasca
Phone: (218) 266-3990
Email: campitasca@msn.com
Web: www.campitasca.com

Freedom Ridge ATV Resort
10694 State Hwy 200
Toll Free: (877) 266-4295
Phone: (218) 266-3938
Email: freedomridge@wcta.net
Web: www.freedomridgeatvresort.com

Itasca State Park
36750 Main Park Dr
Phone: (218) 266-2100
Email: itasca.park@dnr.state.mn.us
Web: www.stayatmnparks.com

Wilderness Bay Resort & Campground
36701 Wilderness Bay Dr
Phone: (218) 732-5608
Email: vacation@wildernessbay.com
Web: www.wildernessbay.com

Bike Rental

Itasca

Itasca Sports Rental
   Phone: (218) 266-2150
   Email: info@itascasports.com
   Web: www.itascasports.com

Festivals and Events

Itasca State Park

July

Butterfly Hike
   At Itasca State Park, a local butterfly en-
   thusiast shows an intro video, then leads
   the group out on a one to two mile hike
   looking for butterflies. Call for date.
   Phone: (218) 266-2100
   Web: www.dnr.state.mn.us

September

Ozawindib Walk
   At Itasca State Park, this public fund-
   raising event named after an Ojibwa
   guide and interpreter, get a t-shirt if
   you walk the one to two mile distance.
   Call for date.
   Phone: (218) 266-2100
   Web: www.dnr.state.mn.us

Lake George

July

Blueberry Festival
   Enjoy a carnival, pie sale, pig roast and
   the Blueberry Ball. Call for date.
   Phone: (218) 266-2915

Itasca State Park

August

Pioneer Farmer's Show
   See grain threshing, lumber sawing,
   shingle making and more the way it was
   done in the old days. Take a ride in a
   horse-drawn covered wagon or model
   railroad made large enough to carry passengers. Check out the world's largest
   display of hot-air engines. Call for date.
   Phone: (218) 657-2233
   Web: pioneerfarmers.wordpress.com

Park Rapids

September

Headwaters 100 Bike Ride
   Follow a well-marked route through the
   lakes area on Wilderness Drive in Itasca
   State Park and the Heartland Trail. The
   ride starts and ends in Park Rapids.
   Fourth Weekend.
   Toll Free: (800) 247-0054
   Phone: (218) 732-4111
   Web: www.parkrapidscvb.com

Alternate Activities

Itasca State Park

Swimming
   A sand beach is located on the North
   Arm of Lake Itasca.
   Phone: (218) 266-2100
   Web: www.dnr.state.mn.us/state_parks/
      itasca/index.html

Boat Rental
   Find motorboat, pontoon, paddleboat,
   kayak and canoe rental located across
   from park headquarters. Excursion
   boats are located below Douglas
   Lodge on Lake Itasca.
   Phone: (218) 266-2100
   Web: www.dnr.state.mn.us/state_parks/
      itasca/index.html

Mississippi Headwaters

Explore the source of the mighty Mississippi River at Itasca State Park. The Mississippi is the third longest river in the world.
Phone: (218) 266-2100
Web: www.dnr.state.mn.us/state_parks/
itasca/index.html

Lake Itasca Tours

Travel part of explorer Schoolcraft's route during a ten mile narrated cruise aboard the Chester Charles. Get a comprehensive overview of the history, wildlife, points of interest and services of Itasca State Park on a naturalist-narrated boat tour to the Headwaters of the Mississippi River.
Phone: (218) 732-5318
Web: www.dnr.state.mn.us/state_parks/
itasca/index.html

Restaurants

Itasca State Park
Mary Gibbs Mississippi Headwaters Restaurant
Phone: (218) 266-2100

Douglas Lodge
Phone: (218) 266-2100

Park Rapids
LaPasta Italian Eatery
Phone: (218) 732-0275
Web: www.dorset-lapasta.com/lapasta.htm

Y Steakhouse
Menu: Fine Dining
Phone: (218) 732-4565
Web: www.ysteakhouse.net

Northern Traditions Backdoor Deli
Phone: (218) 732-5361

Bella Café
Phone: (218) 732-7625

Alternate Activities cont'd

Itasca State Park
Naturalist-Led Programs and Walks
Join naturalist-led walks and programs at Itasca State Park. Get current schedules at the Visitor Center or DNR Calendar on the website.
Phone: (218) 266-2100
Web: www.dnr.state.mn.us/state_parks/
itasca/index.html

Hiking

Explore over thirty miles of hiking trails and the history of the oldest state park in MN. Maps are available at the Visitor Center.
Phone: (218) 266-2100
Web: www.dnr.state.mn.us/state_parks/
itasca/index.html

About The Trail

From Park Rapids to Akeley, the land is quite flat with a mix of pine woodlots, farmland and lakes. The trail passes through a glacial moraine between Akeley and Walker, and the surrounding land becomes hilly and pine forested. The Paul Bunyan Trail joins the Heartland east of Akeley, and the two run together through Walker and north along Highway 371. The Heartland continues to Cass Lake and joins with the MiGeZi Trail.

Trail Highlights

Heartland Park in Park Rapids is a better place to start than the official trailhead on the south side of Highway 34. See the city map. This is Paul Bunyan Country. The theme is overdone, but indulge in a little kitsch and sit in the hand of Paul. He's on one knee for you in the town of Akeley. Akeley also has the Woodtick Theater, featuring country music and other talent from within 100 miles of town. Dorset is a popular starting point on the trail. This little town, barely a wide spot in the road, has Mexican food, Italian food, antique stores, etc.

About The Roads

The two routes between Park Rapids and Nevis feature medium-sized rolling hills and a mosaic of lakes, woods and farmland. Watch and listen for loons on the lakes and check out the moneyed homes along the eastern edge of Fish Hook Lake.

Road Highlights

Highways 12 and 6 between Akeley and Hackensack offer a connector between the Heartland and Paul Bunyan Trails. These are good roads even if you just go out and come back. Highway 12 out of Walker is paved, low traffic and has a shoulder, then turns to gravel at the Hubbard County Line. It's a good ten mile out-and-back route. There is a gravel road connector between Highway 12 and the trail, but the surface is loose, recommended for wide-tired bikes only.

How To Get There

From the Twin Cities take Interstate 94 west to Sauk Centre. Go north on Highway 71 to Park Rapids. Take Highway 34 east from Park Rapids to get to access points along the trail. Park Rapids is about five hours from the Twin Cities. From Duluth take Highway 2 west to Cass Lake, the northernmost town on the trail. Take Highway 371 south to Walker and Highway 34 west from Walker for access points along the trail.

Vital Trail Information:

Trail Distance: 50

Trail Surface: Asphalt

Access Points: Park Rapids, Dorset, Nevis, Akeley, Walker, Cass Lake

Fees and Passes: None

Trail Website: www.dnr.state.mn.us

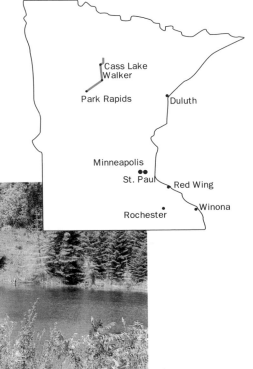

Park Rapids to Cass Lake: 50.1 miles

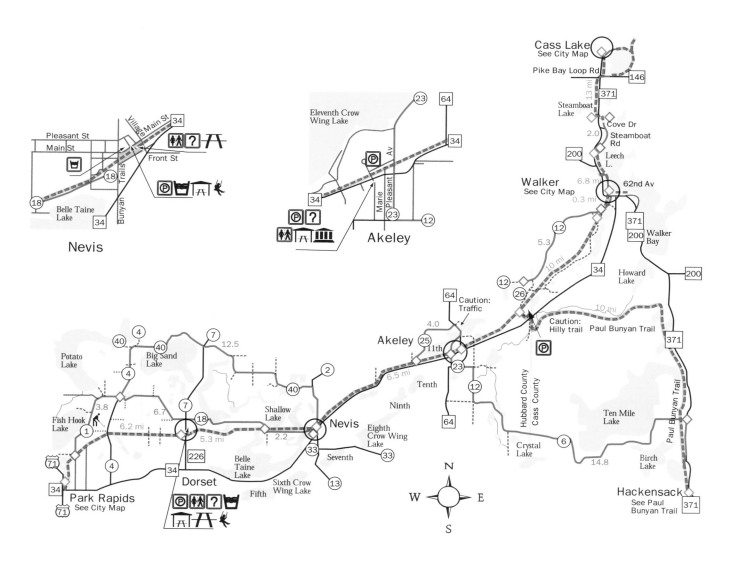

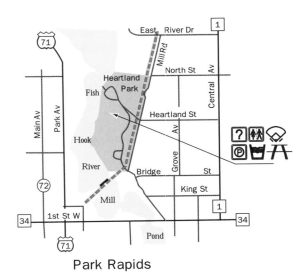

Park Rapids

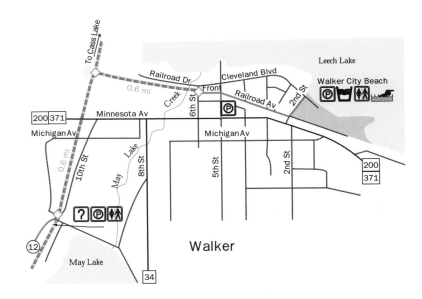

Walker

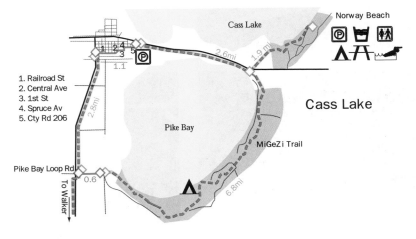

1. Railroad St
2. Central Ave
3. 1st St
4. Spruce Av
5. Cty Rd 206

Cass Lake

Tourist Information

Akeley Civic & Commerce Association
Phone: (218) 652-2600
Web: www.akeleyminnesota.com

DNR Trails and Waterways, Nevis
Phone: (218) 652-4054
Leech Lake Chamber of Commerce
Toll Free: (800) 833-1118
Phone: (218) 547-1313
Fax: (218) 547-1338
Email: walker@eot.com
Web: www.leech-lake.com

Nevis Civic & Commerce Association
Email: brad@nevismn.com
Web: www.nevismn.com

Park Rapids Area Chamber of Commerce
Toll Free: (800) 247-0054
Phone: (218) 732-4111
Fax: (218) 732-4112
Email: chamber@parkrapids.com
Web: www.parkrapids.com

Lodging

Motels/Resorts

Akeley
Crow Wing Crest Lodge
11th Crow Wing Lake
31159 County Rd 23
Toll Free: (800) 279-2754
Phone: (218) 652-3111
Web: www.crowwing.com

Nevis
Nevis Welcome Inn Motel & RV Park
117 Highway 34
P.O. Box 44
Phone: (218) 652-3600
Email: mdslakotah@unitelc.com

Paradise Cove Resort
21428 County 80
Toll Free: (800) 765-2682
Phone: (218) 732-3779
Email: view@visitparadisecove.com
Web: www.visitparadisecove.com

Pine Beach Resort
25082 State 34
Phone: (218) 652-3985
Web: www.pine-beach.com

Park Rapids
King's Cottages Resort/Motel
608 Park Ave N
Phone: (218) 732-4526
Email: kingscottages@unitelc.com
Web: www.kingscottages.org

Riverside Point
700 Park Ave N
Toll Free: (800) 733-9711
Phone: (218) 732-9711
Web: www.riversidepointresort.com

Walker
City Dock Cottages
5th and Leech Lake
Phone: (218) 547-1662

Bed and Breakfast

Nevis
The Park Street Inn
106 Park St
Toll Free: (800) 797-1778
Phone: (218) 652-4500
Email: psi@unitelc.com
Web: www.parkstreetinn.com

Lodging cont'd

Bed and Breakfast

Park Rapids
Dickson Viking Hus B&B
202 E 4th St
Toll Free: (888) 899-7292
Phone: (218) 732-8089
Web: www.parkrapids.com/dickson

Heartland Trail B&B
Rt #3, Box 39
Phone: (218) 732-3252
Email: corbidpj@aol.com
Web: www.heartlandbb.com

Red Bridge Inn B&B
118 N Washington
Toll Free: (888) 733-7241
Phone: (218) 237-7337
Email: redbridgeinn1@arvig.net
Web: www.redbridgeinn.com

Camping

Lake Itasca
Itasca State Park Campground
36750 Main Park Dr
Toll Free: (866) 857-2757
Phone: (218) 266-2100
Email: www.itasca.park@dnr.state.mn.us

Park Rapids
Mantrap Lake State Forest Campground
Off County Rd 104
Phone: (218) 266-2100
Email: itasca.park@dnr.state.mn.us

Walker
Shores of Leech Lake Campground & Marina
6166 Morriss Point NW
Phone: (218) 547-1819
Email: loomis@shoresofleechlake.com
Web: www.shoresofleechlake.com

Bike Rental

Dorset
Heartland Trail B&B
Phone: (218) 732-3252
Email: corbidpj@aol.com
Web: www.heartlandbb.com

Park Rapids
Northern Cycle
Phone: (218) 732-5971

Bike Repair

Park Rapids
Northern Cycle
501 E 1st St
Phone: (218) 732-5971

Festivals and Events

Akeley
June
Paul Bunyan Days
Attend the teen dance on Friday night and adult dance on Saturday night. Take in a fish fry, treasure hunt, pie social, cake walk, kiddy parade and grand parade on Sunday afternoon. Arts, crafts and food booths line the street. Fourth Weekend.
Phone: (218) 652-2600
Web: www.akeleymn.com

Dorset
August
Taste of Dorset
Stroll down the Boardwalk to sample a variety of foods from local Restaurantss. Dorset boasts the reputation of having the most Restaurantss per capita in the USA. First Weekend.
Toll Free: (800) 247-0054
Phone: (218) 732-4111

Nevis
August
Northwoods Triathalon
The quarter mile swim begins and ends at the city beach located on Lake Belle Taine. Bike fourteen miles on paved roads through scenic countryside, and run 5K on the Heartland Trail. Call for date.
Toll Free: (800) 247-0054
Phone: (218) 732-4111
Web: www.nevis.k12.mn.us/nevis/triathlon.html

Park Rapids
July
4th of July Celebration
Firecracker Foot Race. Fireworks at city beach. First Weekend.
Toll Free: (800) 247-0054
Phone: (218) 732-4111
Web: www.parkrapids.com

Festivals and Events cont'd

Park Rapids
July

Hubbard County Shell Prairie Fair
Grandstand shows, demo derby, exhibitors, food vendors, midway, 4-H exhibits. Second Weekend.
Toll Free: (800) 247-0054
Phone: (218) 732-4111
Web: www.parkrapids.com

Summertime Arts and Crafts Festival
Exhibitors, music, food vendors.
Call for dates.
Toll Free: (800) 247-0054
Phone: (218) 732-4111
Web: www.parkrapids.com

August

Antique Tractor Show
Threshing, tractor and horse plowing, shingle making, steam engines, square dance, parade, horse and wagon rides.
Call for dates.
Toll Free: (800) 247-0054
Phone: (218) 732-4111
Web: www.parkrapids.com

September

Fall Fishing Classic
Compete for an $8,000 purse.
First Saturday.
Toll Free: (800) 247-0054
Phone: (218) 732-4111
Web: www.parkrapids.com

Headwaters 100 Bike Ride
Highway 71 plus part of the Heartland Trail. Loops through Itasca State Park.
Fourth Weekend.
Toll Free: (800) 247-0054
Phone: (218) 732-4111
Web: www.parkrapids.com

Walker
July

4th of July
Enjoy a parade, fireworks, food, music, children's games, volleyball, horseshoes and sumo wrestling. First Weekend.
Toll Free: (800) 833-1118
Phone: (218) 547-1313

July

Moondance Jammin Country Fest
At the Moondance Fairgrounds listen in on jam sessions and big name and regional performances. Call for dates.
Toll Free: (877) 666-6526
Phone: (218) 836-2598
Web: www.jammincountry.com

Yikes! Bikes!
Ride eighteen, forty and sixty mile routes using the Heartland and MI-GI-ZI Trails. Third Saturday.
Toll Free: (800) 833-1118
Phone: (218) 547-1313
Web: www.lakesareahabitat org/yikesbikes

August

Cajun Fest
At the Moondance Fairgrounds, check out Cajun style food, parades, dancing and music from Louisiana.
Call for dates.
Toll Free: (877) 544-4879
Web: www.northernlightscasino.com

Festivals and Events cont'd

Walker

September

Annual Ethnic Fest

In downtown Walker, join the celebration of ethnic diversity featuring food vendors, craft demos, entertainment and storytelling. Second Weekend.
Toll Free: (800) 833-1118
Phone: (218) 547-1313
Web: www.leech-lake.com

September

Walker North Country Marathon

10K run/walk, two person team marathon. Third Weekend.
Toll Free: (800) 833-1118
Phone: (218) 547-1313
Web: www.walkernorthcountrymarathon.com

Alternate Activities

Tamarac National Wildlife Refuge

Explore 43,000 acres of sanctuary and breeding ground for migrating birds and other wildlife. The visitor center has hiking trails and a picnic area.
Phone: (218) 847-2641
Web: midwest.fws.gov/Tamarac

Akeley

WoodTick Musical Theatre

Relax at this summer musical theater featuring talent from a 100 mile radius. See website for details.
Toll Free: (800) 644-6892
Phone: (218) 652-4200
Web: www.woodticktheater.com

Paul Bunyan Museum

Located on Main Street behind the statue of Paul Bunyan, the museum contains collection of pictures and artifacts portraying early Akeley history

when the state's largest sawmill was operating.
Phone: (218) 652-4618
Web: www.akeleymn.com

Cass Lake

Chippewa National Forest

Drive the Woodtick Trail, hike the Shingobee Hills or canoe the Boy River.
Phone: (218) 335-8600
Web: www.fs.fed.us/r9/forests/chippewa

La Porte

Forestedge Winery

Taste small-batch organic wines made from blueberry, chokecherry, cranberry, plum, raspberry and rhubarb.
Phone: (218) 224-3535
Web: www.forestedgewinery.com

Park Rapids

Itasca State Park

Visit the source of the Mississippi River, camp, bike, hike and canoe. View stands of old-growth pine over 200 years old. See Itasca Bike Trail.
Phone: (218) 266-2100
Web: www.dnr.state.mn.us/state_parks/itasca

Walker

Shopping, Shopping and More Shopping

Downtown Walker.
Toll Free: (800) 833-1118
Web: www.leech-lake.com

Cass County Museum

Library, archival files, photos, newspapers, also houses Indian Art Museum. See website for hours.
Phone: (218) 547-7251
Web: www.casscountymuseum.org

Restaurants

Akeley

Brauhaus German Restaurants
28234 State Hwy 34
Phone: (218) 652-2478

Dorset

Dorset Café
20456 State 226
Menu: Family Dining
Phone: (218) 732-4072

LaPasta Italian Eatery
Phone: (218) 732-0275
Web: www.dorset-lapasta.com/lapasta.htm

Woodstock North Gifts
Phone: (218) 732-8457

Dorset House
Menu: Homemade Classics
Phone: (218) 732-5556

Companeros
Menu: Mexican
Phone: (218) 732-7624

Park Rapids

Y-Steak House
Menu: Fine Dining
Phone: (218) 732-4565
Web: www.ysteakhouse.net

Walker

The Wharf
Phone: (218) 547-3777

Walker Bay Coffee Co
Phone: (218) 547-1183

Village Square Ice Cream Parlor
Phone: (218) 547-1456
Web: www.villagesquarewalker.com

Zona Rosa
103 5th N
Phone: (218) 547-3558

About The Trail

This former Burlington Northern Rail line is ideal for biking or in-line skating. The trail more or less follows Highway 371 from Backus/Brainerd to Hackensack, then dips and rolls through the Chippewa National Forest before connecting with the Heartland Trail. Most of the small towns along the trail have parks, trailside facilities, and a lake or swimming area. Views include cattail marshes, cedar swamps, small lakes and mixed farmland/woodlot. The stretches near Highway 371 are generally wooded opposite the highway and open towards the highway.

Trail Highlights

From Hackensack to the Chippewa National Forest is flat, then the trail gets very hilly and winds around many sweeping turns. Inexperienced riders and skaters should use caution when entering this segment of the trail. Merrifield to Nisswa: A seven mile blend of farm fields, woodlots and wetlands, the trail has an open feel to it, yet not barren. From Backus to north of Hackensack, the trail passes through fifteen remote miles of cattail marshes and cedar swamp with occasional upland woods. From the south begin your ride at Lion's Park in Merrifield. It has excellent restrooms, sheltered picnic area and children's play area. Check out the swimming area behind the dam at the Pine River Day Use Park. Relax or swim at the city park in Backus.

About The Roads

Roads near the northern end are mostly gravel or heavily traveled. There are more paved lake roads between Baxter and Nisswa, but expect traffic on weekends and holidays.

Road Highlights

Highways 17 and 1 offer a good alternate to the trail between Pequot Lakes and Pine River. See the Heartland Trail for a great connector between Hackensack on this trail and Akeley on the Heartland Trail.

How To Get There

Brainerd is 130 miles northwest of the Twin Cities and 113 miles southwest of Duluth. Follow Highway 210 west about two miles from Brainerd to Highway 371. See city map for trail access at Baxter. All other trail towns, except Merrifield, are along Highway 371. To start at Merrifield take Highway 25 north about seven miles from Brainerd.

Vital Trail Information:

Trail Distance: 58

Trail Surface: Asphalt

Access Points: Baxter, Merrifield, Nisswa, Pequot Lakes, Jenkins, Pine River, Backus, Hackensack, Highway 34

Fees and Passes: None

Trail Website:
www.paulbunyantrail.com

Baxter to Pequot Lakes: 23 miles

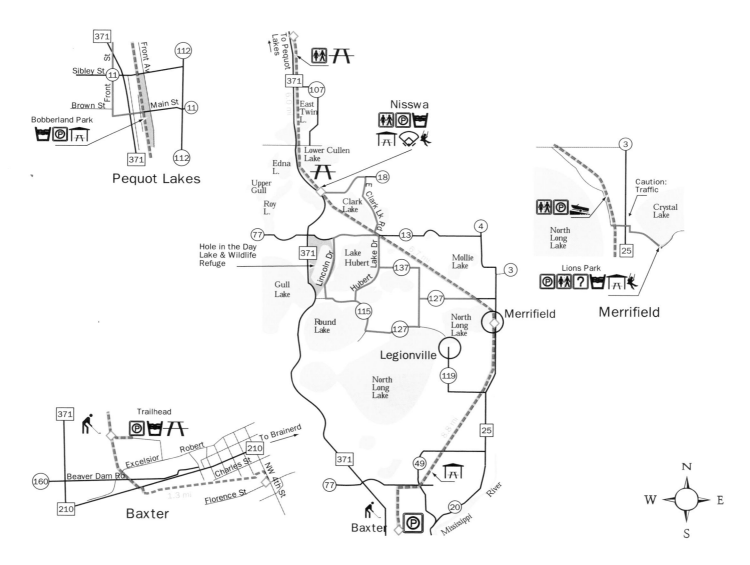

Pequot Lakes

Nisswa

Merrifield

Merrifield

Legionville

Baxter

Baxter

Pequot Lakes to Hackensack: 26 miles

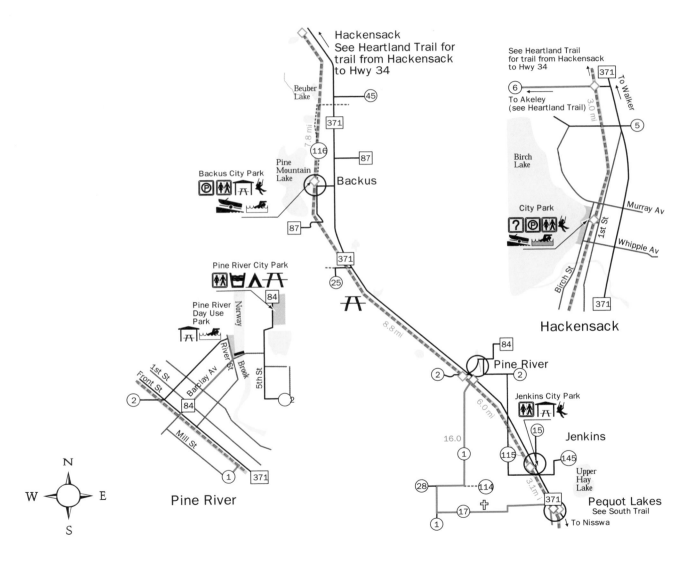

Hackensack
See Heartland Trail for
trail from Hackensack
to Hwy 34

Beuber Lake

45

371

116

87

Pine Mountain Lake

Backus City Park

Backus

87

371

25

Pine River City Park

84

Pine River Day Use Park

Norway

River St

Brook

5th St

1st St

Barclay Av

Front St

2

84

Mill St

1

371

Pine River

8.8 mi

84

Pine River

2

2

Jenkins City Park

6.0 mi

16.0

1

15

Jenkins

115

145

3.1 mi

Upper Hay Lake

28

114

371

Pequot Lakes
See South Trail

1

17

To Nisswa

See Heartland Trail
for trail from Hackensack
to Hwy 34

371

To Walker

6

To Akeley
(see Heartland Trail)

3.0 mi

5

Birch Lake

City Park

Murray Av

1st St

Whipple Av

Birch St

371

Hackensack

N
W · E
S

Tourist Information

Backus City Hall
Phone: (218) 947-3221
Email: clerk@uslink.net
Web: www.backusmn.com

Brainerd Lakes Area Chamber of Commerce
Toll Free: (800) 450-2838
Phone: (218) 829-2838
Email: info@explorebrainerdlakes.com
Web: www.explorebrainerdlakes.com

Cass County Information Web Site
Web: www.co.cass.mn.us

DNR Trails and Waterways, Brainerd
Phone: (218) 828-2557
Web: www.dnr.state.mn.us

Hackensack Chamber of Commerce
Toll Free: (800) 279-6932
Phone: (218) 675-6135
Email: chamber@hackensackchamber.com
Web: www.hackensackchamber.com

Nisswa Chamber of Commerce
Toll Free: (800) 950-9610
Phone: (218) 963-2620
Fax: (218) 963-1420
Email: requests@nisswa.com
Web: www.nisswa.com

Pequot Lakes Tourist Information Bureau
Toll Free: (800) 950-0291
Phone: (218) 568-8911
Web: www.pequotlakes.com
Pine River Information Center
Toll Free: (800) 728-6926
Phone: (218) 587-4000
Email: prcofc@uslink.net
Web: www.pinerivermn.com

Lodging

Motels/Resorts

Backus

Bayside Cabins
206 Rosalind Ave W
Toll Free: (800) 840-3344
Phone: (218) 947-3344
Fax: (218) 947-4144
Email: bayside@uslink.net
Web: www.baysidecabins.com

Mountain View Resort
590 Wood St
Phone: (218) 947-3233
Email: info@mtnviewresort.com
Web: www.mtnviewresort.com

Hackensack

Birch Haven Resort
P.O. Box 243
Phone: (218) 675-6151
Fax: (218) 675-5779
Email: bhresort@uslink.net
Web: www.birchhavenmn.com

Happiness Resort on Ten Mile Lake
4609 Happiness Lane NW
Phone: (218) 675-6574
Email: info@happinessresort.com
Web: happinessresort.com

Hyde-A-Way Bay Resort
3489 Ford Dr NW
Toll Free: (800) 309-5253
Phone: (218) 675-6683
Email: info@hydeawaybay.com
Web: www.hydeawaybay.com

Shady Shores Resort
5445 Lower Ten Mile Lake Rd
Phone: (218) 675-6540
Email: shadyshores@tds.net
Web: www.shadyshoresresorthackensack.com

Merrifield

Train Bell Resort
21489 Train Bell Rd
Toll Free: (800) 252-2102
Phone: (218) 829-4941
Web: www.trainbellresort.com

Nisswa

Good Ol' Days Family Resort
P.O. Box 358
Toll Free: (800) 227-4501
Phone: (218) 963-2478
Email: info@goodoldaysresort.com
Web: www.goodoldaysresort.com

Pequot Lakes

AmericInn Lodge & Suites
Hwy 371 N & County Rd 16
P.O. Box 610
Toll Free: (888) 568-8400
Phone: (218) 568-8400
Email: info@upnorthlodge.com
Web: www.upnorthlodge.com

Bed and Breakfast

Brainerd

Whiteley Creek Homestead
12349 Whiteley Creek Trail
Phone: (218) 829-0654
Email: whiteleycrk@aol.com
Web: www.whiteleycreek.com

Camping

Backus

Lindsey Lake Campground
3781 State Hwy 87 NW
Phone: (218) 947-4728

Brainerd

Crow Wing State Park Campground
3124 State Park Rd
Phone: (218) 825-3075
Web: www.dnr.state.mn.us

Lodging cont'd

Motels/Resorts

Brainerd
Rock Lake State Forest Campground
3124 State Park Rd
Phone: (218) 825-3075

Hackensack
Quietwoods Campground & Resort
4755 Alder Ln NW
Phone: (218) 675-6240
Email: quietwoodsresort@hotmail.com

Pequot Lakes
Tall Timbers Campground
3823 County Rd 17
Phone: (218) 568-4041

Pine River
River View RV Park
3040 16th Ave SW
Phone: (218) 587-4112
Email: riverviewrv@tds.net

Bike Rental

Backus
Bayside Cabins and Bike Rental
206 Rosalind Ave W
Toll Free: (800) 840-3344
Phone: (218) 947-3344
Email: bayside@uslink.net
Web: www.baysidecabins.com

Brainerd
Easy Rider Bicycle & Sport Shop
415 Washington St
Phone: (218) 829-5516
Email: easyride@integra.net
Web: www.easyridersbikes.com

Trailblazer Bikes
Phone: (218) 829-8542

Hackensack
Mike's
Phone: (218) 675-6976

Merrifield
Train Bell Resort
N Long Lake
Toll Free: (800) 252-2102
Phone: (218) 829-4941
Web: www.trainbellresort.com

Nisswa
Trailblazer Bikes
P.O. Box 844
Phone: (218) 963-0699

Pequot Lakes
Bunyan Bike Shuttle and Rental
4655 Pow Wow Point Rd
Phone: (218) 568-8422

Bike Repair

Brainerd
Easy Riders Bicycle and Sport Shop
415 Washington St
Phone: (218) 829-5516
Email: easyride@integra.net
Web: easyridersbikes.com

Trailblazer Bikes
24 Washington St
Phone: (218) 829-8542

Hackensack
Mike's
Phone: (218) 675-6976

Nisswa
Trailblazer Bikes
P.O. Box 844
Phone: (218) 963-0699

Bike Shuttle

Brainerd
Easy Riders Bicycle and Sport Shop
415 Washington Street
Phone: (218) 829-5516
Email: easyride@integra.net
Web: easyridersbikes.com

Pequot Lakes
Bunyan Bike Shuttle and Rental
4655 Pow Wow Point Rd
Phone: (218) 568-8422

Festivals and Events

Backus
May
Annual Smelt Fry
Get your fill at the Backus Fire Hall.
First Weekend.
Phone: (218) 947-3221

Annual Yard Sale
This event is sponsored by the Lions
Club. Memorial Day Weekend.
Phone: (218) 947-3221

Old Timer's Weekend
Stop by this three day event featuring
old time music, horseshoe tournament,
ice cream bars and Sloppy Joe's.
Memorial Day Weekend.
Phone: (218) 947-3221

August
Annual Cornfest
Check out the corn feed, parade,
games, music and talent show (kids and
adult divisions). Second Saturday.
Phone: (218) 947-3221

Festivals and Events cont'd

Brainerd

June

Crow Wing Encampment
The event features a fur trade era encampment with crafts, a shooting demonstration, leather and bead working at Crow Wing State Park following a ten mile canoe trip from Kiwanis Park. Call for dates.
Phone: (218) 825-3075

July

4th of July Celebration
Festivities spread out over several days.
Toll Free: (800) 450-2838
Phone: (218) 829-5278

Art in the Park
See juried artists, entertainment, food and a car show in Gregory Park.
Toll Free: (800) 450-2838
Phone: (218) 829-5278

Hackensack

All Summer

Flea Market
Parking lot of Sacred Heart Church. Second Wednesdays of summer months.
Phone: (218) 675-6135

Kids Fishing Contest
Kids can fish at the city pier from 11:00am to 1:00pm every Tuesday from mid-June to August.
Toll Free: (800) 279-6932
Phone: (218) 675-6135

June

Sweetheart Canoe Derby
See canoe races, food vendors and a craft fair. Third Weekend.
Toll Free: (800) 279-6932
Phone: (218) 675-6135

July

Sweetheart Days
Enjoy the antique car show, parade, horseshoe tourney, carnival and street dance. Festivities are preceded by performances of "Ballad of Lucette," a light operetta at the Community Building. Call for dates.
Toll Free: (800) 279-6932
Phone: (218) 675-6135

Volunteer Fire Dept. Fundraiser BBQ & Dance
Third Weekend.
Toll Free: (800) 279-6932
Phone: (218) 675-6135

August

Northwoods Arts Festival
Regional and local artists gather at the Community and Senior Center. Call for date.
Toll Free: (800) 279-6932
Phone: (218) 675-6135

Nisswa

All Summer

Turtle Races
Watch all the action behind the Chamber of Commerce at 2:00pm every Wednesday afternoon, mid-June through August.
Toll Free: (800) 950-9610
Phone: (218) 963-2620

July

Freedom Day Parade
Celebrate the Fourth of July with a loon calling contest, water wars, food court and parade. No fireworks.
Toll Free: (800) 950-9610
Phone: (218) 963-2620

Garden Club Show
See the flower show that also features a bake sale, plant sale, demo classes and refreshments. Fourth Weekend.
Toll Free: (800) 950-9610
Phone: (218) 963-2620

Majestic Pines Arts Festival
The juried art show also has food concessions. Third Weekend.
Toll Free: (800) 950-9610
Phone: (218) 963-2620

August

Crazy Days
It's a community celebration downtown, including sales, food and a weightlifting competition.
Toll Free: (800) 950-9610
Phone: (218) 963-2620

Festivals and Events cont'd

Pequot Lakes
July
Bean Hole Days
One hundred fifty gallons of Pequot Lakes baked beans are cooked overnight in the ground and served between 12:00pm and 2:00pm. See arts and crafts and the Bobberland Wayside Trail Park. Wednesday following the 4th of July.
Toll Free: (800) 950-0291
Phone: (218) 568-8911
Web: www.pequotlakes.com

July 4th Celebration
Fireworks fly on the night of the 3rd, and the celebration continues through Bean Hole Days. On the 4th see the parade, baby race, liar's contest, bed races, pie eating contest, haystack, greased pole, foot races and food vendors. 4th of July.
Toll Free: (800) 950-0291
Phone: (218) 568-8911
Web: www.pequotlakes.com

September
Pequot Lakes Arts and Crafts Fair
Come for the fair and Taste of Pequot. The event features regional arts and crafts and local food vendors trailside. Third Weekend.
Toll Free: (800) 950-0291
Phone: (218) 568-8911
Web: www.pequotlakes.com

Pine River
All Summer
Duck Races
Decoys only! Race at the Pine River Dam at 1:00pm every Friday from late June to mid-August.
Toll Free: (800) 728-6926
Phone: (218) 587-4000
Web: www.pinerivermn.com

June
Pine River Art Show
Enjoy exhibits, sales, demonstrations and snacks.
Toll Free: (800) 728-6926
Phone: (218) 587-4000

Summerfest
See craft and sidewalk sales, band and gospel music, a parade, golf, softball and horseshoe tournaments, a fly-in breakfast at the airport, the Legion steak fry and firemen's street dance. Fourth Weekend.
Toll Free: (800) 728-6926
Phone: (218) 587-4000

July
Cass County Fair
Times vary, but the fair usually falls on the third weekend in July.
Toll Free: (800) 728-6926
Phone: (218) 587-4000
Web: www.pinerivermn.com

September
Quilt Show
Explore various exhibits, food and music at Pine River churches. Call for festival date.
Toll Free: (800) 728-6926
Phone: (218) 587-2369

Alternate Activities

Brainerd
Vacation Land Family Fun Park
Stay busy with bumper boats, batting cages, NASCAR simulators, Go-Karts, a rock climbing wall and mini golf.
Phone: (218) 454-4386
Web: vacationlandpark.com

This Old Farm Antique Museum
Browse thousands of antiques, including cars, tractors, steam engines, a sawmill, blacksmith shop, shingle mill, log house, one room school house, old time saloon and sweet shop.
Phone: (218) 764-2524
Web: www.thisoldfarm.net

Alternate Activities cont'd

Brainerd

Paul Bunyan Land
Spend some time on rides, attractions, arcades, and miniature golf.
Phone: (218) 764-2524
Web: www.thisoldfarm.net

Northland Arboretum
Go for the hiking trails, picnic area and learning center.
Phone: (218) 829-8770
Web: arb.brainerd.com

Crow Wing County Historical Society
Learn about local logging, railroad and mining history in the old county jail/ sheriff's residence. Call for hours.
Phone: (218) 829-3268
Web: www.rootsweb com/~mncwcghs/hs

Crow Wing State Park
Learn about local logging, railroad and mining history in the old county jail/ sheriff's residence. Call for hours.
Phone: (218) 825-3075
Web: www.dnr.state.mn.us/state_parks/crow_wing

Cass County

Pillsbury State Forest
Come for the camping, swimming, fishing, picnicking and one mile nature trail.
Phone: (218) 825-3075

Crosby

Croft Mine Historical Park
Take a narrated ride into the simulated depths of a mine. Find an entrance to local bike trails at the end of the parking lot.
Phone: (218) 546-5466

Hackensack

Deep Portage Conservation Reserve
See the environmental learning center, nature trails and interpretive center between Longville and Hackensack.
Phone: (218) 682-2325
Web: www.deep-portage.org

Merrifield

River Treat
Spend time canoeing to primitive camp grounds. There are shuttle services for canoe trips from two hours to seven days long. Bring your own or rent.
Phone: (218) 765-3172

Nisswa

Nisswa Family Fun Center
Try the water slides, hot tubs, mini golf, climbing wall, snack stand, children's recreation area and heated wading pool.
Phone: (218) 963-3545
Web: nisswafamilyfun.com

Pequot Lakes

Bump and Putt Family Fun
Enjoy bumper boats, mini golf, water wars, basketball, and the battery powered four-wheeler track for kids.
Phone: (218) 568-8833

Pine River

Canoe the Pine River
Shuttle service available at Doty's RV Park and Pardner's Resort.
Toll Free: (800) 728-6926
Phone: (218) 587-4000
Web: www.pinerivermn.com

Restaurants

Backus

Willard's Saloon & Eatery
121 Front St
Phone: (218) 947-3832

Salty Dog Saloon & Eatery
3380 State Hwy 87
Phone: (218) 947-4446

Hackensack

River House Restaurants & Lounge
222 Hwy 371
Phone: (218) 675-6200

Jenkins

Jenkins VFW Post 3839
3341 Veterans St
Phone: (218) 568-8664

Nisswa

Grand View Lodge
Toll Free: (866) 801-2951
Phone: (218) 963-2234
Web: www.grandviewlodge.com

Pequot Lakes

Pestello's
Hwy 371
Phone: (218) 568-9950

A-Pine Family Restaurants
33039 Old 371
Phone: (218) 568-8353

Pine River

Al's Bakery
215 Barclay
Phone: (218) 587-2545

Red Pine Supper Club and Lounge
2789 Hwy 371
Phone: (218) 587-3818

Cottage Café
300 Barclay Ave
Phone: (218) 587-2588

About The Trail

The trail from Carlton to Duluth has some exceptionally beautiful and historic areas. Smooth enough for in-line skaters, the trail passes over a steep gorge of the St. Louis River, runs along a diversion canal for the hydro-electric plant and winds through impressive rock cuts. Hinckley, the southern terminus, is best known for the Hinckley Fire Storm of September 1, 1894. The trail follows the escape route that carried residents from town to Skunk Lake, an eighteen inch deep water hole where passengers buried themselves in mud and water to escape the intense heat of the fire. For additional information about the fire storm, stop at the Hinckley Fire Museum in downtown.

Trail Highlights

Start in Carlton and pull over a short distance later at one of the bump-out observation platforms on the bridge overlooking the St. Louis River's fast-flowing waters and rocky outcrops. Further east, the trail passes a diversion canal for the hydro-electric plant, touches the northern edge of Jay Cooke State Park, passes through impressive rock cuts and offers a view of Duluth Harbor, then drops down to water level. The eastern edge is a short distance from the Lake Superior Zoo, a favorite stopping point for kids and adults alike. If you have time, try the Alex Laveau Memorial Trail from Carlton to Wrenshall, a pretty little trail with rock cuts, creeks and Jay Cooke State Park all in less than three miles.

About The Roads

The roads near the southern half of the trail are nearly as flat as the trail. Traffic is moderate around Sandstone, less as you get farther north. Highway 61 runs parallel to the trail from Hinckley to Carlton. The northern roads are much more interesting. See trail maps for details.

Road Highlights

Branch out from Wrenshall for quiet, rolling hills and a scenic loop around Chub Lake. Highway 210 through Jay Cooke is very pretty, very hilly and sometimes busy with park traffic. Sandstone's attractive business district has a pleasant feel with its village park, seventy-five-year-old brick front buildings and natural landscape plantings in front of the Evangelical Free Church. The loop around Sturgeon Lake hugs the shoreline for a couple of miles, then heads out into the country before coming back to town. A short out-and-back on Highway 46 will give the best lake views. A combination of roads with paved shoulders connects with a trail through Moose Lake State Park near Moose Lake.

How To Get There

Carlton is east of Interstate 35 on Highway 210 about fiftenn miles from Duluth. To get to the West Duluth trailhead take Interstate 35 to Highway 23 in West Duluth and go southwest. See city map for details. Hinckley is about seventy miles south of Duluth on Interstate 35. Take Highway 48 west from Interstate 35 to Highway 61. See the trail map for details to the trailhead. All other points can be accessed by following Highway 61 north. See the trail map.

Vital Trail Information:

Trail Distance: 70

Trail Surface: Asphalt

Access Points: Hinckley, Finlayson, Willow River, Moose Lake, Carlton, Duluth

Fees and Passes: None

Trail Website: www.munger-trail.com

Hinckley to Sturgeon Lake: 27 miles

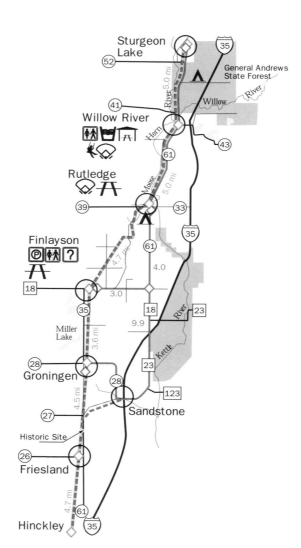

Sturgeon Lake

General Andrews State Forest

Willow River

Rutledge

Finlayson

Miller Lake

Groningen

Sandstone

Friesland

Hinckley

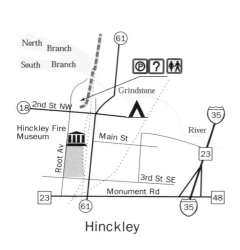

North Branch

South Branch

Grindstone

2nd St NW

Hinckley Fire Museum

Main St

River

Root Av

3rd St SE

Monument Rd

Hinckley

N
W · E
S

Sturgeon Lake to Carlton: 28 miles

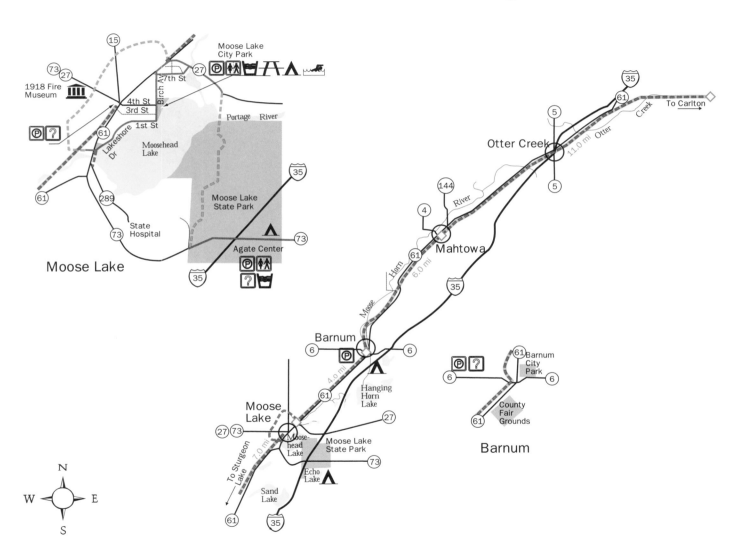

Moose Lake

15
73 27
27
1918 Fire Museum
4th St
3rd St
Birch Av
7th St
Moose Lake City Park
61
1st St
Lakeshore Dr
Portage River
Moosehead Lake
Moose Lake State Park
35
61
289
State Hospital
73
Agate Center
35
73

Mahtowa
144
River
4
61 6.0 mi
Mahtowa
35

Otter Creek
35
61
5
To Carlton
Otter Creek
Otter Creek
11.0 mi
5

Barnum
6
Barnum
6
Moose Horn
4.0 mi
61
Hanging Horn Lake
27

Moose Lake
27 73
Moose Lake
Moosehead Lake
7.0 mi
To Sturgeon Lake
61
Sand Lake
35
Echo Lake
Moose Lake State Park
73

Barnum
6
61
Barnum City Park
6
County Fair Grounds
61

N W E S

Carlton to Duluth: 15.5 miles

Alex Laveau Trail: 5.0 miles

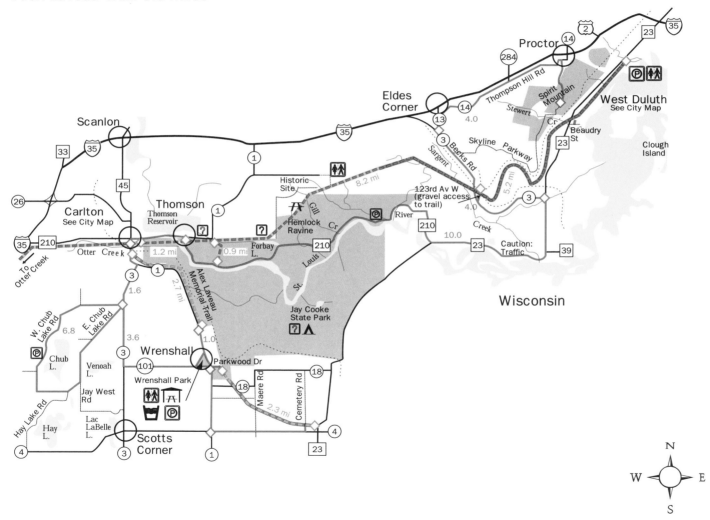

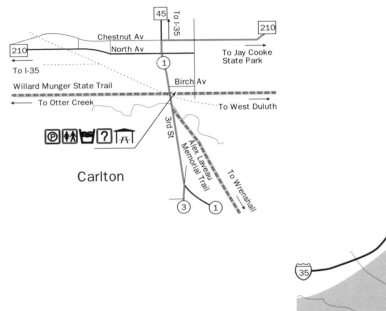

Carlton

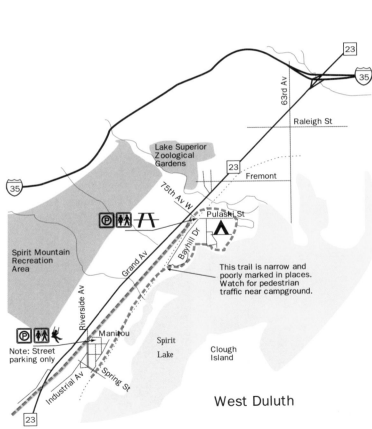

West Duluth

Tourist Information

Carlton Chamber of Commerce
Phone: (218) 384-3322
Web: www.cityofcarlton.com

Cloquet Chamber of Commerce
Toll Free: (800) 554-4350
Phone: (218) 879-1551
Web: www.cloquet.com

Duluth Convention and Visitors Bureau
Toll Free: (800) 438-5884
Phone: (218) 722-4011
Email: cvb@visitduluth.com
Web: www.visitduluth.com
Hinckley Convention and Visitors Bureau
Toll Free: (800) 952-4282
Phone: (320) 384-0126
Email: contactus@hinckleymn.com
Web: www.hinckleymn.com

Moose Lake Chamber of Commerce
Toll Free: (800) 635-3680
Phone: (218) 485-4145
Email: mlchamber@mooselake-mn.com
Web: www.mooselake-mn.com

Munger Trail Towns Association
Email: westwindstudios1@gmail.com
Web: www.munger-trail.com
Sandstone Chamber of Commerce
Phone: (320) 245-2271
Web: www.sandstonechamber.com

Lodging

Motels/Resorts

Barnum
Northwoods Motel & Cottages
3716 Main St
Toll Free: (800) 228-6951
Phone: (218) 389-6951
Email: info@northwoods-motel.com
Web: www.northwoods-motel.com

Carlton
AmericInn Motel
Hwy 210 & I-35
Toll Free: (800) 396-5007
Phone: (218) 384-3535
Fax: (218) 384-3870
Email: carlton.mn@americinn.com
Web: www.americinn.com

Royal Pines Motel
Hwy 210 & I-35
Toll Free: (800) 788-9622
Phone: (218) 384-4242

Duluth
AmericInn Motel & Suites
185 Hwy 2
Toll Free: (800) 396-5007
Phone: (218) 624-1026
Fax: (218) 624-2818
Email: duluth.mn@americinn.com
Web: www.americinn.com

Duluth Spirit Mountain Red Roof Inn
9315 Westgate Blvd
Toll Free: (800) 777-8530
Phone: (218) 628-3691
Email: info@duluthredroofinn.com
Web: www.duluthredroofinn.com

Finlayson
Banning Junction North Country Inn
60671 Hwy 23, I-35 Exit 195
Phone: (320) 245-5284
Email: northcountryinn2006@hotmail.com
Web: www.banningjunction.com

Hinckley
Days Inn
104 Grindstone Court/I-35
P.O. Box 460
Toll Free: (800) 329-7466
Phone: (320) 384-7751
Email: daysinnhinckley@legacyhospitalityinc.com
Web: www.daysinn.com

Moose Lake
AmericInn Lodge & Suites
400 Park Place Dr
Toll Free: (800) 396-5007
Phone: (218) 485-8885
Fax: (218) 485-5750
Email: mooselake.mn@americinn.com
Web: www.americinn.com

Lodging cont'd

Bed and Breakfast

Duluth

A.G. Thomson House
2617 E 3rd St
Toll Free: (877) 807-8077
Phone: (218) 724-3464
Email: info@thomsonhouse.biz
Web: www.thomsonhouse.biz

The Firelight Inn
2211 E 3rd St
Toll Free: (888) 724-0273
Phone: (218) 724-0272
Email: info@firelightinn.com
Web: www.firelightinn.com

The Historic Cotton Mansion
2309 E 1st St
Toll Free: (800) 228-1997
Phone: (218) 724-6405
Web: www.cottonmansion.com

Hinckley

Dakota Lodge B&B
40497 State Hwy 48
Phone: (320) 384-6052
Email: stay@dakotalodge.com
Web: www.dakotalodge.com

Woodland Trails
40361 Grace Lake Rd
Phone: (320) 655-3901
Email: John@WoodlandTrails.net
Web: www.woodlandtrails.net

Camping

Carlton

Jay Cook State Park Campground
780 Hwy 210 E
Toll Free: (888) 646-6367
Phone: (218) 384-4610
Web: www.dnr.state.mn.us

Moose Lake

Gafvert State Forest Campground
4252 County Rd #137
Phone: (218) 485-5420

Moose Lake City Campground
P.O. Box 870
Phone: (218) 485-4761

Moose Lake State Park Campground
4252 County Rd 137
Toll Free: (888) 646-6367
Phone: (218) 485-5420

Red Fox Campground & RV Park
I-35 & Hwy 73
P.O. Box 925
Phone: (218) 485-0341

Sandstone

Banning State Park
I-35, Exit #195
P.O. Box 643
Phone: (320) 245-2668

Sturgeon Lake

Timberline Campground & RV Park
9152 Timberline Rd
Phone: (218) 372-3272
Email: b@timberlineRVpark.com
Web: www.timberlinervpark.com

Bike Rental

Duluth

Willard Munger Inn
7408 Grand Ave
Toll Free: (800) 982-2453
Phone: (218) 624-4814
Email: munger@mungerinn.com
Web: www.mungerinn.com

Bike Repair

Duluth

Boreal Bicycle Works
631 E 8th St
Phone: (218) 722-9291

Ski Hut
1032 E 4th St
Phone: (218) 624-5889
Web: www.theskihut.com

Stewart's Bikes and Sports
1502 E Superior St
Phone: (218) 724-5101
Email: stewarts.duluth@clearwire.net
Web: www.stewartsbikesandsports.com

Twin Ports Cyclery
2914 W 3rd St
Phone: (218) 624-4008

Sandstone

True Value
Phone: (320) 245-2325

Festivals and Events

Barnum
August
Carlton County Fair
Take in exhibits, displays, a talent show, horse races, a demolition derby, games and rides. Check website for dates.
Phone: (218) 389-6737
Web: www.carltoncountyfair.com

Duluth
May
Memorial Day Parade
The parade runs along Grand Avenue in West Duluth.
Toll Free: (800) 438-5884
Phone: (218) 722-4011

June
Grandma's Marathon
A classic among marathons, it runs from Two Harbors to Duluth. Third Saturday.
Phone: (218) 727-0947
Web: www.grandmasmarathon.com

MS 150 Bike Tour
Join this three day event that travels from Duluth to Anoka. See Hinckley.
Toll Free: (800) 582-5296
Phone: (612) 335-7900
Web: bikemnm.nationalmssociety.org

Park Point Art Fair
See fine arts and crafts exhibitions by regional artists and artisans in the recreation area at Park Point. Call for date.
Toll Free: (800) 438-5884
Phone: (218) 428-1916

July
Fourth Fest
Celebrate with food, arts and crafts, nationally known music groups and fireworks in Bayfront Festival Park.
Toll Free: (800) 438-5884
Phone: (218) 722-4011

Festivals and Events cont'd

Duluth

August

Bayfront Blues Festival
Blues and jazz bands play all weekend in open air concerts. Enjoy food vendors and the beer garden at Bayfront Festival Park. Second Weekend.
Toll Free: (800) 438-5884
Phone: (715) 394-6831
Web: www.bayfrontblues.com

Festival of Cultures
Join Duluth's annual celebration of ethnic heritage at Bayfront Festival Park. First Weekend.
Toll Free: (800) 438-5884
Phone: (218) 722-4011
Web: www.duluthfestivalofcultures.com

Finlayson

July

July 4th Celebration
It's a party with a street dance, parade, coronation, fireworks, music, games and a boat parade. July 3rd and 4th.
Phone: (320) 233-6472

Hinckley

June

Annual Grand Celebration Powwow
Hundreds of dancers, singers, and drummers from throughout the Western Hemisphere compete for cash prizes at the Powwow Grounds adjacent to Grand Casino Hinckley. Third Weekend.
Toll Free: (800) 472-6321
Phone: (320) 384-7777
Web: www.grandcasinosmn.com

MS 150 Bike Tour
Stay overnight in Hinckley at West Side Park, where you'll enjoy music, entertainment, food vendors and a city-wide garage sale Second Weekend.
Toll Free: (800) 582-5296
Phone: (612) 335-7900
Web: bikemnm.nationalmssociety.org

July

Corn and Clover Carnival
Watch the grand parade, kiddy parade, pageant, talent show and pedal tractor pull. The carnival also has food and entertainment, antique appraisals, midway rides and games. First weekend after the 4th.
Toll Free: (800) 996-4566
Phone: (320) 384-0126
Web: www.hinckleymn.com

Moose Lake

July

4th of July Carnival
Come for the pancake breakfast, kiddy races, parade, coronation and fireworks.
Toll Free: (800) 635-3680
Phone: (218) 485-4145
Web: www.mooselake-mn.com

Agate Days
Hunt for agates and quarters along Main Street at this gem and mineral show sponsored by the Carlton County Gem & Mineral Club. Second Weekend.
Toll Free: (800) 635-3680
Phone: (218) 485-4145
Web: www.mooselake-mn.com

August

Community Night on the Trail
Kids' games, music, trail run and luminaries are sponsored by Moose Lake Historical Society. Mid-week evening in mid-Aug. Call for exact date.
Toll Free: (800) 635-3680
Web: www.mooselake-mn.com

Sandstone

August

Quarry Days
This event features quarry tours, exhibits, parade, bingo, food stands, children's games and a street dance. Second Weekend.
Phone: (320) 245-2443
Web: www.sandstone.govoffice.com

Willow River

July

Willow River Days
See the coronation, parade, run, softball tournament, dances and food stands. Fourth Weekend.
Phone: (218) 372-3733

Alternate Activities

Carlton

Minnestalgia Winery
Outside McGregor, open for tastes and tours seven days a week.
Toll Free: (866) 768-2533
Phone: (218) 768-2533
Web: www.minnestalgia.com

Alternate Activities cont'd

Carlton

Finke's Berry Farm
Pick your own strawberries in July and blueberries in August.
Phone: (218) 384-4432
Web: www.finkesberryfarm.com

Jay Cooke State Park
Take part in camping, interpretive programs, bike and horse trails, or hike part of the Grand Portage of the St. Louis River.
Phone: (218) 384-4610
Web: www.dnr.state.mn.us

Superior White Water Raft Tours
Experience professionally guided raft tours on the St. Louis River. Minimum age: twelve.
Phone: (218) 384-4637
Web: www.minnesotawhitewater.com

Duluth

North Shore Scenic Railroad
Take a narrated ride on a vintage train. Excursions range from romantic to family fun.
Toll Free: (800) 423-1273
Phone: (218) 722-1273
Web: www.lsrm.org

Berry Pine Farms
Pick your own raspberries and strawberries. Jams and jellies for sale.
Phone: (218) 721-3250

Lake Superior Zoological Gardens
Home to more than twenty-five endangered and threatened species from around the world. Near West Duluth trailhead.
Phone: (218) 733-3777
Web: www.lszoo.org

Lake Superior Marine Museum Association
The museum features film shows, model ships and exhibits. Next to Aerial Lift Bridge.
Phone: (218) 727-2497
Web: www.lsmma.com

Glensheen

Tour the historic Congdon Mansion.
Toll Free: (888) 454-4536
Phone: (218) 726-8910
Web: www.d.umn.edu/glen

St. Louis County Heritage and Art Center
See four museums under one roof, including Lake Superior Railroad Museum, Duluth Children's Museum, St. Louis County Historical Society, Duluth Art Institute, Duluth Playhouse and Duluth Symphony.
Phone: (218) 727-8025
Web: www.duluthdepot.org

Moose Lake

Moose Lake City Beach
Attractions include swimming, a fishing pier and camping.
Phone: (218) 485-4761

Sandstone

Audubon Center of the North Woods
Stay at this residential environmental learning center and retreat on the shores of Grindstone Lake with a 535 acre sanctuary, hiking and learning environments.
Toll Free: (888) 404-7743
Phone: (320) 245-2648
Web: www.audubon-center.org

Banning State Park
Enjoy canoeing, hiking, kayaking, ice cave, quarry ruins and Wolf Creek Falls.
Phone: (320) 245-2668
Web: www.dnr.state.mn.us

Scanlon

River Inn
Summer launch site on St. Louis River for Superior White Water Rafting Tours.
Phone: (218) 384-4637
Web: www.minnesotawhitewater.com

Restaurants

Hinckley
Tobies Restaurants & Bakery
Phone: (320) 384-6174
Web: www.tobies.com

Moose Lake
Poor Gary's Pizza
Phone: (218) 485-8020

Art's Café
Menu: Home Style Cooking
Phone: (218) 485-4602

Blue Bear Café
Phone: (218) 485-8712

Sandstone
Banning Junction
Phone: (320) 245-9989
Web: www.banningjunction.com

Alternate Activities cont'd

Glensheen

Great Lakes Aquarium
You'll love this fresh water aquarium with over thirty interactive exhibits.
Phone: (218) 740-3474
Web: www.glaquarium.org

Hinckley

St. Croix State Park
The park offers camping, swimming, hiking, biking and fishing.
Phone: (320) 384-6591
Web: www.dnr.state.mn.us

Hinckley Fire Museum
Learn about the great fire of 1894 through artifacts, testimony and video. Two blocks from the trailhead.
Phone: (320) 384-7338
Web: www.seans.com/sunsetweb/hinckley

About The Trail

The trail runs through a unique part of Minnesota, where prairie and hardwood forest meet, and it reflects that variety in a scenic blend of lakes, prairie potholes, open farmland and wooded lots, with small towns at seven to ten mile intervals. This is a quiet trail with little highway noise. The pavement is new and smooth enough for in-line skates. The eastern end connects to the Lake Wobegon Trail.

Trail Highlights

Start in Alexandria, the heart of the woodlands and lakes area. Going west, you'll cross a number of channels and culverts connecting lakes. The channels are popular for swimming, boating and fishing. The farther you get east and west of Alexandria, the more open the land becomes. You'll see lots of prairie potholes; small shallow lakes with cattails and wetland grasses, but few trees. Stop in Dalton and wander the grounds of the Lake Regions Threshermen's Show. The old farm machinery and scale model railroad are worth seeing even if the festival isn't in full swing. Start at Delagoon Park just south of Fergus Falls. The park has complete facilities and is easy to find. Access from the park to the trail is via a hard packed gravel trail. OK for bicyclists but difficult for skaters.

About The Roads

The roads take advantage of the rolling terrain and give a nice perspective on the variety of land and its uses in the area. You'll see woodlots, farms, lakes and potholes, sometimes from high above, at other times from lake level. Traffic is low to moderate.

Road Highlights

The northern route from Fergus Falls to Garfield follows the very pretty Otter Tail County Scenic Byway. This is a roller coaster ride with non-stop climbs and dips, some long, but not exceptionally steep. The Lake Osakis route keeps the lake in view much of the way and stays primarily on quiet highways and residential roads. For a short out and back, take Lake Rd along the eastern shore. The road serves numerous lake cottages and small businesses. Inspiration Peak rises 400 ft above the surrounding area. Author Sinclair Lewis frequently visited the peak.

How To Get There

Alexandria is about fifty miles west of St. Cloud on Interstate 94. Take the Highway 29 exit and go north. See the city map of Alexandria for details to the trail. Fergus Falls is about fifty miles west of Alexandria and fifty-five east of Fargo/Moorhead on Interstate 94. Take the Highway 210 exit. See the city map of Fergus Falls for trailhead access.

Vital Trail Information:

Trail Distance: 63

Trail Surface: Asphalt

Access Points: Osakis, Nelson, Alexandria, Garfield, Ashby, Dalton, Fergus Falls

Fees and Passes: None

Trail Website:
www.CentralLakesTrail.com

Fergus Falls to Garfield: 36.3 miles

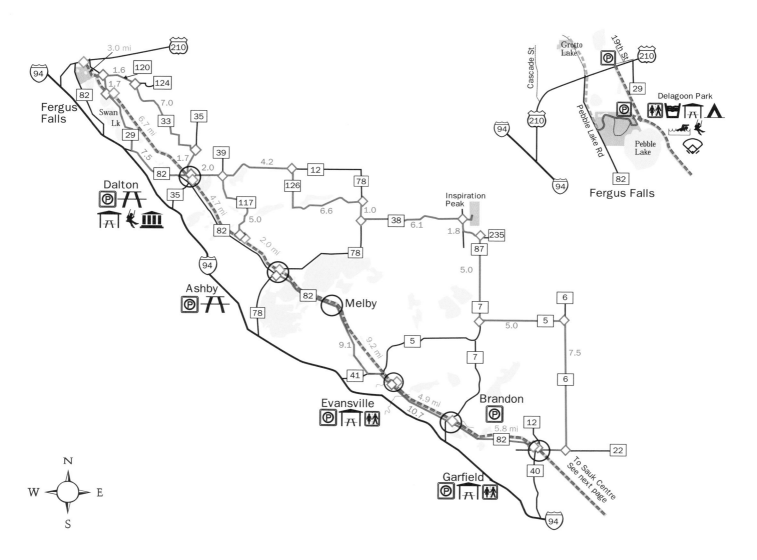

Garfield to Sauk Centre: 26.6 miles

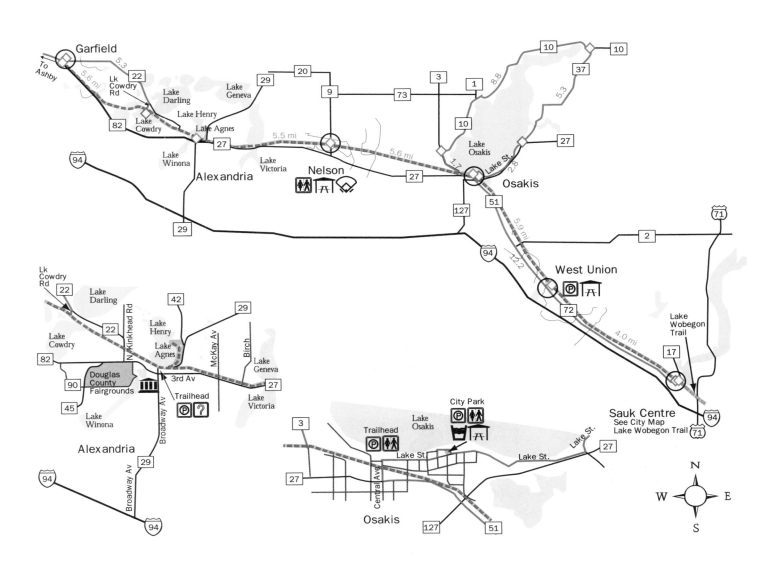

Tourist Information

Alexandria Lakes Area Chamber of Commerce
Toll Free: (800) 235-9441
Phone: (320) 763-3161
Email: alexrecr@rea-alp.com
Web: www.alexandriamn.org

Central LakesTrail
Toll Free: (800) 422-0785
Web: www.lakeosakismn.
com/central_lakes_trail/

Fergus Falls Area Chamber of Commerce
Phone: (218) 736-6951
Web: www.fergusfalls.com

Fergus Falls Convention & Visitors Bureau
Toll Free: (800) 726-8959
Phone: (218) 739-0125
Email: info@visitfergusfalls.com
Web: www.visitfergusfalls.com
Lake Osakis Resort Association
Toll Free: (800) 422-0785
Web: www.lakeosakismn.com

Lodging

Motels/Resorts

Alexandria
AmericInn
4520 Hwy 29 S
Toll Free: (800) 396-5007
Phone: (320) 763-6808
Email: alexandria.mn@americinn.com
Web: www.americinn.com

Broken Arrow Resort
3408 State Hwy 27 E
Toll Free: (800) 729-2202
Phone: (320) 763-4646
Email: mspinner@brokenarrowresort.com
Web: www.brokenarrowresort.com

Butch & Nev's Resort
1810 Geneva Rd
Phone: (320) 762-0898

Days Inn
4810 Hwy 29 S
Toll Free: (800) 329-7466
Phone: (320) 762-1171
Email: daysinnalex@yahoo.com
Web: www.daysinn.com

Geneva Beach Resort
105 Linden Ave
Toll Free: (877) 891-3200
Phone: (320) 763-3200
Email: info@genevabeachresort.com
Web: www.genevabeachresort.com

Holiday Inn
5637 State Hwy 29 S
Toll Free: (888) 465-4329
Phone: (320) 763-6577

L Motel & RV Park
910 State Hwy 27 W
Toll Free: (800) 733-1793
Phone: (320) 763-5121
Email: lmotel@charterinternet.com
Web: www.lmotel.com

Lazy Day Villa
250 Three Havens Dr NE
Toll Free: (888) 850-4569
Phone: (320) 846-1161

Lilac Lodge Resort
114 Lilac Ln
Toll Free: (877) 335-0263
Phone: (320) 763-4440

Lodging cont'd

Motels/Resorts

Alexandria

Shady Lawn Resort
1321 S Darling Dr NW
Phone: (320) 763-3559
Email: shadylawnresort@hotmail.com

Skyline Motel
605 30th Ave W
Toll Free: (800) 467-4096
Phone: (320) 763-3175
Email: info@skylinemotel-mn.com
Web: skylinemotel-mn.com

Sun Valley Resort & Campground
10045 State Hwy 27 W
Phone: (320) 886-5417
Fax: (320) 886-5217
Email: sunvaley@earthlink.net
Web: www.alexandriamn.com/sunvalley

Super 8 Motel
4620 Hwy 29 S
Toll Free: (800) 800-8000
Phone: (320) 763-6552
Web: www.super8.com

Vacationer's Inn
1327 W Lake Cowdry Rd NW
Phone: (320) 763-5011
Email: phish@rea-alp.com
Web: www.alexweb.net/vacationersinn

Val Halla Villa
1301 S Darling Dr NW
Phone: (320) 763-5869
Email: valhalla@rea-alp.com

Viking Trail Resort
2301 County Rd 22 NW
Phone: (320) 763-3602

Fergus Falls

Jewel Motel
1602 Pebble Lake Rd
Phone: (218) 739-5430

Swan Lake Resort
17463 County Hwy 29
Toll Free: (800) 697-4626
Phone: (218) 736-4626
Email: swanlk@prtel.com
Web: www.swanlkresort.com

Osakis

Idlewilde Resort
811 Lake St
Box 299B
Toll Free: (800) 648-1713
Phone: (320) 859-2135
Email: idlewild@midwestinfo.net
Web: www.idlewilde.com

Lakeland Motel
204 W Nokomis St
Phone: (320) 859-4466

Midway Beach Resort/Campground
1821 Lake St E
Toll Free: (800) 367-2547
Phone: (320) 859-4410
Email: info@midwaybeach.com
Web: www.midwaybeach.com

Bed and Breakfast

Alexandria

Cedar Rose Inn
422 7th Ave W
Toll Free: (888) 203-5333
Phone: (320) 762-8430
Web: www.cedarroseinn.com

Lake Le Homme Dieu B&B
441 S Le Homme Dieu Dr NE
Toll Free: (800) 943-5875
Phone: (320) 846-5875
Email: sjradj@rea-alp.com
Web: www.llbedandbreakfast.com

Lodging cont'd

Bed and Breakfast

Alexandria
Pillars Bed & Breakfast
1004 Elm St
Toll Free: (877) 815-2790
Phone: (320) 762-2700
Web: www.pillarsbandb.itgo.com

Ashby
Harvest Inn B & B
200 Melby Ave
Phone: (218) 747-2334
Email: info@harvestinn.net
Web: www.harvestinn.net

Fergus Falls
Bakketopp Hus Bed & Breakfast
20571 Hillcrest Rd
Toll Free: (800) 739-2915
Phone: (218) 739-2915
Email: ddn@prtel.com
Web: www.bbonline.com/
mn/bakketopp

Osakis
Just Like Grandma's B&B
113 W Main
P.O. Box 396
Phone: (320) 859-4504

Camping

Alexandria
L Motel & RV Park
910 State Hwy 27 W
Toll Free: (800) 733-1793
Phone: (320) 763-5121
Email: lmotel@charterinternet.com
Web: www.lmotel.com

Sun Valley Resort & Campground
10045 State Hwy 27 W
Phone: (320) 886-5417
Fax: (320) 886-5217
Email: sunvalley@earthlink.net
Web: www.alexandriamn.com/sunvalley

Lodging cont'd

Camping

Garfield
Oak Park Kampground
9561 County Rd 8 NW
Phone: (320) 834-2345
Email: oakpark@rea-alp.com

Osakis
Midway Beach Resort/Campground
1821 Lake St E
Toll Free: (800) 367-2547
Phone: (320) 859-4410
Email: info@midwaybeach.com
Web: www.midwaybeach.com

Bike Rental

Alexandria
The Bike & Fitness Company
Phone: (320) 762-8493
Email: info@bikeandfitnessco.com
Web: bikeandfitnessco.com

Fergus Falls
Rental Store
Phone: (218) 739-2294

Bike Repair

Alexandria
The Bike & Fitness Company
Phone: (320) 762-8493
Email: info@bikeandfitnessco.com
Web: bikeandfitnessco.com

Fergus Falls
Craig's Bicycle Repair
Phone: (218) 739-2754

Rental Store
Phone: (218) 739-2294

Festivals and Events

Alexandria
May
Awake the Lakes
Kick off summer featuring a street
dance, beer garden, carnival and
children's activities throughout town.
Memorial Day Weekend.
Toll Free: (800) 235-9441
Phone: (320) 763-3161
Web: www.awakethelakes.com

Chain of Lakes Sprint Triathlon
Swim 600 yards in an eight lane,
twenty-five yard pool. Bike thirteen miles
through the Alexandria area countryside along rolling hills. Run three miles
through a residential area and newly
paved trail. First Saturday.
Phone: (320) 529-0884
Web: www.pickleevents.com/colt

June
Vikingland Band Festival
The state's finest marching bands com-
pete in an annual parade. Last Sunday.
Toll Free: (800) 235-9441
Phone: (320) 763-3161
Web: www.marching.com/events/vbf

July
4th of July Fireworks
Celebrate with fireworks, food and
musical entertainment on the lakeside
lawn of Arrowwood Resort along Lake
Darling.
Toll Free: (866) 386-5263
Phone: (320) 762-1124
Web: www.arrowwoodresort.com

Festivals and Events cont'd

Alexandria

July

Art in the Park

City Park is transformed into a market-place of artisans, with crafters, musicians and artists from across the country. This event features traditional and modern arts and crafts, plus music, live entertainment and food. Call for dates.
Phone: (320) 762-8300
Web: www.alexandriaareaarts.org

August

Douglas County Fair

See 4-H exhibits, business exhibits, stock car racing, food vendors, entertainment and the midway. Call for dates.
Phone: (320) 834-4796
Web: www.mndouglascofair.com

September

Grape Stomp & Fall Festival

Tour Carlos Creek Winery's stables, apple orchard and maze. Shop from over 100 wine, food and craft booths. Enjoy crafts, games, food and live music as well as an "I Love Lucy" contest. Call for dates.
Phone: (320) 846-5443
Web: www.carloscreekwinery.com

Dalton

September

Lake Region Pioneer Threshing Show

Peruse historic farm machinery and a French locomotive from World Wars I and II. Watch threshing demonstrations, horse pulls, tractor pulls, sawing demos, homemaker demos, a parade and entertainment. First weekend after Labor Day.
Toll Free: (800) 726-8959
Phone: (218) 739-0125
Web: www.daltonmn.com/threshing.html

Fergus Falls

June

Lincoln Avenue Fine Arts Festival

Enjoy juried exhibitions, hands-on visual arts activities for children, folk music, writers' workshops and other performances. Contact the Center for the Arts. Second full weekend.
Phone: (218) 736-5453
Web: www.fergusarts.org

SummerFest

Come for the kids' activities, parade and arts and crafts sale in downtown Fergus Falls. Second full weekend.
Toll Free: (800) 726-8959
Phone: (218) 739-0125
Web: www.fergusfalls.com

July

West Otter Tail County Fair

Check out 4-H shows, karaoke, a demolition derby, carnival, games, tug-o-war and a watermelon feed. Third Weekend.
Phone: (218) 736-0272
Web: www.otcfair.com

Osakis

June

Osakis Festival

This festival at City Park boasts attractions such as a flea market, craft sale, food vendors, parades, pony rides, a petting zoo, sand pile, money hunt, music and a fire department water fight. Call for dates.
Toll Free: (866) 784-8941
Phone: (320) 859-3777
Web: lakeosakismn.com

July

4th of July Fireworks

At the Osakis Country Club golf course.
Toll Free: (866) 784-8941
Phone: (320) 859-3777
Web: lakeosakismn.com

Alternate Activities

Alexandria

Runestone Museum

Enjoy the stories of the Kensington Runestone, Norse history and many exhibits that demonstrate early pioneer and Native American life of the 1870s. Also see Fort Alexandria's authentic log buildings, country school house, agriculture museum, forty foot Viking Ship replica and a large rotating exhibit which changes annually.
Phone: (320) 763-3160
Web: www.runestonemuseum.org

Theatre L'Homme Dieu

Take in a show at this professional summer theatre. Performances Wednesday through Sunday, mid–June to mid-August.
Phone: (320) 846-3150
Web: www.tlhd.org

Casey's Amusement Park

Drive three great tracks: Naskarts, Indy karts and family and kiddy karts. Also enjoy bumper boats, mini-golf, batting cages and a picnic area. Take in a show at this professional summer theatre. Performances Wednesday through Sunday, mid–June to mid-August.
Phone: (320) 763-7576
Web: www.caseysamusementpark.com

Alternate Activities cont'd

Alexandria

Horseback Riding

Arrowwood Resort guided trail and pony rides.
Toll Free: (866) 386-5263
Phone: (320) 762-1124
Web: www.arrowwoodresort.com

Carlos

Lake Carlos State Park

Sculpted by ancient glaciers, Lake Carlos State Park contains a tamarack bog, marshes, woodland ponds and lakes. The park offers swimming, fishing, boating, camping, hiking and horseback riding.
Phone: (320) 852-7200
Web: www.dnr.state.mn.us

Fergus Falls

Prairie Wetlands Learning Center

This is the first residential environmental education center operated by the U.S. Fish and Wildlife Service. Its focus is on the understanding of prairies and wetlands and consists of 330 acres of native and restored prairie, twenty-eight wetlands and four miles of trails. The visitor center houses a 2,500 square foot exhibit area and the Bluestem Store.
Phone: (218) 736-0938
Web: midwest.fws.gov/pwlc/

A Center for the Arts

Watch theatrical and musical productions, summer children's theater and community orchestra shows.
Phone: (218) 736-5453
Web: www.fergusarts.org

Restaurants

Alexandria

Depot Express

Phone: (320) 763-7712

Country Kitchen

Phone: (320) 763-7128

The Pizza Ranch

Phone: (320) 762-4010
Web: www.pizzaranch.com

Doolittles American Grill

Phone: (320) 759-0885
Web: www.doolittlesRestaurantss.com

Ashby

Ruby's City Restaurants

Phone: (218) 747-2208

Fergus Falls

The Viking Café

Menu: Old Fashioned Food
Phone: (218) 736-6660

Jazzy Fox Bistro

Menu: Classic American
Phone: (218) 998-5299
Web: www.jazzyfoxbistro.com

Garfield

Jo Jo's Café

Phone: (320) 834-2071

Osakis

A.J.'s Restaurants

Menu: Home Cookin'
Phone: (320) 859-3663

Lake Osakis Pub & Grill

Menu: Classic American
Phone: (320) 859-3663
Web: www.lakeosakislodging.com

Tip Top Dairy Bar

Phone: (320) 859-2217

Just Like Grandma's

Phone: (320) 859-4504

About The Trail

Named for the mythical town of Lake Wobegon from Garrison Keillor's "A Prairie Home Campanion," the trail passes through five towns that could easily have been the model for Lake Wobegon. This is a land with deep roots in agriculture. St. Joseph, on the eastern side, has the most lakes and woods near the trail. The rest of the route is mostly flat and wide open so bring sunscreen. The trail comes right up to Interstate 94 between Albany and Freeport, where the noise from the freeway is quite noticeable. The trail has recently been connected with the Central Lakes Trail to create a continuous trail from St. Joseph to Fergus Falls. The Holdingford Spur is worth a trip by itself. It plunges deep into farm country, away from the noise and traffic of Interstate 94. The new addition north of Holdingford passes through wetlands, farm country and woodlots.

Trail Highlights

The fifteen mile stretch from Albany to St. Joseph is the most scenic part of the main trail, with a mix of woods, lakes and prairie. It is also some distance from the interstate and quiet. Holdingford to Highway 10 is very pleasant with a mix of farms, woodlots and wetlands. The churches along the trail are distinctive buildings with beautiful bell towers, and steeples. St. Mary's in Melrose is on the National Register of Historic Places, but be sure to see St. Paul's in Sauk Centre, Sacred Heart in Freeport, Seven Dolors in Albany and the Church of St. Benedict in Avon. Memoryville, near Melrose, is a unique theme park next to the trail.

About The Roads

Mostly paved, low traffic roads through rolling farmland. The terrain breaks up the endless fields of crops enough to keep the routes interesting. The best roads generally skirt a lakeshore or wind along low rises.

Road Highlights

Highway 173 south out of Melrose is a must-ride, even if you only ride to Highway 30, then turn around and ride back to town. It rises and dips as it follows a ridge with scenic views, trees and nice little twists and turns. Highway 154, north of Albany, is a rolling, twisting mix of woodlots and farm fields. Pelican Lake Road, 0.2 miles west of St. Anna, follows the eastern shoreline of Pelican Lake. Small lake cabins line the shore and farm fields butt up against the eastern edge of the road. Quaker Road., east of Albany, is an excellent alternative to the trail. It's best described as quietly beautiful, rather than dramatic. A long, low grassy wetland parallels the north side of the road for miles. Tower Road connects Quaker Road with the trail and is quite hilly and scenic. Traffic is low on both roads.

How To Get There

St. Joseph is about eight miles west of St. Cloud on Interstate 94. All trail towns are directly accessible from the interstate. Take Highway 9 north from Avon to Holdingford. Trail access from US Highway 10 north of Holdingford is poor and not recommended.

Vital Trail Information:

Trail Distance: 59

Trail Surface: Asphalt

Access Points: Sauk Centre, Melrose, Freeport, Albany, Avon, Holdingford, St. Joseph

Fees and Passes: None

Trail Website:
www.lakewobegontrails.com

Sauk Centre to Albany 21.4 miles

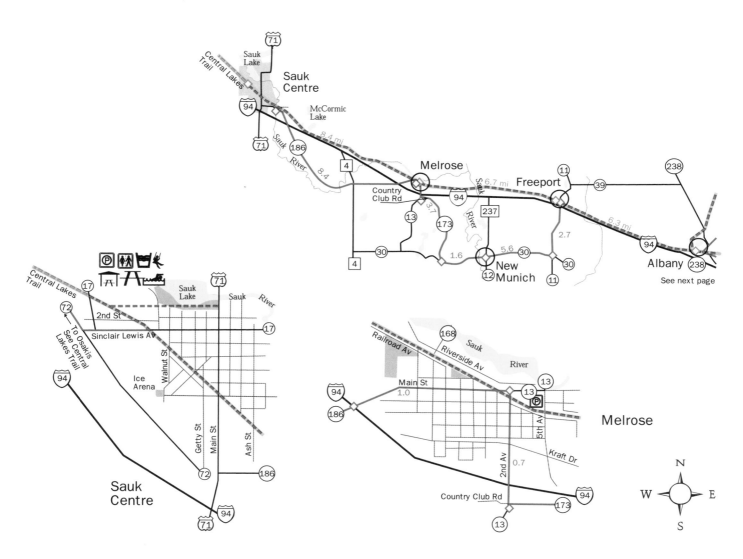

See next page

Albany to St.Joseph: 15 miles

Albany to Hwy 10: 22 miles

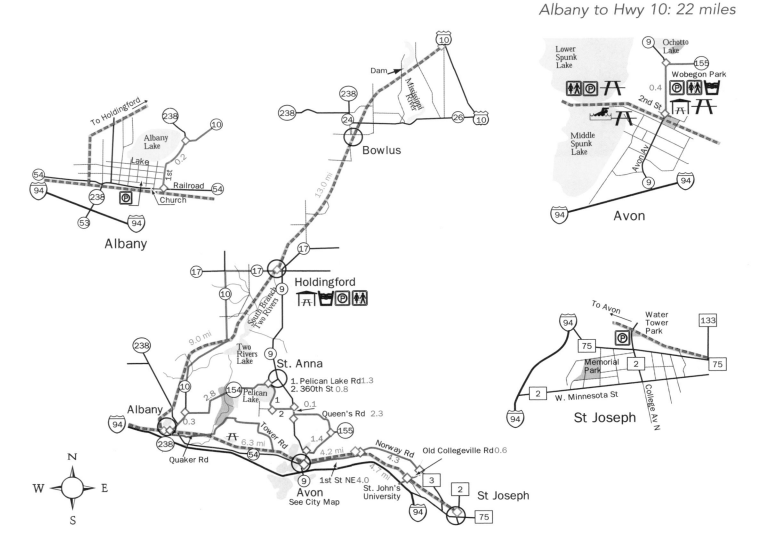

Lower Spunk Lake

Ochotto Lake

9

155

Wobegon Park

0.4

2nd St

Middle Spunk Lake

Avon Av

9

94

94

Avon

To Holdingford

238

10

Albany Lake

1st

Lake

0.2

Railroad

54

54

94

238

Church

94

53

Albany

10

238

238

24

Dam

Mississippi River

26

10

Bowlus

13.0 mi

17

17

17

9

Holdingford

10

South Branch Two Rivers

9.0 mi

238

Two Rivers Lake

9

St. Anna

1. Pelican Lake Rd 1.3
2. 360th St 0.8

10

154 Pelican Lake

1

0.1

2

Queen's Rd 2.3

2.8

Albany

94

0.3

1.4

155

Norway Rd

Old Collegeville Rd 0.6

238

6.3 mi

Tower Rd

4.2 mi

4.3

Quaker Rd

54

1st St NE 4.0

4.7 mi

St. John's University

3

94

Avon
See City Map

9

2

St Joseph

75

To Avon

Water Tower Park

94

75

133

Memorial Park

2

75

2

W. Minnesota St

College Av N

94

St Joseph

Tourist Information

Albany Area Chamber of Commerce
Phone: (320) 845-7777
Fax: (320) 845-2346
Email: albanycc@albanytel.com
Web: www.albanymnchamber.com

Avon Chamber of Commerce
Phone: (320) 249-1550
Email: avonmnchamber@hotmail.com
Web: www.avonmnchamber.com

Holdingford City Hall
Phone: (320) 746-2966
Web: www.holdingfordmn.us

Melrose Chamber of Commerce
Phone: (320) 256-7174
Email: chamber@meltel.net
Web: www.melrosemn.org

Sauk Centre Chamber of Commerce
Phone: (320) 352-5201
Fax: (320) 352-5202
Email: chamber@saukcentrechamber.com
Web: www.saukcentrechamber.com

Lodging

Motels/Resorts

Avon
AmericInn Motel
304 Blattner Dr
Toll Free: (800) 396-5007
Phone: (320) 356-2211
Fax: (320) 356-2211
Email: avon.mn@americinn.com

Sauk Centre
AmericInn Motel
1230 Timberlane Dr
Toll Free: (877) 352-1199
Phone: (320) 352-2800
Fax: (320) 352-2800
Email: manager@americinnsaukcentre.com
Web: www.americinnsaukcentre.com

Palmer House
500 Sinclair Lewis Ave
Toll Free: (866) 834-9100
Phone: (320) 351-9100
Fax: (320) 351-9104
Email: info@thepalmerhousehotel.com
Web: www.thepalmerhousehotel.com

Camping

Melrose
Birch Lake State Forest Campground
Charles Lindbergh State Park
P.O. Box 364
Phone: (320) 616-2525

Sauk River Park
206 N 5th Ave E
Phone: (320) 256-4278

Lodging cont'd

Camping

Monticello
Lake Maria State Park Campground
11411 Clementa Ave NW
Toll Free: (866) 857-2757
Phone: (763) 878-2325
Web: www.dnr.state.mn.us

Sauk Center
Saukinac Campgrounds
21914 Bay Loop
Phone: (320) 352-0037

Bike Rental

Waite Park
Granite City Cycle & Sports
Phone: (320) 251-7540
Email: info@granitecitycycle.com
Web: www.granitecitycycle.com

Bike Repair

St. Cloud
Fitzharris Ski and Sport
P.O. Box 2118
Phone: (320) 251-2844

Rod's Bike Shop
28 Lincoln Ave SE
Phone: (320) 259-1964

Waite Park
Granite City Cycle & Sports
2506 1st St S
Phone: (320) 251-7540
Email: info@granitecitycycle.com
Web: www.granitecitycycle.com

Festivals and Events

Albany
August
> **Heritage Day**
> Enjoy two parades, a firefighters' water fight, beer garden, food vendors, a mini carnival and fireworks. Check website for date. Saturday only.
> Phone: (320) 845-7777
> Web: www.albanymnchamber.com

September
> **Albany Pioneer Days**
> See the tractor-steamer parade, old fashioned arts and crafts, lumber sawing, flour milling, blacksmith shop, model railroad museum and flea market. Check website for dates.
> Phone: (320) 845-7410
> Web: www.albanymnchamber.com

Avon
June
> **Spunktacular Days**
> Get excited for the parade, waterski show, music, beer garden, carnival and 5K run. Third weekend.
> Phone: (320) 356-7922
> Web: www.avonmnchamber.com

Freeport
July
> **Parrish Festival**
> Check out the parade, music, dance, food vendors, beer garden and kids' games. Call for dates.
> Phone: (320) 836-2143

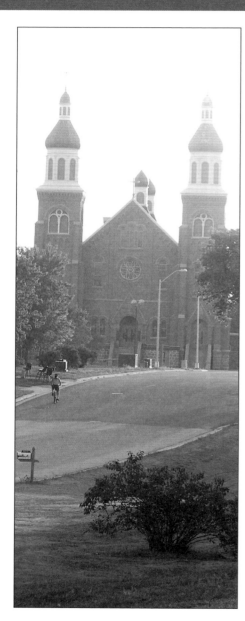

Festivals and Events cont'd

Melrose
July
Independence Day Celebration
Show your patriotism at the parade, carnival rides, food vendors and fireworks in Sauk River Park. Friday and Saturday before the 4th of July.
Phone: (320) 256-7174
Web: www.melrosemn.org

Sauk Centre
July
Sinclair Lewis Days
Shop at craft sales and enjoy the parade, pageant, dance, games and activities for kids. Check website for dates.
Phone: (320) 352-5201
Web: www.saukcentrechamber.com

St. Joseph
July
Tour of Saints Bike Ride
Start at the College of St. Benedict and wind through beautiful central Minnesota. Fifty mile or optional thirty-five mile route. See website for date.
Toll Free: (800) 651-8687
Phone: (320) 363-1311
Web: www.tourofsaints.com

Alternate Activities

Albany
North Park
Stop at the picnic area and playground.
Phone: (320) 845-4244
Web: www.ci.albany.mn.us

Avon
Swimming Beach
Cool off at the beach and observation tower across from the bike trail.
Phone: (320) 356-7922

Melrose
Riverside Park
Take a break at the picnic area and pavilion or stay the night at the campground. Public restrooms available.
Phone: (320) 256-4278

Jaycee Park
The park has a picnic area and playground and is close to the trail.
Phone: (320) 256-4278
Web: www.melrosemn.org

Birch Lake State Forest
Get out and experience camping, boating and hiking trails. The facility is managed by Charles Lindbergh State Park.
Phone: (320) 616-2525
Web: www.dnr.state.mn.us

Alternate Activities cont'd

Albany
Melrose Area Historical Society and Museum
See the large collection of antique memorabilia of the area. The museum is adjacent to the trail.
Phone: (320) 256-4996
Web: www.melrosemnhistory.com

Sauk Centre
Sauk Centre Area Historical Society
Stop at the Bryant Public Library to see the Nineteeth Century artifacts.
Phone: (320) 352-5201
Web: www.saukcentrechamber.com

Sinclair Lewis Museum & Boyhood Home
Across the street from Sinclair Lewis' birthplace, tour the 1880 story-and-a-half home furnished with period furnishings. Open Memorial Day to Labor Day.
Phone: (320) 352-5201
Web: www.saukcentrechamber.com

Restaurants

Albany
Hillcrest Family Restaurants
Phone: (320) 845-2168

Jimmy's Pizza
Phone: (320) 845-4632
Web: www.jimmyspizza.com

Avon
Joseph's
Phone: (320) 356-7880
Web: www.josephsfinedining.com

P.J.'s Supper Club
Phone: (320) 356-7349

Melrose
Rondezvous Grille
Phone: (320) 256-3225

Sauk Centre
River's Edge Dining
Phone: (320) 352-6505

Palmer House Restaurants
Toll Free: (866) 834-9100
Phone: (320) 351-9100
Web: www.thepalmerhousehotel.com

About The Trail

A little gem in the otherwise flat lands of western Minnesota, the trail is in the heart of a glacial moraine, the end point of a vast glacier that pushed south out of Canada. The trail runs flat, but because of the moraine, the sides of the trail slope down into ponds, cattail marshes, rolling hills and wooded pockets of land. The trail has recently been extended to Harwick with the promise of more extensions soon.

Trail Highlights

The most interesting section is from Nest Lake to a few miles north of Highway 40. As you get farther north, the trail leaves the moraine and rolls into flatter, more open lands with little shade and a nearby highway. The southern portion of the trail also moves into flatter land with large farm fields and fewer lakes, still quite attractive, but the northern section sets a pretty high standard by comparison. In-line skaters should stay north of Spicer to avoid gravel road crossings to the south.

About The Roads

Much of the road route follows the Glacial Ridge Trail, a locally designated scenic route that follows the rising and falling terrain of the terminal moraine. There are quite a few hills, some rather tall, but the climbs and descents are moderately steep at the worst. Traffic is low, scenery is high and the roads are in good condition. The round trip from the trail to Sibley State Park is scenic and quiet on well paved roads. You will climb through moraines toward the park and descend on the return.

Road Highlights

Higway 40 winds its way over a large climb in the first mile and a half east of the trail, then drops down to County Road 4 and Indian Beach Road along the eastern shore of Green Lake. Indian Beach Road is a cabin road. It passes small to mid-sized cabins and year 'round homes as it follows the eastern shore back to Spicer. The reward at the end of the loop is a city park with a beach and nearby Restaurantss and drinking establishments. You can also circle Green Lake by starting on the beachfront road in Spicer. A clockwise route keeps you on the lakeside of the road.

How To Get There

Willmar is 100 miles west of the Twin Cities on Highway 12. Turn right on County Road 9 just before Highway 71. County Road 9 becomes 3rd Street NE. Go 1.8 miles north until you cross the trail, turn left and go 0.1 miles to the Willmar Trailhead. The most attractive trailhead is on the north side of Spicer at the Nest Lake Public Water Access. To get to Spicer continue on Highway 12 to Highway 71, go north to the Highway 23 exit. Highway 23 runs into Spicer. Stay on Highway 23 to 73rd Street NE and follow the signs to the public water access. The official Spicer trailhead is one block west of the intersection of County Highway 10 and Highway 23 in Spicer. It's a parking lot. If you go one block east at County Highway 10, you can start at the very popular city beach. Backtrack on the sidewalk and cross at the light to get to the trail.

Vital Trail Information:

Trail Distance: 21

Trail Surface: Asphalt

Access Points: Willmar, Highway 26, Spicer, Nest Lake, New London

Fees and Passes: None

Trail Website: www.dnr.state.mn.us

Willmar to Harwick: 20.5 miles

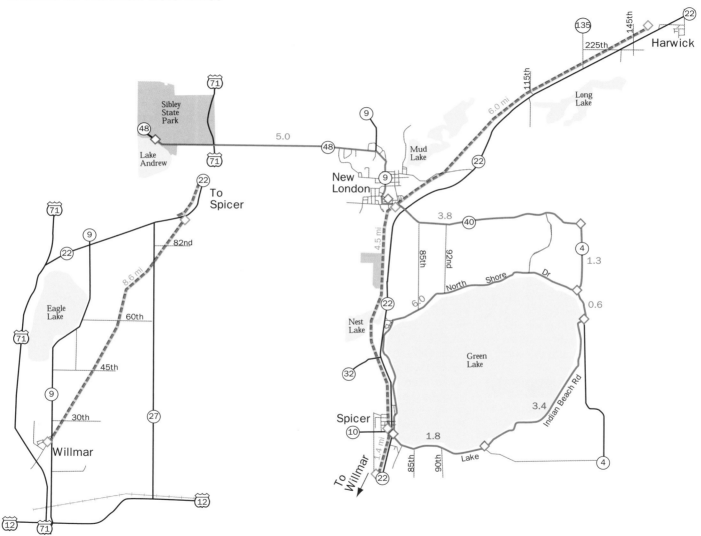

Tourist Information

City of Spicer
Phone: (320) 796-8066
Email: spicer@spicermn.com
Web: www.spicermn.com

New London Chamber of Commerce
Phone: (320) 354-7111
Email: chamber@newlondonmn.com
Web: www.newlondonmn.com/chamber.htm

Willmar Convention and Visitors Bureau
Toll Free: (800) 845-8747
Phone: (320) 235-3552
Email: info@seeyouinwillmar.com
Web: www.seeyouinwillmar.com

Willmar Lakes Area Chamber of Commerce
Phone: (320) 235-0300
Fax: (320) 231-1948
Email: chamber@willmarareachamber.com
Web: www.willmarareachamber.com

Lodging

Motels/Resorts

Spicer
Island View Resort on Nest Lake
5910 132nd Ave NE
Toll Free: (800) 421-9708
Phone: (320) 796-2775
Email: ivr@charterinternet.com
Web: www.islandviewresort-nestlake.com
Lakeview Motel
15150 Hwy 23 NE
Phone: (320) 796-2224
Email: lakeviewmotel@tds.net

Northern Inn Hotel & Suites
154 Lake Ave S
P.O. Box 660
Toll Free: (800) 941-0423
Phone: (320) 796-2091
Web: www.northerninn.com

Park Lane Resort
343 Lake Ave S
Phone: (320) 796-5540
Email: jdnelson11@charter.net
Web: www.parklaneresort.com

Willow Bay Resort
5280 132nd Ave NE
Toll Free: (877) 796-5517
Phone: (320) 796-5517
Email: tjohnson3281@charter.net
Web: www.willowbayresort.com

Ye Old Mill Inn Resort
7911 North Shore Dr
Phone: (320) 796-2212

Willmar
Lakeview Inn
1212 Business Highway 71 N
Toll Free: (800) 718-3424
Phone: (320) 235-3424
Email: info@LakeviewInnMn.com
Web: www.lakeviewinnmn.com

Viking Motel
616 Business Highway 71 N
Toll Free: (800) 835-0176
Phone: (320) 235-5211

Bed and Breakfast

Spicer
Green Lake Inn
152 Lake Ave N
Toll Free: (888) 660-3068
Phone: (320) 796-6523
Email: reservations@thegreenlakeinn.com
Web: www.thegreenlakeinn.com

Spicer Castle
11600 Indian Beach Rd
Toll Free: (800) 821-6675
Phone: (320) 796-5870
Email: spicercastle@spicercastle.com
Web: www.spicercastle.com

Lodging cont'd

Camping

New London
Sibley State Park
800 Sibley Park Rd NE
Phone: (320) 354-2055
Web: www.dnr.state.mn.us

Spicer
Island View Resort on Nest Lake
5910 132nd Ave NE
Toll Free: (800) 421-9708
Phone: (320) 796-2775
Email: ivr@charterinternet.com
Web: www.islandviewresort-nestlake.com

Kandiyohi County Park #5
12381 North Shore Dr
Phone: (320) 796-5564
Email: kandipark5@tds.net
Web: www.kandipark5.com

Stoddard
Glacial Lakes State Park
25022 County Rd 41
Phone: (320) 239-2860
Web: www.dnr.state.mn.us

Bike Rental

Spicer
Spicer Bike and Sports
P.O. BOX 116
Phone: (320) 796-6334
Email: spicerbike_sports@hotmail.com
Web: www.spicerbike-sports.com

Bike Repair

Spicer
Spicer Bike and Sports
P.O. Box 116
Phone: (320) 796-6334
Email: spicerbike_sports@hotmail.com
Web: www.spicerbike-sports.com

Willmar
Rick's Cycling and Sports Center
320 SW 3rd St
Phone: (320) 235-0202

Festivals and Events

New London
May
Historical Society Spring Festival
Learn how to make lefse and rosettes, hot dishes and other home cooked food. Hear bluegrass music. Memorial Day.
Phone: (320) 354-7111

July
New London Water Days
Take in the ski show, food booths, arts and crafts, trolley rides, games, dunking tank and fireworks. Third Weekend.
Phone: (320) 354-7111
Web: www.newlondonmn.com

August
New London Music Fest
Professional musicians perform and teach hands-on workshops. Call for exact weekend.
Phone: (320) 354-0044

Web: www.newlondonmusic.org
New London/New Brighton Antique Car Run
Watch the vintage auto parade, eat at the steak fry dinner at the Legion, and on Saturday drive from New London to New Brighton. Second Weekend.
Phone: (320) 354-7111

Festivals and Events cont'd

Spicer
July
July 4th Celebration
Enjoy a parade, flea market, carnival, helicopter rides, concerts, a street dance and fireworks. Call for dates.
Phone: (320) 796-8066
Web: www.spicermn.com

Willmar
June
Willmar Fests
Come for the parade, water show, firefighters' water fight, block party, coronation, food vendors, carnival and fireworks. Fourth Weekend.
Phone: (320) 979-2268
Web: www.willmarfests.com

August
Kandiyohi County Fair
Enjoy exhibits, food and entertainment. Second Weekend.
Phone: (320) 235-0886
Web: www.kandifair.com

September
Celebrate Art/Celebrate Coffee
Celebrate with original arts and crafts, sales, demos, music, children's arts activities and free gourmet coffee. Call for dates.
Phone: (320) 231-8560
Web: www.dennisbenson.com/cacc

Alternate Activities

New London
Kandiyohi County Park #7
The park has camping, a large swimming area, boat rentals, a store and Restaurants.
Phone: (320) 354-4453

Prairie Woods Environmental Learning Center
Come for weekend family programs and interpretive hiking trails.
Phone: (320) 354-5894
Web: www.prairiewoodselc.org

Shopping
Browse or buy antiques and arts and crafts.

Little Crow Players
Watch performances at the historic theater. Call for schedule.
Phone: (320) 354-7111

Sibley State Park
Activities include camping, an interpretive center, daily programs, swimming, biking and hiking trails, boat and canoe rentals, a volleyball area, horseshoe pits, "Mt. Tom" monument and an observation deck.
Phone: (320) 354-2055
Web: www.dnr.state.mn.us

Spicer
Saulsbury Swimming Beach
Get some sun at the volleyball and basketball courts, picnic area and boat access.
Phone: (320) 796-8066
Web: www.spicermn.com

Willmar
Robbin's Island
Spend a day at the park. Facilities include a swimming beach and biking and walking trails.
Phone: (320) 235-2232

Kandiyohi Historical Society
Visit the 1893 house, antique locomotive and a variety of exhibits.
Phone: (320) 235-1881
Web: www.kandimuseum.com

Restaurants

New London
McKale's
Phone: (320) 354-2007

Jimmy's Pizza
Phone: (320) 354-5683
Web: www.jimmyspizza.com

Hillcrest Restaurants & Truck Stop
Phone: (320) 354-4545

Agape Coffe House
Phone: (320) 354-7017

Riverside Café
Phone: (320) 354-2124

Spicer
Papa's Pizza Place
Phone: (320) 796-2040

Little Crow Country Club
Phone: (320) 354-1111

Green Lake Inn
Phone: (320) 796-6523
Web: www.thegreenlakeinn.com

Melvin's Restaurants
Phone: (320) 796-2195
Web: www.melvinsonthelake.com

O'Neils Bar
Phone: (320) 796-6524
Web: www.oneilsbar.com

Willmar
Willmar Blue Heron
Phone: (320) 235-4448
Web: www.willmarsblueheron.com

Jake's Pizza
Phone: (320) 235-1714

About The Trail

This is the oldest state trail. At only 6 feet wide, the trail is narrow enough to have a full canopy of leaves shading it through the summer. The surface has been re-graded recently. Light use and lack of towns along the trail give it a remarkably remote feeling considering it starts in the West Metro area. The trail has been ex-tended, but the best access point is still East Medicine Lake Beach Park.

Trail Highlights

The eastern end of the trail passes through remnants of the Big Woods and low density residential areas with large wooded lots. The woods continue as a buffer all the way to Watertown, but the land to the north and south opens into ru-ral farmland. Numerous lakes and cattail marshes line the entire length of the trail. An access trail at Crystal Lake Rd goes to Baker Park Reserve with its trail system and park facilities.

About The Roads

Generally low traffic and smooth sur-faced, the roads that parallel the trail of-fer a pleasant return route with medium rolling hills. Traffic is heavier near the parks on weekends and everywhere dur-ing weekday rush hour.

Road Highlights

Highway 26 is an ex-urban road with a mix of residential and farm land, low traffic, smooth surface and rolling hills. Roads in the Wayzata/Orono area pass through quiet residential streets with large houses and big lots. Wander off the beaten path for a look at some beautiful old estates. Baker Park Reserve offers a wide range of recreational facilities, including swim-ming and bike trails. Highway 19 to the Park Reserve is generally low traffic and wide, but can get crowded with vehicles going to the Park. For more route infor-mation on this area, pick up a copy of the Twin Cities Bike Map by Bikeverywhere.

How To Get There

East Medicine Lake Beach Park: Take Highway 169 to the 13th Ave./Plymouth Ave. Exit. Go north on Kilmer, a west frontage road to Highway 169, to 17th Ave. N. Turn left and go to the beach. Parker Lake and Vicksburg Lane access points get you started a little farther west. See the city map for details. Water-town: Take Highway 12 west to Delano, then take Highways 16/27 south. See trail map for details.

Vital Trail Information:

Trail Distance: 24

Trail Surface: Limestone

Access Points: Medicine Lake Beach, Parker's Lake, Vicksburg Lane, Stubb's Bay Park, Watertown

Fees and Passes: None

Trail Website: www.dnr.state.mn.us

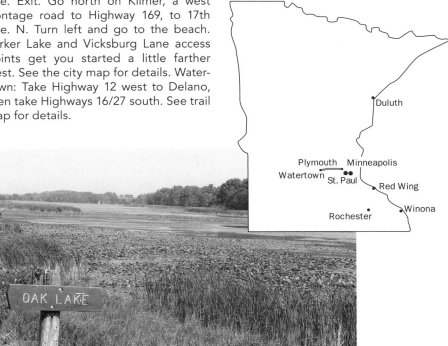

LUCE LINE TRAIL 🏹 Central Minnesota

Medicine Lake to Watertown: 24 miles

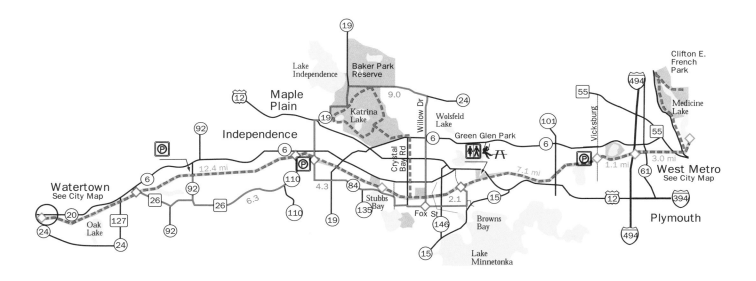

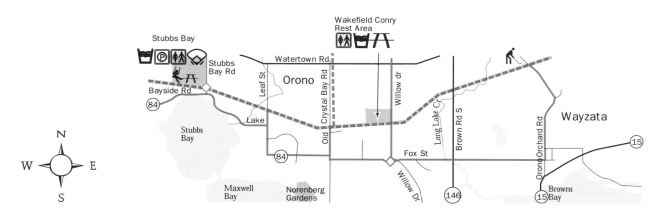

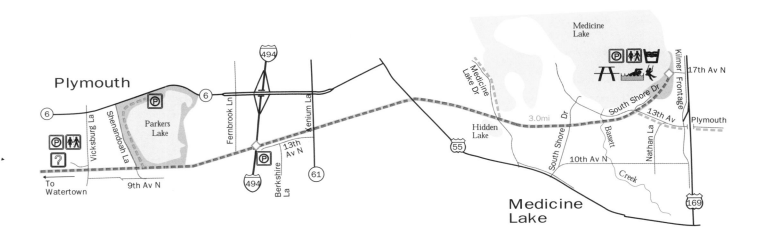

Plymouth

Vicksburg La
Shenandoah La
Parkers Lake
Fernbrook Ln
Xenium La
494
6
6
9th Av N
13th Av N
Berkshire La
494
61
To Watertown

Medicine Lake
Medicine Lake Dr
3.0mi
Hidden Lake
55
South Shore Dr
South Shore Dr
10th Av N
Creek
Bassett
Nathan La
13th Av
Kilmer Frontage
17th Av N
Plymouth
169

Medicine Lake

Watertown

10
27
Lewis Av
Angel Av
Madison St
Mill Av
Territorial St
River
20
Hope Av
White St
To Plymouth
10
Crow
Madison St
To Winsted
(Trail not included in this guide)

N
W · E
S

Tourist Information

City of Maple Plain
Phone: (763) 479-0515
Email: cityhall@mapleplain.com
Web: www.mapleplain.com

DNR Trails and Waterways Area Office
Phone: (952) 826-6769
Web: www.dnr.state.mn.us

Greater Wayzata Chamber of Commerce
Phone: (952) 473-9595
Fax: (952) 473-6266
Email: info@wayzatachamber.com
Web: www.wayzatachamber.com

Long Lake Chamber of Commerce
Phone: (952) 473-1329
Web: www.longlake-orono.org

Northwest Suburban Chamber of Commerce
Phone: (763) 420-3242
Fax: (763) 420-5964
Email: info@nwschamber.com
Web: www.nwschamber.com

Plymouth Park and Recreation
Phone: (763) 509-5200
Fax: (763) 509-5207
Email: recreation@ci.plymouth.mn.us
Web: www2.ci.plymouth.mn.us

Watertown City Offices
Phone: (952) 955-2681
Fax: (952) 955-2695
Email: info@ci.watertown.mn.us
Web: www.ci.watertown.mn.us

Lodging

Motels/Resorts

Plymouth
Comfort Inn Plymouth
3000 Harbor Ln
Toll Free: (877) 424-6423
Phone: (763) 559-1222
Fax: (763) 559-7819
Web: www.comfortinn.com/hotel/mn055

Country Inn & Suites
210 Carlson Pkwy N
Toll Free: (888) 201-1746
Phone: (763) 473-3008
Fax: (763) 473-9005
Web: www.countryinns.com

Camping

Plymouth
Baker Park Reserve
2301 County Rd 19
Phone: (763) 559-6700
Web: www.threeriversparkdistrict.org

Bike Repair

Long Lake
Gear West Ski Bike Run
1786 W Wayzata Blvd
Toll Free: (877) 473-4327
Phone: (952) 473-0377
Email: info@gearwest.com
Web: www.gearwest.com

Maple Grove
Maple Grove Cycle and Fitness
Phone: (763) 420-8878
Email: info@maplegrovecycling.com
Web: www.maplegrovecycling.com

Wayzata
Sports Hut
1175 E Wayzata Blvd
Phone: (952) 473-8843
Web: www.sportshut.com

Festivals and Events

Long Lake
June
Buckhorn Days
This Friday and Saturday historic tribute to the Buckhorn Place offers a fishing tournament, volleyball tournament, carnival, kids' games, music, a waterski show and family fun. Fourth Weekend.
Phone: (952) 473-1329
Web: www.longlake-orono.org

August
Corn Days
Let loose at the corn feed, beer tent, wine tasting, food stands, children's events, music, fun run, parade and bingo at St. George Catholic Church. Second Weekend.
Phone: (952) 475-1329
Web: www.corndays.com

Maple Plain
August
Polo Classic
See the polo and cricket matches, pony rides, picnic, dancing, gourmet food and a fund raiser for Children's Home Society, all at the West End Farm. First Weekend.
Phone: (651) 255-2304

Watertown
July
Rails to Trails Festival
Relax with the fire muster parade, kids' games, pet parade, Taste of Watertown, food fair, fun run and music festival. Check website for dates.
Phone: (952) 955-2681
Web: www.railstotrails.ws

lands and blooming wildflowers in spring. Located at Highway 6 and Brown Road.
Phone: (651) 296-6157

Maple Plain
Baker Park Reserve
Spend a day fishing, swimming, hiking, picnicking, at the play area snacking on concessions and biking.
Phone: (763) 479-2473
Web: www.threeriversparkdistrict.org

Homestead Orchard
Attractions include apple blossom wagon rides, fall raspberry and apple picking, picnic table, hayrides, a petting zoo, pumpkin patch and observation beehive. Check website for more information.
Phone: (612) 290-8024
Web: www.homesteadproduce.com

Orono
Wood-Rill
See this Big Woods old-growth forest in the DNR Scientific and Natural Area located on Old Long Lake Road.
Phone: (651) 296-6157

Plymouth
Clifton E. French Park
The park offers fishing, swimming, hiking, picnicking, a play area, concessions and a bike trail.
Phone: (763) 694-7750
Web: www.threeriversparkdistrict.org

Severs Farm Market and Corn Maze
Buy seasonal summer produce and pick your own pumpkins. The corn maze is open mid-August to Halloween.
Phone: (952) 937-1315
Web: www.severscornmaze.com

Rockford
Lake Rebecca Park Reserve

Festivals and Events cont'd

Wayzata
September
James J. Hill Days
Stay busy with kids' games, an arts and crafts fair, food booths, a parade, historical displays, an antique show and dachshund races. Weekend after Labor Day.
Phone: (952) 473-9595
Web: www.wayzatachamber.com

Alternate Activities

Long Lake
West Hennepin Pioneer Museum
See artifacts from the pioneer days. Open Saturday, 10:00am-4:00pm.
Phone: (952) 473-6557
Web: www.whcpa-museum.org

Wolsfeld Woods
The DNR Scientific and Natural Area boasts 185 acres with hiking trails, wood-

Come to picnic, play in the play area, hit the mountain bike trails or rent a boat.
Phone: (763) 694-7860
Web: www.threeriversparkdistrict.org

Wayzata
Trolley Rides
The free trolley departs from the historic Wayzata Depot and circulates throughout the commercial district from mid-May to mid-October. See Wednesday evening concerts at the depot from June to August.
Phone: (952) 473-9595
Web: www.wayzatachamber.com

Restaurants

Plymouth
Axel's Bonfire
Menu: Southwestern & American
Phone: (763) 398-7408

Wayzata
Culver's Family Restaurants
Phone: (952) 471-7500

Wayzata Legion Post 118
Phone: (952) 473-7678
Web: www.wayzatalegion.com

Wayzata Bar & Grill
Phone: (952) 473-5286

Jade Fountain
Phone: (952) 473-4646

Gianni's Steakhouse
Phone: (952) 404-1100
Web: www.giannis-steakhouse.com

D'Amico & Sons
Phone: (952) 476-8866

Blue Point Restaurants and Oyster Bar
Phone: (952) 475-3636
Web: www.bluepointRestaurantsandbar.com

About The Trail

These two former rail beds may someday become light rail corridors for the western suburbs. Until then, they supply bicycle escape routes to the western edges of the sprawling Twin Cities. The northern route is the older trail. It passes through the old wealth of Lake Minnetonka on its way to Carver Park Reserve. Marinas, mansions and money give way to a mix of rural land and suburban sprawl until the trail ends at the little town of Victoria. Carver Park Reserve is readily accessible from Victoria and worth the visit. The southern trail connects with the Kenilworth and Cedar Lakes Trails. It is possible to ride into Downtown Minneapolis on either of those trails. To the west it passes through a blend of new wealth and middle-class subdivisions with a mix of lakes, parks and restored prairie.

Trail Highlights

Both trails begin in Hopkins, a suburb that has maintained a very comfortable, human-scale downtown. Stop in historic Excelsior for a stroll down Main Street, then take a shaded break at Excelsior Commons on the shore of Lake Minnetonka. Minnetonka has its own system of bike trails. The most interesting trail begins behind the Minnetonka High School and runs down to Purgatory Park, a six mile round trip including the trail through Purgatory Park. See trail map for details. The southern LRT trail skirts Shady Oak Lake and Lake Riley. The last two miles drop quickly toward the Bluff Creek Dr. trailhead. The one mile extension southwest of the trailhead runs through hillside fields, then ends abruptly at Highway 212. The trail is not well maintained west of Bluff Creek Dr.

About The Roads

Expect traffic on the roads in this area. For more information about road and trail routes in this area, pick up a copy of the Twin Cities Bike Map by Bikeverywhere.

Road Highlights

Smithtown Road offers a quiet alternate to the trail. Low rolling hills and large estates dot this short stretch of road.

How To Get There

Hopkins is just off Highway 169 west of Minneapolis. Take Excelsior Boulevard (Highway 3) west about half a mile to 5th Ave. S. The southern trail begins at the back of the park-and-ride lot on the south side of Excelsior Boulevard. You can park here for the north trail as well and take 5th Avenue S. to half a block north of Main Street. The trail begins behind a row of bushes. See the city map for details. See the trail map for highway routes to other access points along the north and south trails.

Vital Trail Information:

Trail Distance: 27

Trail Surface: Limestone

Access Points: North: Hopkins, Excelsior, Victoria, South: Hopkins, Edenvale Park, Miller Park, Lake Riley Park, Chaska

Fees and Passes: None

Trail Website:
www.threeriversparkdistrict.org

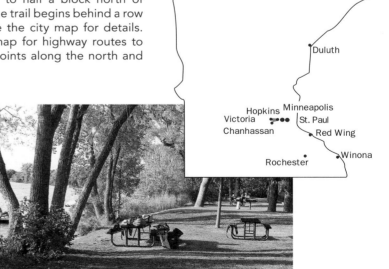

SW REGIONAL LRT TRAILS ⚲ Central Minnesota

North: Hopkins to Victoria: 15.4 miles

South: Hopkins to Chanhassen: 11.1 miles

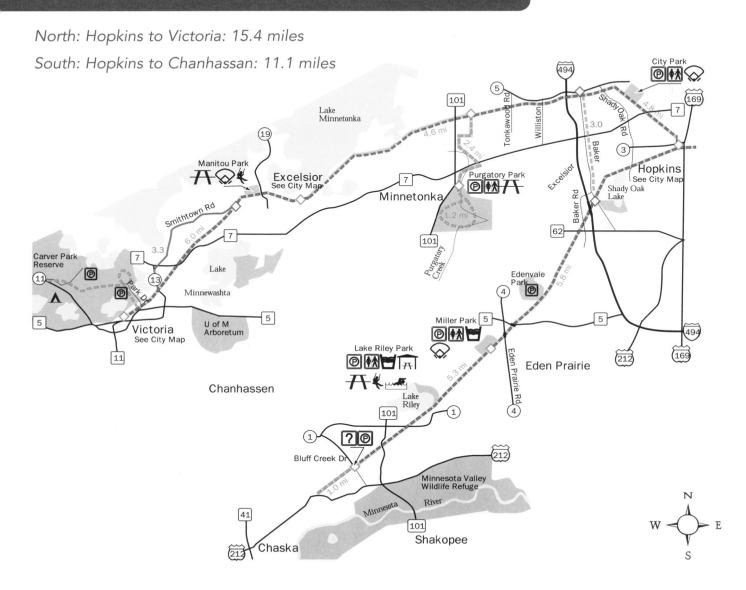

City Maps

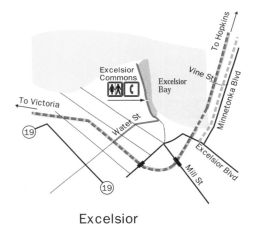

Excelsior

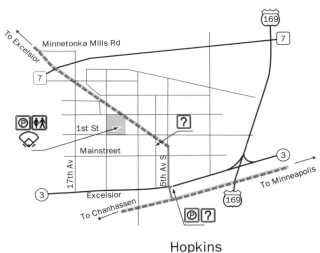

Hopkins

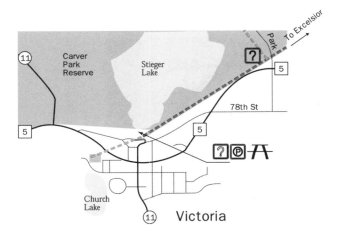

Victoria

Tourist Information

Chaska Chamber of Commerce
Phone: (952) 448-5000
Fax: (952) 448-4261
Email: chaska@chaskaareachamber.org
Web: www.chaskaareachamber.org

City of Hopkins
Phone: (952) 935-8474
Web: www.hopkinsmn.com

Eden Prairie Chamber of Commerce
Phone: (952) 944-2830
Fax: (952) 944-0229
Email: adminj@epchamber.org
Web: www.epchamber.org
Eden Prairie City Hall
Phone: (952) 949-8300
Email: communications@edenprairie.org
Web: www.edenprairie.org

Excelsior Area Chamber of Commerce
Phone: (952) 474-6461
Fax: (952) 474-3139
Web: www.southlake-excelsiorchamber.com

Twin West Chamber of Commerce
Phone: (763) 450-2220
Fax: (763) 450-2221
Email: info@twinwest.com
Web: www.twinwest.com

Lodging

Motels/Resorts

Chanhassen
Country Inn & Suites by Carlson
591 W 78th St
Toll Free: (888) 201-1746
Phone: (952) 937-2424
Fax: (952) 934-1945
Email: cx_chan@countryinns.com
Web: www.countryinns.com

Bed and Breakfast

Chaska
Bluff Creek B&B
1161 Bluff Creek Dr
Toll Free: (800) 445-6958
Phone: (952) 445-2735
Email: lindsay_lein@yahoo.com
Web: www.bluffcreekbb.com

The Peacock Inn
314 Walnut St
Phone: (952) 368-4343
Email: joyce@peacockinn.net
Web: www.peacockinn.net

Camping

Victoria
Carver Park Reserve
7200 Victoria Dr
Phone: (763) 559-6700
Email: feedback@threeriversparkdistrict.org
Web: www.threeriversparkdistrict.org

Bike Rental

Chaska
Get Your Gear Outfitters
700 N Chestnut St
Phone: (952) 448-9911
Email: getanswers@getyourgear.net
Web: www.getyourgear.net

Bike Repair

Chanhassen
Bokoo Bikes
550 Lake Dr
Phone: (952) 934-6468
Email: info@bokoobikes.com
Web: www.bokoobikes.com

Bike Repair cont'd

Chaska

Get Your Gear Outfitters
700 North Chestnut St
Phone: (952) 448-9911
Email: getanswers@getyourgear.net
Web: www.getyourgear.net

St. Louis Park

Bikemasters
3540 Dakota Ave
Phone: (952) 848-0481
Hoigaards, Inc
3550 S Hwy 100
Toll Free: (800) 266-8157
Phone: (952) 929-1351
Email: info@hoigaards.com
Web: www.hoigaards.com

Festivals and Events

Chaska

July

River City Days
Come for the music, arts and crafts show, kids' games and food booths in City Square Park. Fourth Weekend.
Phone: (952) 448-5000
Web: www.chaskarivercitydays.com
Eden Prairie

June

Lions Club Schooner Days Festival
At Round Lake Park, enjoy family activities, carnival rides and a softball tourney. First Weekend in June or Last Weekend in May.
Phone: (952) 949-8300
Web: www.eplions.org

MN Festival of Jazz on the Prairie
Staring Lake Amphitheater. Usually Second Sunday.
Phone: (952) 949-8450

July

4th of July Celebration
Stop by Round Lake and Staring Lake Parks for a triathlon, softball tourney, mixed doubles tennis and fireworks.
Phone: (952) 949-8450
Web: www.edenprairie.org

August

Eden Prairie Lions Club Corn Feed
The Corn Feed is at Round Lake Park. First Saturday.
Web: www.eplions.org/

September

SunBonnet Day
Stuff yourself at the old-fashioned ice-cream social at Cummins Grill Homestead. Usually Second Weekend.
Phone: (952) 949-8450
Web: www.edenprairie.org

Excelsior

May

Memorial Day Parade
See the patriotic program and parade.
Phone: (952) 474-6461
Web: www.southlake-excelsiorchamber.com

June

Art on the Lake
Browse the work of 200 juried artists from all over the U.S. Don't miss the food, music and kids' activities at Commons Park on Lake Minnetonka. Second Weekend.
Phone: (952) 474-6461
Web: www.southlake-excelsiorchamber.com

Festivals and Events cont'd

Excelsior

July

Old-Fashioned Fourth of July

Celebrate with a kids' parade, kids' fishing contest, sand castle contest, 10K fun run, food and entertainment and an evening performance by the Minnesota Orchestra. Watch fireworks off Excelsior Bay.
Phone: (952) 474-6461
Web: www.southlake-excelsiorchamber.com

September

Apple Day

The festival has apples, antiques, art, accessories, an autumn harvest, entertainment and family fun. Call for date.
Phone: (952) 474-6461
Web: www.southlake-excelsiorchamber.com

Hopkins

July

Raspberry Festival

It's a ten day celebration, including a golf tournament, parade, kids' fishing contest, music in the park, softball, volleyball, a bike race, tent dances and a five mile run. Second Weekend.
Phone: (952) 931-0878
Web: www.hopkinsraspberryfestival.com

Alternate Activities

Chanhassen

Minnesota Landscape Arboretum

Spend the afternoon in over a thousand acres of rolling hills, grand vistas, display gardens, and plant collections. Take the three mile drive/bike, trek along the hiking trails and dine at picnic facilities or the Restaurants.
Phone: (952) 443-1400
Web: www.arboretum.umn.edu

Eden Prairie

Eden Prairie Summer Theater

Check out the talent at Staring Lake Amphitheater, 7:00pm Wednesday, Friday and Sunday evenings mid-June through mid-August.
Phone: (952) 949-8450
Web: www.edenprairie.org

Summer Concert Series

Enjoy a show at Staring Lake Amphitheater. Middle to end of June. Check web site for details.
Phone: (952) 949-8450
Web: www.edenprairie.org

Excelsior

Water Street Shops

Stroll along antique and specialty shops, Restaurantss, the Minnesota Transportation Museum and an old train depot.
Phone: (952) 474-6461
Web: www.excelsiorchamber.com

Alternate Activities cont'd

Minnetrista

Lake Minnetonka Regional Park
A day at the beach includes swimming, a play area and a boat launch.
Phone: (763) 694-7754
Web: www.threeriversparkdistrict.org

Victoria

Grimm Farm
Located in Carver Park, the historic farmhouse is under construction as an interpretive center.
Phone: (763) 559-6700
Web: www.threeriversparkdistrict.org

Carver Park Reserve
The park offers 3,300 acres of marsh, tamarack swamp, rolling hills, wooded areas, lots of lakes, camping, hiking, biking, in-line skating, fishing, bird watching, picnic areas, a fishing pier, boat launch and access to the LRT Trail.
Phone: (763) 559-6700
Web: www.threeriversparkdistrict.org

Lowry Nature Center
Located within Carver Park Reserve, the center has hiking trails, free Sunday afternoon family programming and a "Habitat" educational play area.
Phone: (763) 694-7650
Web: www.threeriversparkdistrict.org

Boorsma Farm
Pick your own strawberries and raspberries at this farmer's market.
Phone: (952) 443-2068
Web: www.localharvest.org/farms/M5903

Restaurants

Excelsior

318 Café
Menu: Coffee House by day, Wine Bar by night
Phone: (952) 401-7902
Web: www.three-eighteen.com

Hopkins

Mainstreet Bar & Grill
Phone: (952) 938-2400
Web: www.mainstreetbar.com

The Big 10 Restaurants & Bar
Phone: (952) 930-0369
Web: www.big10Restaurants.com/hopkins.htm

Michelangelo Café
Phone: (952) 938-2211

The Depot Coffee House
Menu: Coffee and bakery products. Student run. Located on the trail in Hopkins
Phone: (952) 938-2204
Web: www.hopkinsmn.com/depot/index.html

Minnetonka

Snuffy's Malt Shop
Phone: (952) 475-1850
Web: www.snuffysmaltshop.com

Schlotzsky's
Phone: (952) 933-9775
Web: www.schlotzskys.com

Market Bar-B-Que
Phone: (952) 475-1770
Web: www.marketbbq.com

About The Trail

The Gateway provides an urban escape route from near downtown St. Paul to the countryside at Pine Point Park. The trail is very popular, for good reasons, and heavily used by bicyclists, in-line skaters and walkers, especially on weekends and holidays.

Trail Highlights

The western end, in St. Paul, passes golf courses, parks, cemeteries and other green spaces. Spur trails circle through Phalen Park near Keller and Phalen Lakes. The central portion runs along Highway 36 and is not attractive, but it does offer ice cream and fast food stops near the trail. North of Highway 36 the trail moves into a semi-rural area with lakes, fields and trees. Here it becomes quite attractive, especially so close to the urban center. The trailhead at Pine Point has bathrooms, running water and some shade.

About The Roads

Flat to low rolling, the roads toward the northeastern end of the trail pass mostly through farm fields and wide open spaces. Traffic is generally low but can spike occasionally or change because of new developments in the ex-urban lands around the city. For more road information, refer to the Twin Cities Bike Map by Bikeverywhere.

Road Highlights

Take an out-and-back loop to Square Lake Park, about four and a half miles northeast of the Pine Point Trailhead. The lake is pretty, clear and usually quiet. The park has a public beach and bathhouse. Withrow is a quiet little town just beyond the relentless urban sprawl. Traffic on Highways 9 and 66 will vary with the time of day and day of the week. The Demontreville Loop circles and passes between lakes, trees and housing developments. The little spur between Lakes Demontreville and Olson is at water's edge and passes through an older development with mature trees and narrow roads.

How To Get There

See city and trail maps for details.

Vital Trail Information:

Trail Distance: 17

Trail Surface: Asphalt

Access Points: Cayuga St. (St. Paul, street parking), Arlington Ave., Phalen-Kellor Park, Hadley Ave, Pine Point Park

Fees and Passes: None. Pine Point Park has a $5.00 per day vehicle permit fee. Pay at the pay box in the parkig lot.

Trail Website: www.gatewaytrailmn.org

St. Paul to Pine Point Park: 17 miles

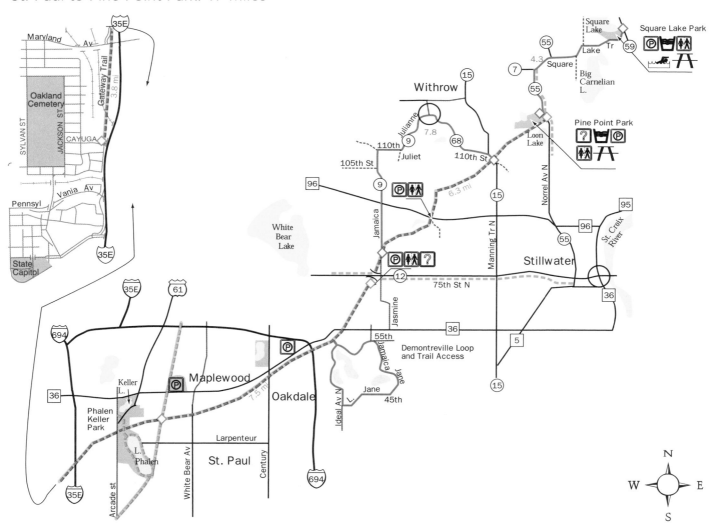

Tourist Information

DNR
Toll Free: (888) 646-6367
Phone: (651) 296-6157
Email: info@dnr.state.mn.us
Web: www.dnr.state.mn.us

Greater Stillwater Chamber of Commerce
Phone: (651) 439-4001
Fax: (651) 439-4035
Email: info@ilovestillwater.com
Web: www.ilovestillwater.com

St. Paul Convention and Visitors Bureau
Toll Free: (800) 627-6101
Phone: (651) 265-4900
Web: www.stpaulcvb.org
The Gateway Trail Association
Email: info@gatewaytrailmn.org
Web: www.gatewaytrailmn.org

Lodging

Bed and Breakfast

Marine-on-St. Croix
ASA Parker House
17500 St. Croix Trail N
Phone: (651) 433-5248
Email: asaparkerhouse@aol.com
Web: www.asaparkerbb.com

Stillwater
Aurora Staples Inn
303 N 4th St
Toll Free: (800) 580-3092
Phone: (651) 351-1187
Web: www.aurorastaplesinn.com

The Ann Beane Mansion
319 W Pine St
Toll Free: (877) 837-4400
Phone: (651) 430-0355
Fax: (651) 351-0861
Web: www.annbeanmansion.com

The Elephant Walk
801 W Pine St
Toll Free: (888) 430-0359
Phone: (651) 430-0359
Email: info@elephantwalkbb.com
Web: www.elephantwalkbb.com

The James A. Mulvey Inn
622 West Churchill St
Toll Free: (800) 820-8008
Phone: (651) 430-8008
Email: info@jamesmulveyinn.com
Web: www.jamesmulveyinn.com

The Rivertown Inn
306 W Olive St
Phone: (651) 430-2955
Fax: (651) 430-2206
Email: rivertown@rivertowninn.com
Web: www.rivertowninn.com

The William Sauntry Mansion
626 N 4th St
Toll Free: (800) 828-2653
Phone: (651) 430-2653
Email: sauntryinn@aol.com
Web: www.sauntrymansion.com

Camping

Hastings
Afton State Park
6959 Keller Ave S
Phone: (651) 436-5391
Web: www.dnr.state.mn.us

Marine on the St.Croix
William O'Brien State Park
16821 O'Brien Trail N
Phone: (651) 433-0500
Web: www.dnr.state.mn.us

Bike Rental

Oakdale
Gateway Cycle
Phone: (651) 777-0188
Email: bill@gatewaycycle.com
Web: www.gatewaycycle.com

Bike Repair

Maplewood
Strauss Skates and Bicycles
  1751 E Cope Ave
  Phone: (651) 770-1344
  Web: www.strausskatesandbicycles.com

Oakdale
Gateway Cycle
  Phone: (651) 777-0188
  Email: bill@gatewaycycle.com
  Web: gatewaycycle.com

Festivals and Events

St. Paul
May
  Cinco de Mayo Mexican Fiesta
  Join the party with a parade, food and
  entertainment on the West side of St.
  Paul. First Weekend.
  Toll Free: (800) 627-6101
  Phone: (651) 222-6347
  Web: www.districtdelsol.com

  Festival of Nations
  This is a multicultural celebration at the
  RiverCentre. Check website for dates.

Toll Free: (800) 627-6101
Phone: (651) 265-4800
Web: www.festivalofnations.com

June
  Grand Old Day
  This all day street festival draws huge
  crowds every year. Activities include
  music, food, crafts, a parade and
  shopping along Grand Avenue. First
  Weekend.
  Toll Free: (800) 627-6101
  Phone: (651) 699-0029
  Web: www.grandave.com

Festivals and Events cont'd

St. Paul

July

A Taste of Minnesota
This 4th of July celebration at the State Capitol grounds has music, food and fireworks. Check website for all dates.
Toll Free: (800) 627-6101
Phone: (651) 772-9980
Web: www.tasteofmn.org/

August

Irish Fair of Minnesota
Experience Irish music, dancing, food and crafts on Harriet Island. Second Weekend.
Toll Free: (800) 627-6101
Phone: (952) 474-7411
Web: www.irishfair.com

Minnesota State Fair
Come to one of the largest state fairs in the U.S. Fourth Weekend.
Toll Free: (800) 627-6101
Phone: (651) 288-4400
Web: www.mnstatefair.org

Stillwater

May

Rivertown Art Fair
The fair has arts, crafts, food and entertainment in Lowell Park. Check website for dates.
Phone: (651) 430-2306
Web: www.rivertownartfestival.com

July

Fourth of July
Fireworks on the St. Croix.
Phone: (651) 439-4001
Web: www.ilovestillwater.com

Lumberjack Days
Watch exhibitions, competitions, parade, 10K and half marathon runs, a craft fair, food vendors, music, kids' games and rides and fireworks: Check website for dates.
Phone: (651) 430-2306
Web: www.lumberjackdays.com

Summer Tuesdays
Check out market sales, food, outdoor concerts and a featured movie all overlooking the river. Tuesday evenings from mid-July to the end of August. See website for details.
Phone: (651) 439-4001
Web: www.ilovestillwater.com

September

Oktoberfest
Go German with polka bands and food at Gasthaus Bavarian Hunter. Check website for dates.
Phone: (651) 439-7128
Web: www.gasthausbavarianhunter.com

October

Fall Colors Fine Art and Jazz Festival See juried fine art, jazz bands and food vendors at Lowell Park. First Weekend.
Phone: (651) 439-4001
Web: www.ilovestillwater.com

Alternate Activities

Marine on St. Croix

William O'Brien State Park

Spend time camping, hiking, participating in interpretive programs, canoeing (rentals available), swimming or picnicking.
Toll Free: (888) 646-6367
Phone: (651) 433-0500
Web: www.dnr.state.mn.us

St. Paul

Fitzgerald Theater

Here is the home of Garrison Keillor's "A Prairie Home Companion" and other popular MPR shows. Check website for dates of shows and other events.
Phone: (651) 290-1200
Web: www.fitzgeraldtheater.org

Capitol City Trolley

Ride along on historical tours of downtown St. Paul. Thursdays by reservation only.
Phone: (651) 223-5600
Web: www.capitalcitytrolleys.com

Farmers Market

290 East 5th Street. Saturday and Sunday mornings, May to November.
Phone: (651) 227-8101
Web: www.stpaulfarmersmarket.com

Minnesota Historical Society

Take in exhibits and demonstrations from Minnesota's past and present. Check website for events and tours at all society sites statewide.
Toll Free: (800) 657-3773
Phone: (651) 296-6126
Web: www.mnhs.org

Minnesota Museum of American Art

A diverse collection of American Art, including paintings, crafts and sculptures, is located in the impressive Landmark Center.
Phone: (651) 266-1030
Web: www.mmaa.org

Minnesota Children's Museum

Kids under ten years old and their families will love this interactive children's museum.
Phone: (651) 225-6000
Web: www.mcm.org

Minnesota State Capitol Tours

Tour the House, Senate, Supreme Court and governor's reception room.
Toll Free: (800) 657-3773
Phone: (651) 296-2881
Web: www.mnhs.org

Paddleford Packet Boat Company

The Sternwheeler riverboat cruises on the Mississippi from Harriet Island.
Toll Free: (800) 543-3908
Phone: (651) 227-1100
Web: www.riverrides.com

Down In History Tours

Take several tours, including the popular St. Paul Gangster Tour; haunts and hideouts of America's most notorious gangsters, the Rivers and Roots Tour, The Caves Tour and The Victorian Tour.
Phone: (651) 292-1220
Web: www.wabashastreetcaves.com

Science Museum of Minnesota

Explore hands-on science exhibits, a world-class collection of fossils and artifacts and the Omnitheater.
Toll Free: (800) 221-9444
Phone: (651) 221-9444
Web: www.smm.org

Alternate Activities cont'd

Marine on St. Croix
Phalen Keller Park
Enjoy picnic areas, walking and bike trails, swimming and Wheelock Parkway at Arcade Street.
Phone: (651) 632-5111
Web: www.ci.stpaul.mn.us/depts/parks

Como Park Zoo and Conservatory
See zoological exhibits, botanical gardens and daily interpretive talks.
Phone: (651) 487-8200
Web: www.comozooconservatory.org

Stillwater
Wolf Brewery Caves
10,000 square feet of caves, open for afternoon tours, Spring through Fall
Phone: (651) 292-1220
Web: www.wabashastreetcaves.com

Historic Tours
Explore Stillwater, Minnesota's oldest town, by narrated trolley tours. Check website for details.
Phone: (651) 430-0352
Web: www.stillwatertrolley.com

Rockin' R Ranch
Come for carriage and hay rides, riding lessons and trail rides.
Phone: (651) 439-6878
Web: www.ilovestillwater.com

Northern Vineyards
The vineyard in downtown Stillwater offers wine tasting and tours by appointment.
Phone: (651) 430-1032
Web: www.northernvineyards.com

Nature's Nectar
Try local honey, comb honey, beeswax products and honey sticks for instant energy. Call ahead for hours.
Phone: (651) 439-8793

Antique shopping
Downtown Stillwater is Minnesota's antique mecca.
Phone: (651) 439-4001
Web: www.ilovestillwater.com

Aamodt's Apple Farm
Pick your own apples. Also experience hayrides and hot air balloon rides.
Phone: (651) 439-3127
Web: www.aamodtsapplefarm.com
White Bear Lake

Pine Tree Apple Orchards of White Bear Lake
Pick your own strawberries, apples and pumpkins. There are wagon rides and hiking in the orchards.
Phone: (651) 429-7202
Web: www.pinetreeappleorchard.com

Restaurants

Maplewood
Taste of India
Menu: Authentic Indian
Phone: (651) 773-5477
Web: www.tasteofindiamn.com

St. Paul
Jimmy John's
Menu: Gourmet Sandwiches
Phone: (651) 647-1999
Web: www.jimmyjohns.com

Trattoria da Vinci
Phone: (651) 222-4050
Web: www.trattoriadavinci.com

Stillwater
Gasthaus Bavarian Hunter
Menu: German
Phone: (651) 439-7128
Web: www.gasthausbavarianhunter.com

Dock Café
Menu: Fine Dining
Phone: (651) 430-3770
Web: www.dockcafe.com

Brine's Restaurants & Bar
Phone: (651) 439-7556
Web: www.brines-stillwater.com

Stone's Restaurants & Lounge
Phone: (651) 439-1900
Web: www.stonesstillwater.com

BT Doyle's Rib Joint
Menu: Barbeque
Phone: (651) 439-2852
Web: www.doylesribjoint.com

About The Trail

This former Chicago Great Western Rail Line runs along the south side of the Cannon River from Cannon Falls to Red Wing. Views from the trail include panoramic overlooks near Cannon Falls and intimate river bottom near Red Wing. The trail drops at a steady rate from Cannon Falls on the west to Red Wing on the east. Watch for old railway mileposts and a wide variety of wildflowers.

Trail Highlights

The bluffs come right up to the trail on the south and the river drops away to the north between Cannon Falls and Anderson Memorial Rest Area, creating spectacular panoramic views of the river and a damp micro environment supporting ferns, mosses and lichens. The city trail in Cannon Falls has scenic stretches. The city trail along Hay Creek in Red Wing is quite scenic and worth exploring.

About The Roads

This is bluff country. The marked routes are hilly, smooth, low traffic and rural in character. Ride all the way from end to end or cut back to the trail at the halfway point near Welch Village. Roads to the north of the Cannon River tend to be gravel. Expect to climb from the trail to all road routes.

Road Highlights

County Road 1 climbs from the Mississippi River Valley in Red Wing to the rural highlands of Goodhue County. Once out of the river valley, expect rolling ridge top to the town of White Rock, then more pronounced up and down to Highway 25. Traffic is heavy near Red Wing, so consider the alternate route laid out in the Red Wing City Map. Highway 25 climbs long and steadily out of Cannon Falls, then settles into rolling ridge top to Highway 1. Highway 7 connects the trail to the tiny town of Vasa via a long climb, then rolls up and down to Highway 1. Check out the Vasa Museum and the nearby Lutheran Church on the hill. The cemetery next to the church has tombstones dating back to the middle 1800s. Baypoint Park, one mile west of the Red Wing Trailhead, has great facilities and a marina.

How To Get There

Cannon Falls is off Highway 52, about midway between the Twin Cities and Rochester. Red Wing is forty-five miles southeast of St. Paul on Highway 61. To get to Welch Village, at the midpoint of the trail, take Highway 7 south from Highway 61, about eight miles west of Red Wing. Watch for the Welch Village signs. See city maps for directions to trailheads in Cannon Falls and Red Wing.

Vital Trail Information:

Trail Distance: 20

Trail Surface: Asphalt

Access Points: Cannon Falls, Welch Village, Red Wing

Fees and Passes: Wheel Pass $3.00/day, $12.00 per season. No charge for children under 18

Trail Website:
www.cannonvalleytrail.com

CANNON VALLEY TRAIL ☙ Central Minnesota

Cannon Falls to Red Wing: 20 miles

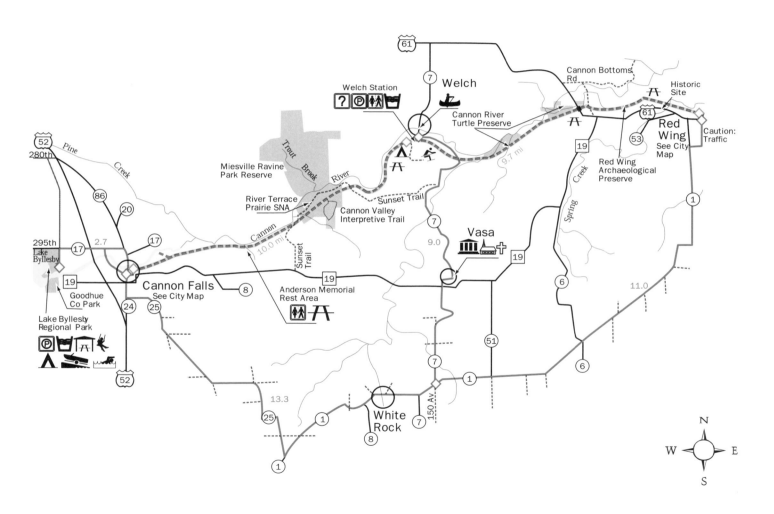

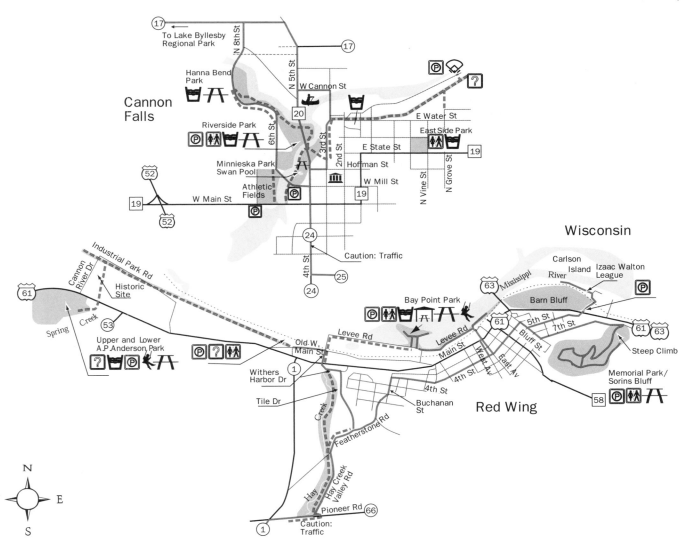

Cannon Falls

(17) ← To Lake Byllesby Regional Park

N 8th St
N 5th St
(17)

Hanna Bend Park

W Cannon St

Cannon Falls

20

Riverside Park

6th St
3rd St
2nd St

E Water St

East Side Park

E State St
(19)

Minnieska Park Swan Pool

Hoffman St

W Mill St

(52)
19
(52)

W Main St

Athletic Fields

19

N Vine St
N Grove St

Wisconsin

(24)

4th St

Caution: Traffic

(24)
(25)

Industrial Park Rd

Cannon River Dr

(61)

Historic Site

Spring Creek

(53)

Upper and Lower A.P. Anderson Park

Carlson Island

(63) Mississippi River

Izaac Walton League

Barn Bluff

Bay Point Park

Levee Rd

Levee Rd

(61)

5th St
7th St

Bluff St

(61)(63)

Steep Climb

Old W. Main St

Main St

West Av
East Av

Memorial Park/ Sorins Bluff

Withers Harbor Dr

(1)

4th St

Tile Dr

Creek

4th St

Buchanan St

Red Wing

58

Featherstone Rd

Hay Creek

Hay Creek Valley Rd

Pioneer Rd (66)

(1)

Caution: Traffic

N
W ◆ E
S

Tourist Information

Cannon Falls Chamber of Commerce
Phone: (507) 263-2289
Email: tourism@cannonfalls.org
Web: www.cannonfalls.org

Cannon Valley Trail, Cannon Falls
Phone: (507) 263-0508
Email: info@cannonvalleytrail.com
Web: www.cannonvalleytrail.com

Cannon Valley Trail, Welch
Phone: (507) 263-0508
Email: info@cannonvalleytrail.com
Web: www.cannonvalleytrail.com

Red Wing Chamber of Commerce
Toll Free: (800) 762-9516
Phone: (651) 388-4719
Email: chamber@redwingchamber.com
Web: www.redwingchamber.com

Red Wing Visitor and Convention Bureau
Toll Free: (800) 498-3444
Phone: (651) 385-5934
Fax: (651) 388-3900
Email: visitorscenter@redwing.org
Web: www.redwing.org

Lodging

Motels/Resorts

Cannon Falls
Caravan Motel
Hwy 52
31913 64th Ave
Phone: (507) 263-4777
Web: www.caravanmotel.net

Red Wing
AmericInn
1819 Old West Main
Toll Free: (866) 385-0018
Phone: (651) 385-9060
Fax: (651) 385-8139
Email: redwing.mn@americinn.com
Web: www.americinnmn.net

Nichols Inn & Suites
1750 Hwy 61
Phone: (651) 388-6633
Email: nicholsredwing@charterinternet.com
Web: www.nicholsinn.com

St. James Hotel
406 Main St
Toll Free: (800) 252-1875
Phone: (651) 388-2846
Email: info@st-james-hotel.com
Web: www.st-james-hotel.com

Bed and Breakfast

Cannon Falls
Quill and Quilt
615 W Hoffman St
Toll Free: (800) 488-3849
Phone: (507) 263-5507
Email: info@quillandquilt.com
Web: www.quillandquilt.com

Red Wing
Candlelight Inn
818 W 3rd St
Toll Free: (800) 254-9194
Phone: (651) 388-8034
Email: info@candlelightinn-redwing.com
Web: www.candlelightinn-redwing.com

Moondance Inn
1105 W 4th St
Toll Free: (866) 388-8145
Phone: (651) 388-8145
Email: info@moondanceinn.com
Web: www.moondanceinn.com

Lodging cont'd

Motels/Resorts

Red Wing
The Golden Lantern Inn
721 East Ave
Toll Free: (888) 288-3315
Phone: (651) 388-3315
Email: info@goldenlantern.com
Web: www.goldenlantern.com

Camping

Cannon Falls
Cannon Falls Campground
30365 Oak Ln
Toll Free: (888) 821-2267
Phone: (507) 263-3145
Web: www.cannonfallscampground.com

Lake Byllesby Regional Park Campground
7650 Echo Point Rd
Phone: (507) 263-4447

Frontenac
Frontenac State Park
Phone: (651) 345-3401
Web: www.dnr.mn.us

Lake City
Dorer Memorial Hardwood State Forest
1801 S Oak
Phone: (651) 345-3216

Red Wing
Hay Creek Valley Campground
31655 Hwy 58 Blvd
Toll Free: (888) 388-3998
Phone: (651) 388-3998
Email: pat.oneill@rivervalleyinc.com

Welch
Hidden Valley Campground
27173 144 Avenue Way
Phone: (651) 258-4550
Email: gekko@redwing.net
Web: www.hvcamping.com

Bike Rental

Cannon Falls
Cannon Falls Canoe & Bike
Toll Free: (877) 882-2663
Phone: (507) 263-4657
Email: williaml@mchsi.com
Web: www.cannonfallscanoeandbike.com

Red Wing
The Route
401 W Levee St
Phone: (651) 388-1082
Email: eric@theroute.net
Web: www.theroute.net

Bike Repair

Cannon Falls
Hjermstad Trustworthy Hardware
Phone: (507) 263-2611

Bike Repair cont'd

Red Wing
The Route
401 W Levee St
Phone: (651) 388-1082
Email: eric@theroute.net
Web: www.theroute.net

Bile Shuttle

Cannon Falls
Cannon Falls Canoe & Bike
Toll Free: (877) 882-2663
Phone: (507) 263-4657
Email: williaml@mchsi.com
Web: www.cannonfallscanoeandbike.com

Festivals and Events

Cannon Falls
All Summer
Farmers Market
Buy your fresh produce on Saturdays during growing season at the downtown city parking lot.
Phone: (507) 263-2289
Web: www.cannonfalls.org
Voices of the Valley
Natural and cultural resource people along the trail answer questions on a variety of topics. May through September. First Saturday.
Phone: (507) 263-2289

May
Memorial Day Parade
See the parade and service at Colvill Memorial.
Phone: (507) 263-2289
Web: www.cannonfalls.org

July
Cannon Valley Fair
The fair offers a parade, carnival, harness racing, exhibits and fireworks. First Weekend.
Phone: (507) 263-2289
Web: www.cannonfalls.org

Little Log House Antique Power Show
Check out the antique and classic tractor show, flea market, craft sale, and the replica of the famed Hastings Spiral Bridge. Call for dates.
Phone: (507) 263-2289
Web: www.cannonfalls.org

August
Cruisin' Days
See the Friday night '50s car cruise and dance, Saturday merchant Crazy Days and Sunday classic car show. First Weekend.
Phone: (507) 263-2289
Web: www.cannonfalls.org

September
Community Wide Garage Sale
Third Saturday after Labor Day.
Phone: (507) 263-2289
Web: www.cannonfalls.org

Red Wing
May
100 Mile Garage Sale
Residents and stores in fourteen river towns around Lake Pepin participate in a huge garage sale spectacular. First Weekend.
Toll Free: (888) 999-2619
Web: www.redwingchamber.com

July
Red Wing Collectors' Society
The Red Wing Pottery Show has auctions, sales and seminars for adults and children. Second Weekend.
Toll Free: (800) 977-7927
Web: www.redwingcollectors.org

August
River City Days
Enjoy the parade, family events, arts and crafts, carnival and fireworks at Bay Point Park. First Weekend.
Toll Free: (800) 498-3444
Phone: (651) 385-5934

October
Fall Festival of Arts
This juried art festival features seventy-five artists, a Minnesota book fair, film festival, music, children's activities, food and entertainment downtown. Second Weekend.
Toll Free: (800) 498-3444
Phone: (651) 388-7569
Web: www.redwing.org

Alternate Activities

Cannon Falls
Cannon River Winery
The winery offers wine tastings as well as guided and walking tours of the scenic vineyard in the beautiful Sogn Valley. The gift shop offers one-of-a-kind wine-related gifts and artwork made by Minnesota artists.
Phone: (507) 263-7400
Web: www.cannonriverwinery.com

Cannon Falls Historical Museum
Learn about local history. Call library for hours.
Phone: (507) 263-4080
Web: www.citlink.net/~cfmuseum

Downtown Cannon Falls
Twenty-nine downtown properties are listed on the National Registry of Historic Places.
Phone: (507) 263-2289
Web: www.cannonfalls.org

Alternate Activities cont'd

Cannon Falls

Countryside Antique Mall
Find over fifty antique dealers under one roof.
Phone: (507) 263-0352
Web: www.csamantiques.com

Frontenac

Frontenac State Park
Check out wooded bluffs with scenic views, camping, boating, fishing and picnic areas. Explore Old Frontenac historic river town.
Phone: (651) 345-3401
Web: www.dnr.state.mn.us

Red Wing

Barn Bluff and Sorin's Bluff
Hike miles of trails on the bluffs overlooking Red Wing and the Mississippi River.
Phone: (800) 498-3444
Web: www.redwing.org

Levee Park
Downtown on the Mississippi River, find the docking site for Mississippi steamboats.
Toll Free: (800) 498-3444
Phone: (651) 385-5934
Web: www.redwing.org

Antique Shopping and Architecture Walking Tour
Take a walk downtown.
Toll Free: (800) 498-3444
Phone: (651) 385-5934
Web: www.redwing.org

Historic Pottery District
Old West Main Street boasts Antique Alley, Redwing Pottery salesroom, Pottery Place, factory outlets, specialty shops, eateries and antique dealers.
Toll Free: (800) 498-3444
Phone: (651) 385-5934
Web: www.rwpotteryplace.com

Sheldon Theatre
See the oldest municipally owned theater in the United States. Check website for events and details.
Toll Free: (800) 899-5759
Phone: (651) 388-8700
Web: www.sheldontheatre.com

Goodhue County Historical Society
This kid-friendly historical museum has exhibits that include archaeology, early immigration and settlers, local clay industry, a rural school room and more. Check website for details.
Phone: (651) 388-6024
Web: www.goodhuehistory.mus.mn.us

Restaurants

Cannon Falls

Lorentz Meats & Deli
Phone: (507) 263-3618
Web: www.lorentzmeats.com

Dairy Inn
Phone: (507) 263-4141

Pizza Man
Phone: (507) 263-5553

Stone Mill Coffee House & Eatery
Phone: (507) 263-2580

Brewster's Bar & Grill
Phone: (507) 263-5020

Red Wing

Staghead
Phone: (651) 388-6581

Lily's Coffee House & Flowers
Phone: (651) 388-8797
Web: www.lilyscoffeehouse.com

Braschler's Bakery & Coffee Shop
Phone: (651) 388-1589
Web: www.pressenter.com/~braschlr

Randy's Restaurants
709 Main St
Phone: (651) 388-1551

Liberty's Restaurants & Lounge
303 W 3rd St
Phone: (651) 388-8877
Web: www.libertysonline.com

Smokey Row Café & Bakery
Phone: (651) 388-6025
Web: www.jennylindbakery.com

About The Trail

Running from a narrow, wooded valley called "Wardlaws Ravine" in Mankato through Sakatah Lake State Park and to the edge of Faribault, this trail passes through a number of attractive small towns and skirts large and small lakes. In-line skaters should be cautious at road and driveway crossings, they are often gravel. Trail towns offer parks, museums, and historic buildings.

Trail Highlights

The western section from Mankato to Madison Lake has the most diversity. It climbs through the heavily wooded, narrow valley of Wardlaws Ravine, then opens up to wildflowers and farmland on the way to Madison Lake. The Elysian trail access is set in a pleasant little park with drinking water, modern bathrooms and a sheltered picnic area. The trail stops at each edge of Waterville, but the road route connector is well marked and follows quiet residential streets. Pull off the trail at Sakatah State Park and head up to the lake for a pleasant break. Do the same a few miles farther east at Morristown, where a short side trip will take you to the historic dam site and a quiet park along the Cannon River. The trail east of Morristown follows Highway 60 and loses some of its charm as a result.

About The Roads

The roads near the middle and eastern portions of the trail offer the best riding. They undulate over low to medium rollers past farm fields and woodlots and skirt a number of midsized lakes. The routes on the trail map offer only a hint of the road riding options in this area. The roads near Mankato tend to have more, and faster moving, traffic.

Road Highlights

The wide range of cutting and milling tools in the steam powered Geldner Saw Mill are visible even when the museum is closed because of wide mesh steel grated doors. The mill is on the west edge of German Lake, northwest of Elysian. Highway 131, on the north edge of Sakatah Lake, is a quiet, winding road with great views of Sakatah Lake State Park across the water. The roads north of the trail between Morristown and Faribault pass through gently rolling farmland and offer a great alternate to the trail.

How To Get There

Take the Highway 60 exit off Interstate 35 at Faribault. The nearest trail access is at the Dairy Queen just west of the interstate. See the city map. All trail towns can be accessed from Highway 60 as you head west. The Mankato trailhead is near the eastern edge of Mankato. Take the Highway 22 exit off Highway 14. Go north to Lime Valley Road. The trailhead is on the left, 0.2 miles north on Lime Valley Road.

Vital Trail Information:

Trail Distance: 38

Trail Surface: Asphalt

Access Points: Faribault, Warsaw, Morristown, Sakatah Lake State Park, Waterville, Elysian, Madison Lake, Mankato

Fees and Passes: None

Trail Website:
www.dnr.state.mn.us/state

SAKATAH SINGING HILLS TRAIL ⚑ Southern Minnesota

Faribault to Mankato: 39 miles

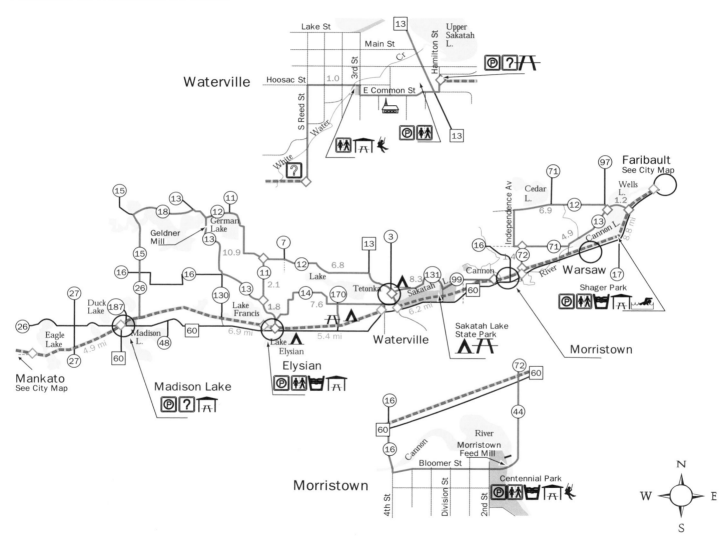

City Maps

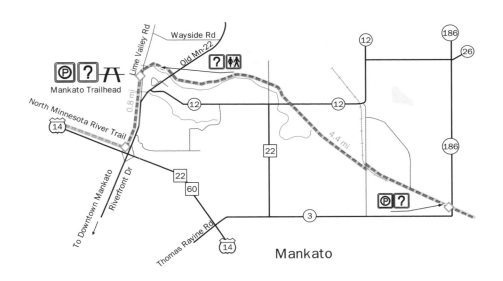

Lime Valley Rd

Wayside Rd

Old Mn-22

Mankato Trailhead

North Minnesota River Trail

14

To Downtown Mankato

Riverfront Dr

Thomas Ravine Rd

22

60

14

0.8 mi

12

12

22

3

4.4 mi

12

186

26

186

Mankato

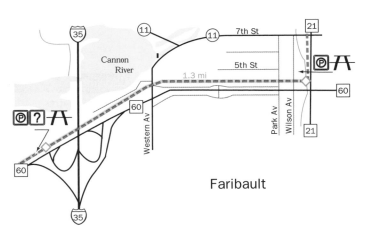

35

11

11

7th St

21

Cannon River

5th St

1.3 mi

60

Western Av

Park Av

Wilson Av

60

21

35

60

Faribault

N
W — E
S

Tourist Information

Elysian Tourism Center
Toll Free: (800) 507-7787
Phone: (507) 267-4040
Web: www.elysianmn.com

Faribault Chamber of Commerce
Toll Free: (800) 658-2354
Phone: (507) 334-4381
Web: www.faribaultmn.org

Mankato Area Convention and Visitors Bureau
Toll Free: (800) 657-4733
Phone: (507) 345-4519
Fax: (507) 345-4451
Email: info@greatermankato.com
Web: www.mankato.com

Morristown City Hall
Phone: (507) 685-2302
Fax: (507) 685-2632
Email: motown@cvtel.net
Web: www.ci.morristown.mn.us

Sakatah Singing Hills State Trail Office
Toll Free: (800) 507-7787
Phone: (507) 267-4040
Web: www.dnr.state.mn.us

Waterville Chamber of Commerce
Phone: (507) 362-4609
Email: lmesk@frontiernet.net
Web: www.watervillemn.com

Lodging

Motels/Resorts

Faribault
AmericInn Motel & Suites
1801 Lavender Dr
Toll Free: (800) 397-5007
Phone: (507) 334-9464
Fax: (507) 334-0616
Email: faribault.mn@americinn.com
Web: www.americinn.com

Days Inn
1920 Cardinal Ln
Toll Free: (800) 329-7466
Phone: (507) 334-6835
Fax: (507) 333-4636
Web: www.daysinn.com

Galaxie Inn & Suites
1400 4th St NW
Toll Free: (888) 334-9294
Phone: (507) 334-5508
Email: bhanuthanki@hotmail.com
Web: www.galaxieinn.com

Select Inn
4040 Hwy 60 W
Toll Free: (800) 641-1000
Phone: (507) 334-2051
Web: www.selectinn.com

The Lyndale Motel
904 Lyndale Ave N
Toll Free: (800) 559-4386
Phone: (507) 334-4386

Mankato
Holiday Inn Downtown
101 E Main St
Box 3386
Toll Free: (800) 465-4329
Phone: (507) 345-1234

Waterville
Lakeview Resort
14972 Sakatah Lake Rd
P.O. Box 164
Phone: (507) 362-4616
Email: Lakevieww1@aol.com
Web: www.mnlakeviewresort.com

Sakatah Bay Resort Motel
815 E. Paquin St
Phone: (507) 362-8980
Email: fun@sakatahbay.com
Web: www.sakatahbay.com

Lodging cont'd

Bed and Breakfast

Mankato
Butler House
704 S Broad St
Phone: (507) 387-5055
Email: butler1@hickorytech.net
Web: www.butlerhouse.com

Camping

Elysian
Silver's Resort
108 S 1st St
P.O. Box 205
Phone: (507) 267-4694

Faribault
Camp Faribo Campground/RV Park
21851 Bagley Ave
Toll Free: (800) 689-8453
Phone: (507) 332-8453

Morristown
Maiden Rock Campground
P.O. Box 326
Toll Free: (800) 657-4776
Phone: (507) 685-4430
Email: mrw@campmaidenrock.com
Web: www.campmaidenrock.com

Waterville
Kamp Dels
14842 Sakatah Lake Rd
Phone: (507) 362-8616
Web: www.kampdels.com

Lakeview Resort
14972 Sakatah Lake Rd
P.O. Box 164
Phone: (507) 362-4616
Email: Lakevieww1@aol.com
Web: www.mnlakeviewresort.com

Sakatah Lake State Park Campground
50499 Sakatah Lake State Park Rd
Phone: (507) 362-4438
Web: www.dnr.state.mn.us

Bike Rental

Mankato
The Spoke
819 Carney Ave
Phone: (507) 625-2453
Email: info@spokebikes.com
Web: www.spokebikes.com

Waterville
Ron's Hardware Hank
229 E Main
Phone: (507) 362-4308

Bike Repair

Faribault
The Village Pedaler
311 Central Ave
Phone: (507) 331-2636

Mankato
Scheels Sport Shop
1850 AdamsSt #404
Phone: (507) 386-7767
Web: www.scheelssports.com

The Spoke
819 Carney Ave
Phone: (507) 625-2453
Email: info@spokebikes.com
Web: www.spokebikes.com

Waterville
Ron's Hardware Hank
229 E Main
Phone: (507) 362-4308

Festivals and Events

Elysian
July
Fourth of July Festival
This three day celebration is packed with a parade, kids' fishing contest, kids' tractor pull, milk jug regatta, pageant, dance, car show and flea market.
Phone: (507) 267-4708
Web: www.elysianmn.com

Rookies' Triathlon
Seven age categories compete in a 0.4 mile swim, eight mile bike and four mile run. Saturday after the 4th.
Phone: (507) 267-4708
Web: www.elysianmn.com

Faribault
All Summer
Farmers Market
Get fresh produce at Central Park every Wednesday afternoon and Saturday morning during growing season.
Phone: (507) 334-4381

Festivals and Events con't

Faribault

June

Heritage Days
Celebrate the diverse heritage and cultures that comprise Faribault with a parade, carnival, street dance, arts and crafts show, volleyball and softball tourneys, a kids' fishing contest, bike tour, truck pull and tours of historic buildings. Third Weekend.
Toll Free: (800) 658-2354
Phone: (507) 334-4381
Web: www.faribaultmn.org

July

Rice County Free Fair
Enjoy food, derby races, a coronation and a rodeo at this five day event at the fairgrounds. Third Weekend.
Toll Free: (800) 658-2354
Phone: (507) 339-8888
Web: www.ricecountyfair.net

September

Faribault Airfest
This hot air balloon exhibition, which features an antique aircraft display, glider demonstrations, airplane rides and food vendors, takes place at the Municipal Airport. Check website for dates.
Toll Free: (800) 658-2354
Phone: (507) 334-4381
Web: www.faribaultairfest.com

Tree Frog Music Festival
Don't miss music, art, food: twenty diverse music acts, original art, food booths, beer garden and childrens' activities at Teepee Tonka Park. Check website for dates.
Toll Free: (800) 658-2354
Phone: (507) 334-4381
Web: www.treefrogmusic.org

October

Business Expo & Taste of Faribault
Sample food from local vendors at the Faribault Ice Arena. Call for date.
Toll Free: (800) 658-2354
Phone: (507) 334-4381
Web: www.faribaultmn.org

Madison Lake

July

Paddlefish Days
See the parade, street dance, tractor pull, food fair, fun run and fire department open house. Fourth Weekend.
Phone: (507) 243-3011
Web: www.madisonlake.govoffice2.com

Mankato

July

Mankato Vikings Training Camp
Swing by Blakeslee Field at Minnesota State University – Mankato. End of July through mid–August.
Toll Free: (800) 657-4733
Phone: (507) 345-4519
Web: www.vikings.com

North Mankato Fun Days
This community celebration features food, a parade, high school marching bands, a horseshoe tournament and entertainment. Check website for dates.
Toll Free: (800) 657-4733
Phone: (507) 345-4519
Web: www.greatermankato.com

September

Mankato Mdewakanton Powwow
Enjoy American Indian food, crafts, ceremonial dancing and singing at Land of Memories Park. Second or Third Weekend.
Toll Free: (800) 657-4733
Phone: (507) 345-4519
Web: www.greatermankato.com

Morristown

June

Dam Days
Experience the twilight parade on Friday, the carnival, family events, kids' parade, lawn mower pull, car show and American Legion steak fry.
First Weekend.
Phone: (507) 685-2302
Web: www.ci.morristown.mn.us

August

City-Wide Garage SalesMaps are available at the community hall. First Saturday.
Phone: (507) 685-2302
Web: www.ci.morristown.mn.us

Waterville

June

Bullhead Days
The festival has a pageant, carnival, grand parade, kids' parade, food stands (including deep-fried bullhead), a demolition derby, 10K run and bike race, tractor pull, mud drag races and a kids' fishing contest. Second Weekend after Memorial Day.
Phone: (507) 362-4609
Web: www.watervillemn.com

Alternate Activities

Elysian

Okaman Cervidae Elk Farm
View a majestic herd of elk at the restored historic farm.
Phone: (507) 267-4054
Web: www.okamanonline.com

Klondike Hill
The highest point in three counties offers a beautiful panoramic view and one of the first Jesse James gang campsites.
Phone: (507) 267-4708
Web: www.elysianmn.com

Le Sueur County Historical Society and Museum
Displays and tours. Open weekends.
Phone: (507) 267-4620
Web: www.frontiernet.net/~lchsmuseum

Elysian City Park and Beach
The park has a public swimming beach, sand volleyball courts and picnic shelters.
Phone: (507) 267-4708
Web: www.elysianmn.com

Faribault

Rice County Historical Society Museum
See various exhibits and tour the Alexander Faribault House and an historical one room log cabin school. Call for hours.
Phone: (507) 332-2121
Web: www.rchistory.org

Faribault Art Center
Local artists put their work on display. Check out pottery and basket making in downtown Faribault.
Phone: (507) 332-7372

Faribault Mills
Tour the mill and shop the outlet store.
Toll Free: (800) 448-9665
Phone: (507) 334-1644
Web: www.faribowool.com

River Bend Nature Center
Explore forests, prairies, wetlands, riverbanks and nine miles of marked trails. Call for programs.
Phone: (507) 332-7151
Web: www.rbnc.org

Mankato

Highland Summer Theater
Presents four musicals and plays during the summer season at Minnesota State University. Call for a brochure.
Phone: (507) 389-6661
Web: www.msutheatre.com

Blue Earth County Historical Society
Take in various exhibits at the Blue Earth County heritage Center and at the Hubbard House, a restored Victorian home.
Phone: (507) 345-5566
Web: www.rootsweb.com/~mnbechs

Minneopa State Park
Native prairie area boasts the only major waterfall in southwestern Minnesota plus hiking and bird watching, an interpretive drive, an old stone mill and vanished village, camping, picnicking and a paved bike trail.
Phone: (507) 389-5464
Web: www.dnr.state.mn.us

Waterville

Minnesota Fish Hatchery
Located two miles west of Waterville on County Road 14. Call for tours.
Phone: (507) 362-4223

Sakatah Lake State Park
The park has camping, picnicking, hiking, canoe and boat rentals, a playground, swimming, fishing, an interpretive center and five miles of trails
Phone: (507) 362-4438
Web: www.dnr.state.mn.us

Restaurants

Faribault

El Tequila Mexican Restaurants
Phone: (507) 332-7490

The Depot Bar and Grill
Phone: (507) 332-2825

Bernie's Grill
Phone: (507) 334-7476

Signature Bar & Grill
Phone: (507) 331-1657

Boston's Gourmet Pizza
Phone: (507) 331-3255
Web: www.bostons-pizza.com

Monte's Steak House
Phone: (507) 333-9393
Web: www.montessteakhouse.com

Mankato

Coffee Hag
Phone: (507) 387-5533

McGoff's Irish Pub & Eatery
Phone: (507) 387-4000

Charley's Restaurants & Lounge
Phone: (507) 388-6845
Web: www.charleysRestaurantsmankato.com

BW-3
Phone: (507) 625-9464

Applebee's
Phone: (507) 386-1010

Warsaw

Channel Inn
Phone: (507) 685-4622

About The Trail

The two trails combine to create an eleven mile trail from the Sakatah Singing Hills Trailhead to the small town of Rapidan. Along the way you follow the banks of the Minnesota River past low sandstone outcrops and along the base of a high concrete levee. A short transition takes you under a low, active railroad trestle and through residential neighborhoods to the start of the Red Jacket Trail. From here south, the trail quickly enters a rural countryside of small woodlots, open fields and the low hills of Mt. Kato Ski Resort. The crown jewel of the trail is a long, high trestle over the Le Sueur River. The trail ends at Huffy Road, but don't stop there. Ride out to Rapidan Road, then a few blocks south to Rapidan and the vine smothered Peddler, a gift and food store that is open when they hack the vines away from the doors.

Trail Highlights

The trestle is the focal point of the trail. If you don't have much time, start in Weagel Park or Red Jacket Trail Park. If you want to see the trestle from the top and bottom, first take the lower trail to Red Jacket Trail Park. Check out the trestle from the observation area, then look for the trail that drops down to the river and crosses under Highway 66. Follow it under the highway and up the other side for a view similar to that in the historic picture at the observation point. Continue across the bridge on Highway 60 on the bike path. After you cross under the trestle, take a right turn and another right up to the trail. Turn right at the trail and cross the trestle for views from the top. Sandstone outcrops line one side of the northern end of the North Minnesota

River Trail creating an intimate feel to the trail. Farther south, the trail changes character as it runs between a high concrete levee wall and a riprap slope to the Minnesota River. Neither beautiful, nor ugly, it's just a bit odd and likely to get very hot on a sunny summer afternoon. The high wall makes the trail feel narrower than it is.

About The Roads

This area has some very promising low traffic, paved roads. All of the roads shown are excellent. If you love road riding, check with local riders or a bike shop. You should get plenty of good advice.

Road Highlights

The ride from the south end of the trail to Rapidan Dam County Park is very pleasant. The park is small but comfortable, and a small convenience store in the park has a vending machine and other food. Return via Highways 34 and 33 to the South Route Trail, follow the trail to Stolzman Road, then return to Mankato. Makes a very pleasant loop.

How To Get There

Mankato is southwest of the Twin Cities off Highway 169. Go east on Highway 14 across the Minnesota River and watch for the Sakatah Singing Hills Trailhead sign (Lime Valley Road). The trailhead is a short distance north of the highway. If you prefer a southern start stay on Highway 169 to County Highway 90. Go east on Highway 90 to County Highway 66. Go north on Highway 66 to get to Weagel Park or go south to Red Jacket Trail Park.

Vital Trail Information:

Trail Distance: 11

Trail Surface: Asphalt

Access Points: Sakatah Singing Hills Trailhead Mankato, Sibley Park, Weagel Park, Red Jacket Trail Park, Rapidan

Fees and Passes: None

Trail Website:
www.co.blue-earth.mn.us/dept/parks/redjacket.php

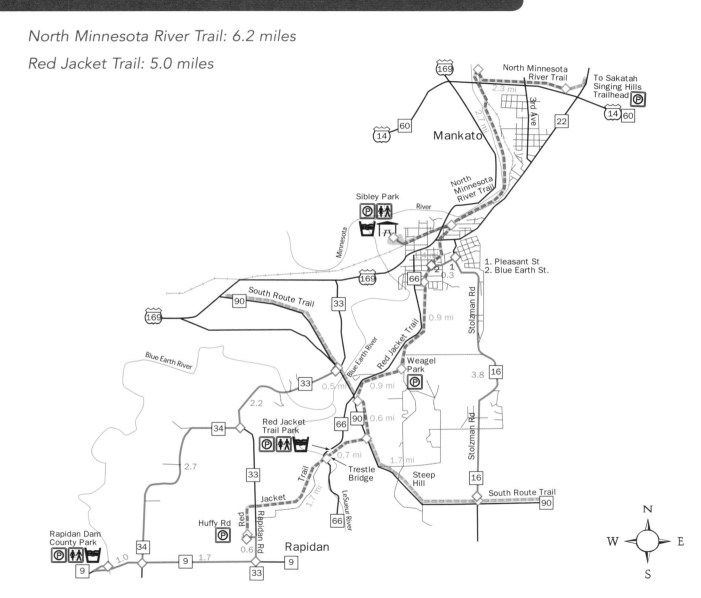
North Minnesota River Trail: 6.2 miles

Red Jacket Trail: 5.0 miles

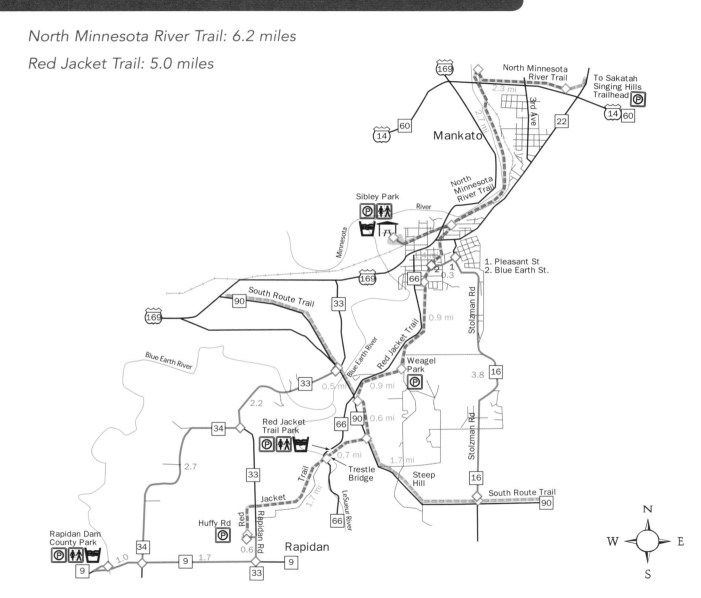

North Minnesota River Trail

To Sakatah Singing Hills Trailhead

Mankato

Sibley Park

Minnesota

River

1. Pleasant St
2. Blue Earth St.

South Route Trail

Blue Earth River

Red Jacket Trail

Weagel Park

Stolzman Rd

Red Jacket Trail Park

Trestle Bridge

Steep Hill

South Route Trail

Blue Earth River

LeSueur River

Huffy Rd

Red

Jacket

Rapidan Rd

Rapidan

Rapidan Dam County Park

2.3 mi · 2.7 mi · 0.3 · 0.9 mi · 3.8 · 0.5 mi · 0.9 mi · 0.6 mi · 1.7 mi · 0.7 mi · 1.7 mi · 2.2 · 2.7 · 1.0 · 1.7 · 0.6

Tourist Information

Greater Mankato Chamber & Convention Bureau
Toll Free: (800) 657-4733
Phone: (507) 345-4519
Fax: (507) 345-4451
Email: info@greatermankato.com
Web: www.greatermankato.com

Lodging

Motels/Resorts

Mankato
AmericInn
240 Stadium Rd
Toll Free: (800) 634-3444
Phone: (507) 345-8463
Web: www.americinnmankato.net

Fairfield Inn
141 Apache Pl
Phone: (507) 386-1220
Web: www.marriott.com
Riverfront Inn
1727 N Riverfront Dr
Phone: (507) 388-1638

Bed and Breakfast

Mankato
The Butler House B&B
704 S Broad S
Phone: (507) 387-5055
Email: butler1@hickorytech.net
Web: www.butlerhouse.com

Camping

Mankato
Land of Memories Park
Phone: (507) 387-8649
Minneopa State Park
54497 Gadwall Rd
Phone: (507) 389-5464
Web: www.dnr.state.mn.us

Bike Repair

Mankato
Broken Spoke
Phone: (507) 278-4320

Flying Penguin Outdoor Sports
Phone: (507) 345-4754

University Cycle Inc.
Phone: (507) 345-1144
Email: coolworld@mankatobikeshop.com
Web: www.mankatobikeshop.com

Festivals and Events

Mankato
June
National Brew Fest
Enjoy free samples of 100 of America's finest craft beers, sample the food court and groove at the music festival in downtown Mankato. Fourth Weekend.
Toll Free: (800) 657-4733
Phone: (507) 345-4451
Web: www.greatermankato.com

Solstice
Local and regional musicians, artists, crafts and food vendors will keep you entertained. Check website for dates.
Toll Free: (800) 657-4733
Phone: (507) 388-2506
Web: www.solsticemankato.com

Festivals and Events cont'd

Mankato
July
North Mankato Fun Days
Partake in a parade, horseshoe tournament, food, bingo, petting zoo, car show and fireworks. First Weekend.
Toll Free: (800) 657-4733
Phone: (507) 345-4451
Web: www.greatermankato.com

August
Hickory Street Ribfest
Twenty five bands on two stages entertain gamers and ribbers from across the country as they compete for cash and prizes. First Weekend.
Toll Free: (800) 657-4733
Phone: (507) 345-4451
Web: www.greatermankato.com

Alternate Activities

Mankato
Mount Kato
Offers seven miles of mountain bike trails for novice to expert rider. Trails are eighty percent wooded and single track.
Toll Free: (800) 668-5286
Phone: (507) 625-3363
Web: www.mountkato.com

Carnegie Art Center

The center hosts monthly gallery exhibitions featuring the work of regional artists, sponsors art education programs and runs the Broad Street Gallery Gift Shop.
Phone: (507) 625-2730

Elk's Nature Center

This is a unique 150 acre tract designed solely for passive recreation. Periodic special interest events are offered for adults and children at no cost.
Toll Free: (800) 657-4733
Phone: (507) 387-8585

Restaurants

Mankato

Pizza Man
Phone: (507) 344-8898

Eastern Buffet
Phone: (507) 625-8889

Neighbors Italian Bistro
Phone: (507) 625-6776

Hub Coffee House Café
Phone: (507) 388-4822

Rapidan Dam Café
Phone: (507) 546-9997

Peddler of Rapidan Restaurants
Menu: Irregular hours. Call ahead.
Phone: (507) 278-4808

Alternate Activities cont'd

Mankato

North Links Golf Course

The par 72, 18 hole course has four sets of tees and features the area's #1 driving range and two hole practice course with a chipping green and bunker. A pro shop, golf carts and lounge are also available.
Phone: (507) 947-3355
Web: www.northlinksgolf.com

Victory Bowl

An ultra modern bowling center features automatic scoring with 3-D color graphics, computer controlled bumpers for the kids and the Thunder Alley Sound & Light show.
Phone: (507) 387-7991
Web: www.victorybowl.com

About The Trail

This short, popular trail has two great access points at Pine Island and Douglas and a surprising number of amenities. The trail passes primarily through flat, rich agricultural land and ends on the north side of Rochester. Rochester sprawls around the southern end of the trail. Many spur trails to housing developments have made this a popular destination for walkers and cyclists.The Mayo Clinic and most of the city's services are ten miles from the trailhead.

Trail Highlights

Watch for irregular knobs of land protruding above the landscape about 3.5 miles south of Pine Island, followed by a slight rise into a wooded hillside. The trailhead in Douglas provides a pleasant, shaded rest stop.

About The Roads

Flat near the north and south ends of the trail, hilly and scenic just north of Douglas, these rural, lightly traveled roads cross the trail and pass near it but offer an entirely different look at the land.

Road Highlights

Going north from Douglas, County Road 3 climbs for about a mile to a ridgetop with great overviews of the valley below. Then it's up and down for another half dozen miles until payback time with a long, swift, scenic descent into the flatlands. Finish by entering the south end of Pine Island. See the city map for a route through town to the trailhead.

How To Get There

Pine Island is just off Highway 52 about seventy miles south of the Twin Cities. Take the Highway 11 exit. Trailhead is half a mile west of the highway. See the city map. Rochester is eighty miles south of the Twin Cities on Highway 52. Take the 19th Street NW exit and go west 0.6 miles to Valleyhigh Drive. Turn right. Valleyhigh becomes Olmsted County Highway 4. Continue to the trailhead. The distance from the intersection of 19th and Valleyhigh Drive to the trailhead is 1.3 miles. See the city map.

Vital Trail Information:

Trail Distance: 13

Trail Surface: Asphalt

Access Points: Pine Island, Douglas, Rochester

Fees and Passes: None

Trail Website:
www.dnr.state.mn.us/state

Pine Island to Rochester: 13 miles

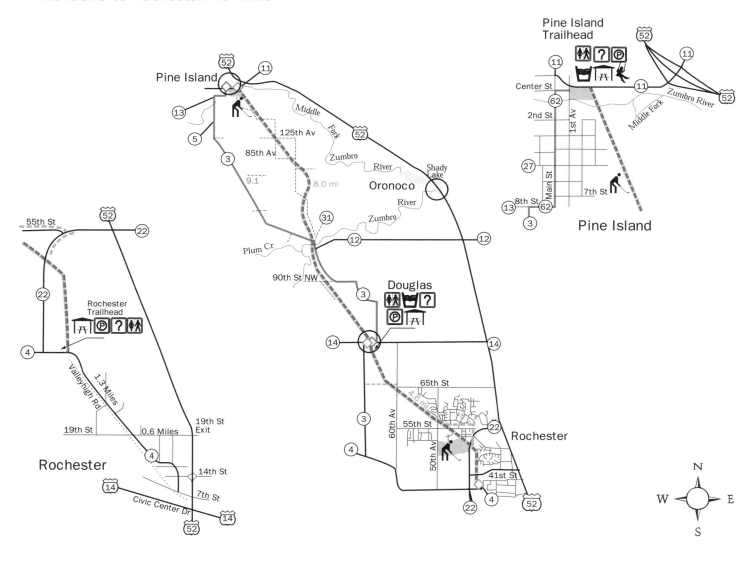

Tourist Information

City of Pine Island
Phone: (507) 356-4591
Fax: (507) 356-8230
Email: piclerk@pitel.net
Web: cc.pineislandmn.com

Rochester Convention and Visitors Bureau
Toll Free: (800) 634-8277
Phone: (507) 288-4331
Fax: (507) 288-9144
Email: info@rochestercvb.org
Web: www.rochestercvb.org

Lodging

Motels/Resorts

Rochester
Comfort Inn
5708 Bandel Rd NW
Toll Free: (877) 424-6423
Phone: (507) 289-3344
Fax: (507) 292-0963
Web: www.choicehotels.com

Country Inn & Suites
4323 Hwy 52 N & W Frontage Rd
Toll Free: (888) 201-1746
Phone: (507) 285-3335
Email: rochestercis@tharaldson.com
Web: www.countryinns.com

Kahler Inn & Suites
9 3rd Ave NW
Toll Free: (800) 533-1655
Phone: (507) 285-9200
Email: bseitl@sunstonehotels.com
Web: www.kahler.com

Camping

Pine Island
Wazionja Campground
6450 120th St NW
Phone: (507) 356-8594

Rochester
Willow Creek Campground & RV Park
5525 Hwy 63 S
Phone: (507) 281-0304
Web: www.willowcreeksite.com

Bike Rental

Rochester
Silver Lake Boat & Bike Rental
Phone: (507) 261-9049
Email: richard.aaronandjeab@gmail.com
Web: www.silverlakefun.com

Bike Repair

Rochester
Bicycle Sports, Inc.
1400 5th Pl NW
Phone: (507) 281-5007
Email: gritman@bicyclesportsinc.com
Web: www.bicyclesportsinc.com

Honest Bike Shop
431 4th Ave SE
Phone: (507) 288-8888
Web: www.honestbikeshop.com

Rochester Cycling and Fitness
1211 NW 7th St
Phone: (507) 289-7410
Email: info@cycling-fitness.com
Web: www.cycling-fitness.com

Festivals and Events

Rochester
All Summer
Down by the Riverside Concerts
Watch free evening concerts in Mayo Park by various musical groups. Mid-July through mid-August. Call for schedule.
Toll Free: (800) 657-3980
Phone: (507) 328-2200
Web: www.riversideconcerts.com

Festivals and Events cont'd

Rochester

May

Med City Marathon
Run the marathon and two & four person relay. Sunday before Memorial Day.
Toll Free: (800) 634-8277
Phone: (507) 288-4331
Web: www.medcitymarathon.com.

June

Mayowood Family Festival
Tour the Mayowood Mansion and several private gardens. Last Saturday in June.
Toll Free: (800) 634-8277
Phone: (507) 282-9447
Web: www.olmstedhistory.com

Rochesterfest
Party at the street dance and parade with live music, food vendors and family entertainment. Weeklong celebration, mid-June.
Toll Free: (800) 634-8277
Phone: (507) 285-8769
Web: www.rochesterfest.com

July

4th of July Celebration
The Water Ski Club performs at Silver Lake. Check out food vendors and fireworks. First Weekend.
Toll Free: (800) 634-8277
Phone: (507) 288-4331
Web: www.rochestercvb.org

Olmsted County Fair
Enjoy exhibits, food and entertainment at the fairgrounds. Check website for dates.
Toll Free: (800) 634-8277
Phone: (507) 282-0519
Web: www.olmstedcountyfair.com

August

Greek Festival
Come for the music, food and dance. Call for info and location.
Toll Free: (800) 634-8277
Phone: (507) 282-1529
Web: www.greekfestrochester.com

September

Fall Harvest Fest
Nature related activities and crafts, canoeing, a rock climbing wall, minnow races, live music and a food wagon will keep you entertained at the Quarry Hill Nature Center. Check website for date.
Phone: (507) 281-6114
Web: www.qhnc.org

Olmstead County Gold Rush Days
See the antique show, flea market and food vendors at the fairgrounds three times each year. Check website for dates.
Phone: (507) 288-0320
Web: www.iridescenthouse.com

Alternate Activities

Rochester

Rochester Art Center
Browse fine arts and crafts and ongoing exhibits. Free admission.
Phone: (507) 282-8629
Web: www.rochesterartcenter.org

Silver Lake Park
Get some exercise by biking, roller-blading, jogging, paddle boating and canoeing (for rent). Also try picnicking, then swing by the children's adventure playground or outdoor pool.
Phone: (507) 328-2525
Web: www.ci.rochester.mn.us

Olmsted County History Center & Museum
See pictures, maps, diaries, exhibits, a restored pioneer log cabin and a one room schoolhouse.
Phone: (507) 282-9447
Web: www.olmstedhistory.com

Mayo Clinic Tours
Join a behind-the-scenes walking tour to learn about Mayo's historical origins, art and architecture. Monday through Friday at 10:00am.
Phone: (507) 538-0440
Web: www.mayoclinic.com

Sekapp Orchard
Pick your own strawberries and raspberries.
Phone: (507) 282-4544

Quarry Hill Nature Center
The center has hiking trails, a bike trail that connects to town, interactive displays and exhibits, a 1,700 gallon aquarium, live bee display and a life-size model T-Rex head.
Phone: (507) 281-6114

Web: www.qhnc.org

Restaurants

Pine Island

Dominic's Pizzaria
Phone: (507) 356-8008

Rochester

Culvers of Rochester
Phone: (507) 281-8538
Web: www.culversofrochester.com

Wong's Café
Phone: (507) 288-3730

Michaels Steaks, Chops & Seafood Restaurants
Phone: (507) 288-2020

Newt's
Menu: American Style
Phone: (507) 289-0577
Web: www.cccrmg.com/newts.htm

The Redwood Room
Menu: Gourmet Mediterranean and European
Phone: (507) 281-2978
Web: www.cccrmg.com/redwoodroom.htm

City Market
Menu: Deli
Phone: (507) 536-4748
Web: www.zcitymarket.com

About The Trail

A former Milwaukee Road railbed running through the blufflands and Amish country of southeast Minnesota, the trail follows and crosses the Root River as it passes beneath towering bluffs. The scenery is exceptional and the wildlife abundant. Expect to see hawks and vultures riding wind currents near the bluffs, wild turkeys in the woods, and deer in the open fields. Lanesboro, with its entire Main Street designated a historic district, is the best-known town on the trail, but Rushford offers a unique museum in its two story depot, Whalan is known for its pies and the Houston Trailhead is a combination Nature Center, restroom and shower facility.

Trail Highlights

Check out the Karst landscape near Fountain. Karst is a type of topography characterized by sinkholes, caves and underground channels. The Harmony-Preston Valley Trail begins just east of the Isinours Unit. See Harmony-Preston Valley Trail for details. The dam and road cut on the western edge of Lanesboro create a dramatic first impression of the trail if you start from Lanesboro and ride west. East of Lanesboro, the trail hugs the Root River for some miles as it squeezes between the bluffs and the river. For a change of pace, start and end your trip in Houston. The trail is very scenic and underused between Rushford and Houston.

About The Roads

From the Valley of the Root River to the top of the bluffs, the roads will lead you through all the terrain that you only see from the trail. The options are endless, sometimes the hills will feel the same. Roads are low traffic with generally good asphalt, but watch for Amish vehicles, buffalo farms and forty mile per hour descents off the bluffs. Expect to climb in any direction as you go away from the Root River.

Road Highlights

Highway 13 from Houston climbs steeply through a couple of ten mph switchbacks to the ridgetop. Highway 30 is quite flat from Arendahl to several miles east of Highway 25, then begins a rapid descent towards Rushford. The first few miles of the descent pass through a narrow, intimate valley. Highways 21 and 10, south of the trail, have been re-paved recently. The climb from Lanesboro to Highway 12 is long and fairly steep. Watch for the buffalo farm at the intersection of Highways 10 and 12.

How To Get There

Fountain, the western terminus, is about thirty miles south of Rochester on Highway 52. Continue on Highway 52 to Highway 16 for access to Lanesboro and other towns along the trail. From the east, take Interstate 90 west from Le Crescent about twenty-five miles to Highway 16. Rushford is about ten miles south of Interstate 90 on Highway 16. See trail and city maps for details.

Vital Trail Information:

Trail Distance: 43

Trail Surface: Asphalt

Access Points: Fountain, Lanesboro, Whalan, Peterson, Rushford, Houston

Fees and Passes: None

Trail Website: www.rootrivertrail.org

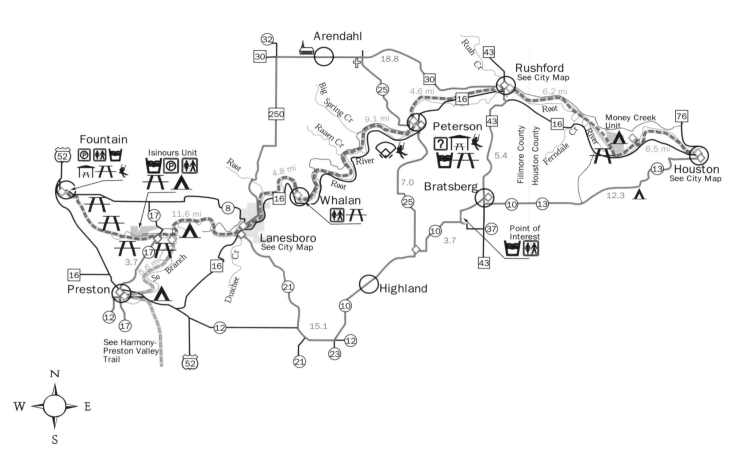
Fountain to Houston: 43 miles

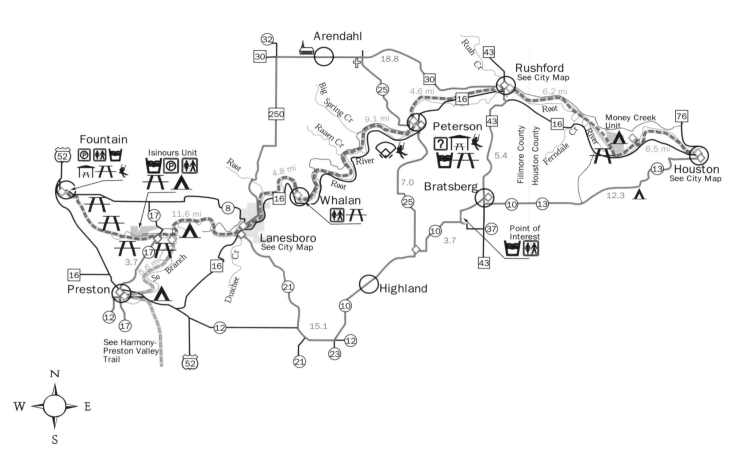

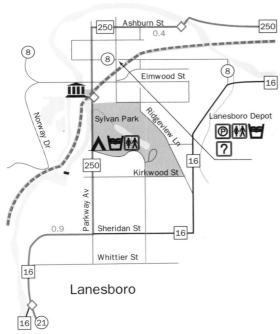

Lanesboro

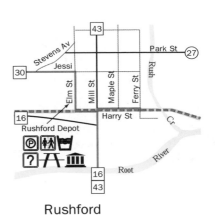

Rushford

Houston

Green Gables Inn
303 W Sheridan St
Toll Free: (800) 818-4225
Phone: (507) 467-2936
Email: green@acegroup.cc
Web: www.lanesboroweb.
com/greengables/

Peterson
Geneva's Hideaway
87 Centennial St
Toll Free: (877) 727-4816
Phone: (507) 875-7733
Email: genevas@acegroup.cc
Web: www.genevashideaway.com

Wenneson Historic Inn
425 Prospect St
Phone: (507) 875-2587
Email: wenneson@acegroup.cc
Web: www.wennesonhistoricinn.com

Bed and Breakfast

Houston
Addie's Attic B&B
117 South Jackson St
P.O. Box 677
Phone: (507) 896-3010
Web: www.bbonline.com/mn/addies/

The Bunkhouse
501 S Jefferson
Phone: (507) 896-2080
Email: jaschultz@acegroup.cc
Web: www.houstonbunkhouse.com

Lanesboro
Berwood Hill Inn
22139 Hickory Rd
Toll Free: (800) 803-6748
Phone: (507) 765-2391
Email: indulge@berwood.com
Web: www.berwood.com

Tourist Information

City of Fountain
Phone: (507) 268-4923
Web: www.bluffcountry.com/fountain.htm

Historic Bluff Country
Toll Free: (800) 428-2030
Phone: (507) 886-2230
Email: hbc@harmonytel.net
Web: www.bluffcountry.com

Houston Nature Center
Phone: (507) 896-4668
Email: nature@acegroup.cc
Web: www.houstonmn.com

Lanesboro Chamber of Commerce
Toll Free: (800) 944-2670
Phone: (507) 467-2696
Web: www.lanesboro.com

Rushford Area Chamber of Commerce
Phone: (507) 864-3338
Email: chamber@acegroup.cc
Web: www.rushfordchamber.com

Lodging

Motels/Resorts

Lanesboro
Brewster's Red Hotel
106 Parkway Ave S
Phone: (507) 467-2999
Email: info@brewstersredhotel.com
Web: www.brewstersredhotel.com

Eagle Cliff Campground & Lodging
3 miles east of Lanesboro on Hwy 16,
RR1, PO Box 344
Phone: (507) 467-2598
Web: www.eaglecliff-campground.com

Lodging cont'd

Bed and Breakfast

Lanesboro

Cady Hays House
500 Calhoun Ave
Phone: (507) 467-2621
Email: cadyhbb@acegroup.cc
Web: www.cadyhayeshouse.com

Cozy Quilt Cottage
RR2 Box 9
Phone: (507) 467-2458
Email: weaveab@acegroup.cc

Habberstad House Bed and Breakfast
706 Fillmore Ave S
Phone: (507) 467-3560
Email: habrstad@acegroup.cc
Web: www.habberstadhouse.com

Hillcrest Hide-away B&B
404 Hillcrest St E
Toll Free: (800) 697-9902
Phone: (507) 467-3079
Email: hillcresthideaway@yahoo.com
Web: www.hillcresthideaway.com

Historic Scanlon House
708 Parkway Ave S
Toll Free: (800) 944-2158
Phone: (507) 467-2158
Email: ScanlanBB@aol.com
Web: www.scanlonhouse.com

Mrs. B's Inn & Restaurants
101 Parkway Ave N
P.O. Box 411
Toll Free: (800) 657-4710
Phone: (507) 467-2154
Email: mrsbsinn@earthlink.net
Web: www.mrsbsinn.com

The Inn at Sacred Clay Farm
23234 Grosbeak Rd
Toll Free: (866) 326-8618
Phone: (507) 467-9600
Email: sacredclayfarm@acegroup.cc
Web: www.sacredclayfarmbandb.com

Rushford

Meadows Inn B&B
900 Pine Meadows Ln
Phone: (507) 864-2378
Email: meadowsinn@acegroup.cc
Web: www.meadowsinn.com

River Trail Inn
202 S Mill St
Toll Free: (800) 584-6764
Phone: (507) 864-7886
Web: www.rivertrailinn.com

Sweet Dreams B&B
32796 Sorum Rd
Phone: (507) 864-2462

Camping

Houston

Cushon's Peak Campground
18696 Hwy 16
Phone: (507) 896-7325
Email: camppeak@acegroup.cc
Web: www.camppeak.com

Lanesboro

Eagle Cliff Campground & Lodging
3 miles east of Lanesboro on Hwy 16,
RR1, PO Box 344
Phone: (507) 467-2598
Web: www.eaglecliff-campground.com

Sylvan Park/Riverview Campground
202 Parkway Ave S
P O Box 333
Phone: (507) 467-3722

Peterson

Peterson RV Campground
P.O. Box 11
Phone: (507) 875-2587
Email: campground@petersonmn.org
Web: www.petersonmn.org/campground.htm

Preston

The Old Barn Resort
Rt 3, Box 57
Toll Free: (800) 552-2512
Phone: (507) 467-2512
Email: info@barnresort.com
Web: www.barnresort.com

Rushford

North End Park
City Park in Rushford
Phone: (507) 864-3338

Bike Rental

Lanesboro

Eagle Cliff Campground
Rt 1 Box 344
Phone: (507) 467-2598
Web: www.eaglecliff-campground.com

Bike Rental cont'd

Lanesboro
Little River General Store
P.O. Box 317
Toll Free: (800) 994-2943
Phone: (507) 467-2943
Web: www.lrgeneralstore.com

Root River Outfitters
109 Parkway Ave S
Phone: (507) 467-3400
Email: rro@acegroup.cc
Web: www.rootriveroutfitters.com

Rushford
Geneva's Hideaway
307 Industrial Dr
Toll Free: (877) 727-4816
Phone: (507) 875-7733
Email: genevas@acegroup.cc
Web: www.genevashideaway.com

Bike Repair

Lanesboro
Little River General Store
P.O. Box 317
Toll Free: (800) 994-2943
Phone: (507) 467-2943
Web: www.lrgeneralstore.com

Festivals and Events

Houston
May
Bluff Country Bird Festival
Sponsored by Eagle Bluff Environmental Learning Center, the festival offers opportunities to see Sandhill Cranes, Tennessee Warblers, Tufted Titmice, Sora Rails and more. Check website for details.
Toll Free: (800) 428-2030
Phone: (507) 886-2230
Web: www.bluffcountry.com

July
Hoedown Days
Come for the flea market, quilt display, antique cars and tractors, soapbox derby, live music and parade.
Last full weekend.
Phone: (507) 896-3010
Web: www.houstonhoedown.com

Lanesboro
All Summer
Farmers Market
Find fresh produce, baked goods and crafts by Amish farmers. Wednesday evenings and Saturday mornings, May through October in Sylvan Park.
Toll Free: (800) 944-2670
Phone: (507) 467-2696
Web: www.lanesboro.com

June
Art in the Park
Check out artisans and crafters, entertainment, demos, food, children's activities and a photography contest. Father's Day.
Toll Free: (800) 944-2670
Phone: (507) 467-2696
Web: www.lanesboro.com

August
Buffalo Bill Days
There is a parade, flea market, brat and beer garden, live theater, volleyball and softball tourneys, a dance and pony rides. First Weekend.
Toll Free: (800) 944-2670
Phone: (507) 467-2696
Web: www.lanesboro.com

October
Fall Fest
Spend the day doing harvest activities for all ages, a cookie walk and wagon rides. First Saturday.
Toll Free: (800) 944-2670
Phone: (507) 467-2696
Web: www.lanesboro.com

Rushford
July
Rushford Days Celebration
This party has food, a street dance, flea market, softball tournament, craft fair and entertainment. Third Weekend.
Phone: (507) 864-7820
Web: www.rushford.govoffice.com

Whalan
May
Standstill Parade and Sykkle Tur
The parade doesn't move; the spectators do! Also see the Lefse and soap making demos, church food and antique bicycles. Call for date.
Toll Free: (800) 944-2670
Phone: (507) 467-2696

Alternate Activities

Fountain
Fillmore County History Center
A collection of artifacts that describes the heritage of Fillmore County includes a huge tractor collection, airplane memorabilia and genealogy services (weekdays only).
Phone: (507) 268-4449
Web: www.fillmorecountyhistory.wordpress.com

Houston
Houston Nature Center
See REBART, recycled bike art, over the weekend before Labor Day, the Summer Solstice Celebration and free nature programs every Saturday at 7:00pm. Restrooms, showers and visitor information located in the Center.
Phone: (507) 896-4668
Web: www.houstonmn.com/Nature/nature2.htm

Alternate Activities cont'd

Lanesboro

Eagle Cliff Campground
Rent canoes, kayaks or inner tubes.
Phone: (507) 467-2598
Web: www.eaglecliff-campground.com

Cornucopia Art Center
Local and regional artists display their
work at year 'round exhibits.
Phone: (507) 467-2446
Web: www.lanesboroarts.org

State Fish Hatchery
Take a self-guided tour of the largest
trout hatchery in Minnesota. Open
Monday through Friday.
Phone: (507) 467-3771
Web: www.dnr.state.mn.us

Scenic Valley Winery
Taste and buy wine and browse the gift
shop.
Toll Free: (888) 965-0250
Phone: (507) 467-2958
Web: www.scenicvalleywinery.com

**Eagle Bluff Environmental
Learning Center**
Book a reservation to come and experi-
ence four and a half miles of hiking
trails, a bat condominium, raptor view-
ing from the bluffs and treetop-high
ropes course.
Toll Free: (888) 800-9558
Phone: (507) 467-2437
Web: www.eagle-bluff.org

Commonweal Theatre Company
Watch a show, from Shakespeare to mu-
sicals and more, at this live professional
theater. Call for schedule.
Toll Free: (800) 657-7025
Phone: (507) 467-2525
Web: www.commonwealtheatre.org

Peterson

1877 Peterson Station Museum
The museum is close to the trail. Call
for hours.
Phone: (507) 875-2551

Geneva's Hideaway
Rent canoes and inner tubes.
Toll Free: (877) 727-4816
Phone: (507) 875-7733
Web: www.genevashideaway.com

Rushford

Rushford Historic Depot
See the depot, schoolhouse, church
and jail, all next to the trail.
Phone: (507) 864-3338

Restaurants

Lanesboro

Mrs. B's Inn & Restaurants
Toll Free: (800) 657-4710
Phone: (507) 467-2154
Web: www.mrsbsinn.com

Old Village Hall Restaurants
111 Coffee St
Phone: (507) 467-2962
Web: www.oldvillagehall.com

Auntie's Café
Phone: (507) 467-4567

The Aroma Pie Shoppe
618 Main St
Phone: (507) 467-2623
Peterson

Judy's Country Café
Phone: (507) 875-2424

Preston

Old Barn Resort
Rt 3 Box 57
Toll Free: (800) 552-2512
Phone: (507) 467-2512
Web: www.barnresort.com/Restaurants.htm

Rushford

Stumpy's Restaurants
Phone: (507) 864-7156
Web: stumpys.net/

The Creamery
Phone: (507) 864-7214
Web: www.the-creamery.com

McGeorge's Steak & Burger
Phone: (507) 864-7654

About The Trail

A spur off the Root River Trail, it has enough character to merit independent status. The trail begins near the Isinours Unit near the west end of the Root River Trail and follows the south branch of the Root to Preston. From Preston it follows Camp Creek south for several miles, then climbs quickly to the top of the ridge near Harmony. This trail crosses the creek many times and runs neither flat nor straight, making it a welcome addition to the trails of Minnesota.

Trail Highlights

Camp Creek is a quiet trout stream running through small woodlots and along the edge of farms and horse pastures. It's almost always shaded and quiet. Watch for small, seldom used concrete access bridges across the creek. If you don't feel up to climbing to Harmony, consider a bike shuttle to the town and an effortless ride down from the hilltop to the edge of Camp Creek. North of Preston, the trail has all the charm and more variety of terrain than any section of the Root River Trail. For a short side trip follow the one mile Trout Run Trail along the Root River in Preston.

About The Roads

From hilltop to river bottom, expect a large change in elevation including either steep climbs or quick descents. Traffic on Highway 22 near Harmony and Highway 17 near Preston is moderate. Highway 15 and the two mile section of Highway 22 that is gravel are low traffic and very scenic.

Road Highlights

Highway 17 was recently paved and is very smooth. It has moderate traffic and follows a scenic ridgeline until it drops into Preston. If you don't mind some gravel, ride Highways 15 and 22 south from Preston. The route follows a valley creating an intimate, scenic ride. The gravel section is about two miles long on Highway 22.

How To Get There

Preston is about forty miles south of Rochester on Highway 52. Continue south on Highway 52 to Harmony for a hilltop start.

Vital Trail Information:

Trail Distance: 18

Trail Surface: Asphalt

Access Points: Preston, Harmony, Root River Trail at Isinours Unit

Fees and Passes: None

Trail Website:
www.dnr.state.mn.us/state_trails

Isinours Unit to Harmony: 17.6 miles

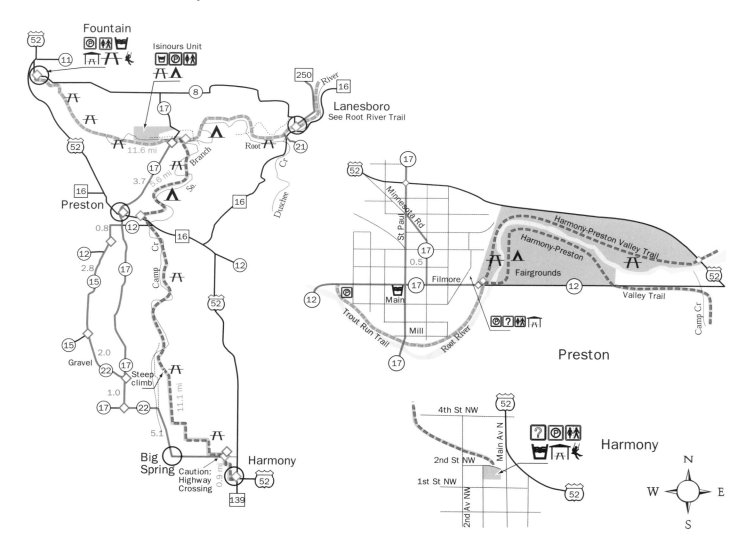

Fountain

Isinours Unit

Lanesboro
See Root River Trail

Root

S. Branch

Duschee Cr

Preston

Camp Cr

Gravel

Steep climb

11.1 mi

Big Spring

Caution: Highway Crossing

0.9 mi

Harmony

52

Minnesota Rd

St Paul St

Filmore

Main

Mill

Trout Run Trail

Root River

Harmony-Preston Valley Trail

Harmony-Preston

Fairgrounds

Valley Trail

Camp Cr

Preston

4th St NW

Main Av N

2nd St NW

1st St NW

2nd Av NW

Harmony

N
W — E
S

Tourist Information

Harmony Visitor Information
Toll Free: (800) 247-6466
Phone: (507) 886-2469
Email: visit@harmonytel.net
Web: www.harmony.mn.us

Historic Forestville
Phone: (507) 765-2785
Email: forestville@mnhs.org
Web: www.mnhs.org

Preston Area Tourism Association
Toll Free: (888) 845-2100
Phone: (507) 765-2153
Email: preston@prestonmn.org

Lodging

Motels/Resorts

Harmony
Country Lodge Motel
525 Main Ave N
P.O. Box 656
Toll Free: (800) 870-1710
Phone: (507) 886-2515
Email: ctrylodg@harmonytel.net
Web: www.countrylodgeinnharmonymn.com

Preston
The Old Barn Resort
Rt 3, Box 57
Toll Free: (800) 552-2512
Phone: (507) 467-2512
Email: info@barnresort.com
Web: www.barnresort.com

Bed and Breakfast

Preston
Jailhouse Inn
109 Houston St NW
PO Box 422
Phone: (507) 765-2181
Email: innkeepers@jailhouseinn.com
Web: www.jailhouseinn.com

Camping

Harmony
Harmony Campground
Phone: (507) 886-2469

Preston
Fillmore County Fairgrounds Camping
413 Fillmore Street E
Phone: (507) 765-2425

Maple Springs Campground, Inc.
21606 Co. 118
Phone: (507) 352-2056
Email: maplecamp@hmtel.com
Web: www.maplespringscampground.com

The Old Barn Resort
Rt 3, Box 57
Toll Free: (800) 552-2512
Phone: (507) 467-2512
Email: info@barnresort.com
Web: www.barnresort.com

Bike Rental

Harmony
Kingsley Merchantile
Phone: (507) 886-2323

Preston
Brick House Coffee House
104 E Main St
Phone: (507) 765-9820

Root River Outfitters
Rt 3 Box 57
Phone: (507) 467-3400
Email: rro@acegroup.cc
Web: www.rootriveroutfitters.com

Festivals and Events

Forestville
All Summer
Forestville Bread and Butter Day
Watch demonstrations of 1899 domestic arts such as baking and butter making. Check website for dates.
Toll Free: (800) 657-3773
Phone: (507) 765-2785
Web: www.mnhs.org

July
4th of July at Forestville
Enjoy music, speeches and children's games at Historic Forestville, located in Forestville State Park.
Toll Free: (800) 657-3773
Phone: (507) 765-2785
Web: www.mnhs.org

Evening of Leisure
Experience summer leisure activities of 1899 through music, toys, games and food in Historic Forestville.
Check website for dates.
Toll Free: (800) 657-3773
Phone: (507) 765-2785
Web: www.mnhs.org

October
Harvest Day
Come for the corn harvest, apple cider pressing, quilting bee and heirloom seed saving. It's only on Saturday.
Check website for dates.
Toll Free: (800) 657-3773
Phone: (507) 765-2785
Web: www.mnhs.org

Harmony
July
4th of July
Stay busy with the parade, kids' games and fireworks.
Toll Free: (800) 247-6466
Phone: (507) 886-8122
Web: www.harmony.mn.us

October
Fall Foliage Fest
Take in Amish tours, horse and wagon rides, food vendors, shopping, a scarecrow contest, toad races, sheep shearing and spinning and a fish fry at the Legion. Check website for date.
Toll Free: (800) 247-6466
Phone: (507) 886-8122
Web: www.harmony.mn.us

Preston
May
Trout Days
Enjoy the parade, bike ride, craft show, food vendors, street dance and car show. Third Weekend.
Toll Free: (888) 845-2100
Phone: (507) 765-2100
Web: www.preston.org

July
Fillmore County Fair
Explore exhibits, food and entertainment. Third Weekend.
Toll Free: (888) 845-2100
Phone: (507) 765-2100
Web: www.fillmorecountyfair.com

September
Fall Foliage
On Saturday only go for a hay wagon ride, feast on chicken BBQ and browse city-wide garage sales. Fourth Weekend.
Toll Free: (888) 845-2100
Phone: (507) 765-2100
Web: www.preston.org

Alternate Activities

Forestville

Forestville/Mystery Cave State Park
The park has trout fishing, camping, a seventeen mile shared hiking and horseback trail system and tours of Mystery Cave, the longest cave in Minnesota.
Phone: (507) 352-5111
Web: www.dnr.state.mn.us

Historic Forestville
See the daily living history program with costumed interpreters. Located in Forestville State Park.
Toll Free: (888) 727-8386
Phone: (507) 765-2785
Web: www.mnhs.org

Harmony

Harmony Roller Rink
Lace up your roller skates at this indoor rink.
Phone: (507) 886-4444

Harmony Toy Museum
See over 4,000 toys on display.
Toll Free: (800) 247-6466
Phone: (507) 886-8122
Web: www.harmony.mn.us

Niagara Cave
On daily guided tours see the sixty foot underground waterfall, and stop by the gift shop.
Toll Free: (800) 837-6606
Phone: (507) 886-6606
Web: www.niagaracave.com

Austin's Goat Farm
Two hundred baby angora goats produce mohair for knitters to create a variety of hand-crafted pieces. Stop by the gift shop on your tour.
Phone: (507) 886-6731
Web: www.bluffcountry.com/austins.htm

Slim's Wood Shed
Enjoy the woodcarving museum/workshop, hand carved circus caricatures display, woodcarving supplies and gift shop.
Phone: (507) 886-3114
Web: www.slimswoodshed.com

Michel's Amish Tours
Take a tour with your personal guide through Amish country.
Toll Free: (800) 752-6474
Phone: (507) 886-5392

Amish Country Tours
Go on minibus and car tours of Amish farms.
Toll Free: (800) 752-6474
Phone: (507) 886-2303
Web: www.shawcorp.com/amish

Preston

Preston Apple and Berry Farm
Find bedding plants and garden seeds in April and May. Pick your own strawberries in June, raspberries in August and September, and apples August to January.
Phone: (507) 765-4486
Web: www.bluffcountry.com/appleberry.htm

Restaurants

Harmony

Harmony House
57 Main Ave N
Phone: (507) 886-4612

Wheelers Bar & Grill
Menu: American Style
Phone: (507) 886-4444

Sugar Plum
Menu: Sweets, Drinks, Sandwiches
Toll Free: (877) 886-2409
Phone: (507) 886-2666

Preston

Branding Iron
Phone: (507) 765-3388

Brick House on Main Coffeehouse
104 Main St SE
Toll Free: (888) 999-1576
Phone: (507) 765-9820

Bowlwinkles Cantina
Phone: (507) 765-2522

Old Barn Resort
Rt 3 Box 57
Toll Free: (800) 552-2512
Phone: (507) 467-2512
Web: www.barnresort.com

About The Trail

Madeline Island is three miles off the shores of Bayfield, Wisconsin, in the heart of the Apostle Islands of Lake Superior. Access via a ferry. Explore the island town of La Pointe, then circle the island for great views of Lake Superior and intimate wanders through deep forest. Lake Superior chills the island through June. The best times to visit are July through September.

Trail Highlights

There is no formal trail through Madeline Island, but a paved shoulder on Middle Road is designated for bikes only and leads to the most popular destination on the Island, Big Bay State Park.

About The Roads

Madeline Island is almost flat, with a few small rises. Traffic is restricted to forty miles per hour on the whole island and the speed limit is generally observed. The roads have low traffic, are well maintained and wander through dense forest and along the shores of Lake Superior.

Road Highlights

Big Bay Road, between Big Bay Town Park and School House Road, has the best views of Lake Superior. South Shore Drive is quiet and remote as it wanders through deep woods. The park roads in Big Bay State Park are scenic and low traffic. North Shore Drive and the roads connecting to it are gravel. The surface is generally well maintained, but wide tires are recommended. The island has approximately thirty miles of roads, and most are worth riding.

How To Get There

Take Interstate 35 to Duluth and cross into Wisconsin on Highway 2. Go east on Highway 2 to Highway 13 south and follow Highway 13 around the Bayfield Peninsula to Bayfield. Take the Madeline Island Ferry from Bayfield to the Island. Highway 63 through northwest Wisconsin offers a more direct route, but it is usually two lanes and runs through numerous small towns.

Vital Trail Information:

Trail Distance: 6

Trail Surface: Paved Shoulder

Access Points: LaPointe

Fees and Passes: None

Trail Website:
www.madelineisland.com

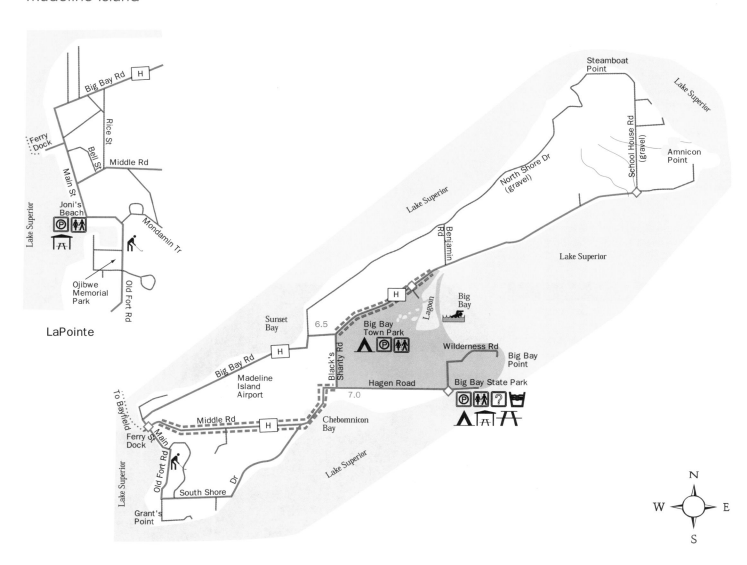
Madeline Island

LaPointe

Big Bay Rd   H

Rice St

Ferry
Dock

Bell St

Middle Rd

Main St

Lake Superior

Joni's
Beach

Mondamin Tr

Old Fort Rd

Ojibwe
Memorial
Park

Sunset
Bay

6.5

Big Bay Rd   H

Madeline
Island
Airport

Black's Shanty Rd

7.0

Middle Rd   H

Chebomnicon
Bay

To Bayfield

Ferry
Dock

Main St

Old Fort Rd

South Shore Dr

Grant's
Point

Lake Superior

Lake Superior

Big Bay
Town Park

H

Lagoon

Big
Bay

Benjamin Rd

Lake Superior

Wilderness Rd

Hagen Road

Big Bay
Point

Big Bay State Park

North Shore Dr
(gravel)

Lake Superior

Steamboat
Point

School House Rd
(gravel)

Amnicon
Point

Lake Superior

Lake Superior

N
W   E
S

Tourist Information

Bayfield Chamber of Commerce
Toll Free: (800) 447-4094
Phone: (715) 779-3335
Email: chamber@bayfield.org
Web: www.bayfield.org

Madeline Island Chamber of Commerce
Toll Free: (888) 475-3386
Phone: (715) 747-2801
Email: vacation@madelineisland.com
Web: www.madelineisland.com

Madeline Island Ferry Line
Phone: (715) 747-2051
Email: vacation@madelineisland.com
Web: www.madferry.com

Lodging

Motels/Resorts

Bayfield
Harbor's Edge Motel
331 N Front St
Phone: (715) 779-3926
Email: info@harborsedgemotel.com
Web: www.harborsedgemotel.com

La Pointe
The Inn on Madeline Island
P.O. Box 93
Toll Free: (800) 822-6315
Phone: (715) 747-6315
Fax: (715) 747-6345
Email: theinn@madisland.com
Web: www.madisland.com

Bed and Breakfast

Bayfield
Apostle Island Rentals
Toll Free: (800) 842-1199
Phone: (715) 779-3621
Email: rental@apostleislands.com
Web: www.apostleisland.com

Greunke's First St. Inn
17 Rittenhouse Ave
P.O. Box 768
Toll Free: (800) 245-3072
Phone: (715) 779-5480
Email: judith@greunkesinn.com
Web: www.greunkesinn.com

Isaac Wing House
17 S 1st St
Toll Free: (800) 382-0995
Phone: (715) 779-3363
Email: Info@Isaacwinghouse.com
Web: www.isaacwinghouse.com

Old Rittenhouse Inn
301 Rittenhouse Ave
Toll Free: (800) 779-2129
Phone: (715) 779-5111
Web: www.rittenhouseinn.com

The Bayfield Inn
20 Rittenhouse Ave
Toll Free: (800) 382-0995
Phone: (715) 779-3363
Email: info@thebayfieldinn.com
Web: www.bayfieldinn.com

La Pointe
Bog Lake Outfitters
P. O. Box 341
Phone: (715) 747-2685
Email: boglakeotftr@yahoo.com
Web: www.madelineisland.com/boglake

Brittany Cottages
Old Fort Rd
P.O. Box 458
Phone: (715) 747-5023
Fax: (715) 747-6263
Email: coolepark@cheqnet.net
Web: www.brittanycabins.com

Lodging cont'd

Bed and Breakfast

La Pointe

Cadotte's Cottages
P.O. Box 103A
Phone: (715) 747-3075
Email: cado@cheqnet.net

Marshcroft Lodge
1360 Middle Rd
Toll Free: (800) 243-5283
Phone: (715) 373-2122
Email: nwcoftsp@nwcoffeemills.com
Web: www.marshcroft.com

Woods Manor
P.O. Box 7
Toll Free: (800) 966-3756
Phone: (715) 747-3102
Email: tundra@islandelegance.com
Web: www.islandelegance.com

Camping

Bayfield

Apostle Islands Area Campground
85150 Trailer Ct Rd
Phone: (715) 779-5524

Dalrymple Park
Bayfield City Hall
North Hwy 13
Phone: (715) 779-5712

Lodging cont'd

Camping

La Pointe
Big Bay State Park
P.O. Box 589
Bayfield 54814
Toll Free: (877) 303-9663
Phone: (715) 747-6425
Email: Mark.Eggleson@wisconsin.gov
@dnr.state.wi.us
Web: www.dnr.state.wi.us

Big Bay Town Park
Toll Free: (888) 475-3386
Phone: (715) 747-2801
Email: vacation@madelineisland.com
Web: www.madelineisland.com

Bike Rental

Bayfield
Trek & Trail
Toll Free: (800) 354-8735
Phone: (715) 779-3595
Email: trek@trek-trail.com
Web: www.trek-trail.com

La Pointe
Motion to Go
Phone: (715) 747-6585
Email: drgoldo@cheqnet.net
Web: www.motion-to-go.com

Bike Repair

Ashland
Bay City Cycles
412 Main St
Phone: (715) 682-2091

Festivals and Events

Bayfield
May
Bayfield in Bloom
A month-long celebration of blooming wildflowers and orchards features plant sales; special gardeners' seminars and workshops, the Apple Blossom walk/run, garden, orchard and wildflower tours, special lodging packages and retail and Restaurants discounts. Mid-May through mid-June.
Toll Free: (800) 447-4094
Phone: (715) 779-3335
Web: www.bayfield.org

June
Lake Superior Big Top Chautauqua
Relax in this 850 seat tent theatre. A seventy night summer season of concerts, variety shows and original historical musicals includes national acts and runs from mid-June to early September.
Toll Free: (888) 244-8368
Phone: (715) 373-5552
Web: www.bigtop.org

Schubert Festival
Enjoy a concert of baroque music to celebrate the Blessing of the Fleet. Call for dates.
Toll Free: (800) 447-4094
Phone: (715) 779-3335
Web: www.bayfield.org

July
Bayfield Festival of the Arts
Over 100 artists from nine states gather in Memorial Park on the shores of Lake Superior for a juried arts and crafts show, demonstrations and sales. Fourth Weekend.
Toll Free: (800) 447-4094

Phone: (715) 779-3335
Web: www.bayfield.org

Fourth of July Celebrations
Join your fellow Americans with fireworks and a strawberry shortcake social, a parade, live music and speeches. Fireworks launch from Madeline Island.
Toll Free: (800) 447-4094
Phone: (715) 779-3335
Web: www.bayfield.org

September
Apostle Annual Lighthouse Celebration
Three weeks of special lighthouse cruises and lighthouse tours, featuring all seven historic lighthouses of the Apostle Islands, begin the Wednesday after Labor Day.
Toll Free: (800) 779-4487
Phone: (715) 779-3335
Web: www.lighthousecelebration.com

October
Bayfield Apple Festival
Features 46 orchards and food booths, kids' carnival, "Monster Mural," Venetian Boat Parade and Grand Parade with the 600 member "Mass Band" playing "On Wisconsin." First Weekend.
Toll Free: (800) 447-4094
Phone: (715) 779-3335
Web: www.bayfield.org
La Pointe

October
Madeline Island Fall Festival
You'll find local artist displays, demonstrations, pumpkin carving, a kids' costume parade, a celebration of fall colors, community and art. Call for date.
Toll Free: (888) 475-3386
Phone: (715) 747-2801
Web: www.madelineisland.com

Alternate Activities

Bayfield

Bayfield Apple Company
See Wisconsin's largest raspberry crop. Pick raspberries in the summer, taste apples in the fall and purchase ciders, jams, jellies and fruit butters.
Toll Free: (800) 363-4526
Phone: (715) 779-5700
Web: www.bayfieldapple.com

Farmers Market
Find the market on the corner of 3rd and Manypenny, Saturday mornings from mid-June to mid-October.
Toll Free: (800) 447-4094
Phone: (715) 779-3335

Bayfield Maritime Museum
Learn about 150 years of Bayfield history with hands-on demonstrations of commercial fishing, boatbuilding, lighthouses, sailor crafts and shipwrecks.
Toll Free: (800) 323-7619
Phone: (715) 779-9919
Web: www.apostleisland.com/4.htm

Trek & Trail
Choose from a variety of day and overnight kayak guided trips around the Apostle Islands National Lakeshore. See sea caves, secluded white sand beaches, old shipwrecks, historic lighthouses and a variety of wildlife.
Toll Free: (800) 354-8735
Phone: (715) 779-3595
Web: www.trek-trail.com

Alternate Activities cont'd

Bayfield

Apostle Islands National Lakeshore

Visit the other twenty-one Apostle Islands, pristine sand beaches, spectacular sea caves, old-growth forests, bald eagles, black bears and the largest collection of lighthouses anywhere in the National Park System. You'll also find great sailing, boating, kayaking and hiking. Permits are required for camping, and reservations are recommended. The visitor center is a short walk from the Bayfield end of the ferry.
Phone: (715) 779-3397
Web: www.nps.gov/apis

Apostle Island Cruise Service

Choose from a variety of narrated cruises including island shuttles, sunset cruises and lighthouse tours.
Toll Free: (800) 323-7619
Phone: (715) 779-3925
Web: www.apostleisland.com

Adventures in Perspective

These adventures specialize in guided trips and kayak rentals in the Apostle Islands National Lakeshore; instructional clinics, half day shipwreck tours, full day sea cave tours and overnight extended tours. Ferry pick-ups available.
Toll Free: (866) 779-9503
Phone: (715) 779-9503
Web: www.livingadventure.com

La Pointe

Capser & Meech Hiking Trails

The Madeline Island Wilderness Preserve; inland forest land for public enjoyment; Capser & Meech and two rustic, ungroomed trails are approximately half a mile from the ferry.
Toll Free: (888) 475-3386
Phone: (715) 747-2801
Web: www.madelineisland.com

Bog Lake Outfitters

Specializing in guided trips and kayak rentals in the Apostle Islands National Lakeshore; instructional clinics, half-day shipwreck tours, full day sea cave tours, and overnight extended tours, Ferry pick-ups available.
Phone: (715) 747-2685
Web: www.madelineisland.com/boglake

Sandstrom Center for the Arts

Visit the historical twenty acre Sandstrom farmstead and orchard. Art classes and workshops are available for children and adults.
Phone: (715) 747-2054

La Pointe Center Art Guild & Gallery

Peruse showcases of local and regional artists in a variety of media. See summer lectures, films and gallery exhibits, too.
Phone: (715) 747-3321

Madeline Island Historical Museum

Look at prehistoric relics from the days of Ojibwa habitation, trade goods, missionaries' effects and tools of the lumbering and maritime industries.
Phone: (715) 747-2415
Web: www.wisconsinhistory.org

Big Bay State Park

Check out the 1.5 mile sandy beach, picnic area, more than nine miles of hiking trails, bird and wildlife watching, and interpretive programs during summer months.
Phone: (715) 747-6425
Web: www.dnr.state.wi.us

Restaurants

Bayfield

Hurricane Hut & Ice Cream Shoppe

Phone: (715) 779-5522

Wild Rice

Menu: Fine Dining
Phone: (715) 779-9881
Web: www.wildriceRestaurants.com

Maggie's

Menu: Seafood and More
Phone: (715) 779-5641
Web: www.maggies-bayfield.com

Groove Haus Bistro & Brew

Phone: (715) 779-7004
Web: users.bandzoogle.com/Griffin/index.cfm

Ethel's at 250

Phone: (715) 779-0293
Web: www.ethelsat250.com

Egg Toss Bakery Café

Phone: (715) 779-5181
Web: www.eggtoss-bayfield.com

La Pointe

Grampa Tony's

Menu: Family Dining
Phone: (715) 747-3911

The Beach Club

Menu: Casual Dining
Phone: (715) 747-3955
Web: www.beachclubmadeline.com

The Pub Restaurants & Wine Bar

Toll Free: (800) 822-6315
Phone: (715) 747-6322
Web: www.madisland.com

Lotta's Lakeside Café

Phone: (715) 747-2033
Web: www.lottascafe.com

About The Trail

This former SOO Line railroad bed follows Highway 35 from St. Croix Falls to Danbury. Small towns dot the trail at four to seven mile intervals providing plenty of access points and opportunities to start or stop. I saw more variety of wildlife on this trail than any other, in part because I rode sections in a light rain when no one else was on the trail.

Trail Highlights

Frederic has endorsed the trail. The town has rebuilt the historic depot and developed other facilities for bicyclists. Coon Lake Park, about half a mile east of the trail in Frederic, offers a shady, restful lakeside stop. See the city map. The trail skirts several lakes and passes through bogs and cattail marshes for several miles north and south of Siren. At the far north end, the trail makes a high crossing of the Yellow River just south of Danbury. Although the improved surface ends at Highway 77 in Danbury, it is worth walking or riding a fat tired bike 0.4 miles north to the bridge over the St. Croix River. The bridge, about 300 feet long and 100 feet above the river, overlooks a pristine portion of the St. Croix. ATVs and other motorized vehicles are allowed on this stretch, so proceed with caution.

About The Roads

Polk and Burnett counties offer a wide selection of beautiful, low traffic roads. Northern roads wind around lakes and weave through forests. Southern roads undulate through a mix of farmland and woodlots. Hills can be long, but the grade is usually mild to intermediate. Ride one way on the trail and return by the roads for an interesting mix of scenery and topography.

Road Highlights

The eastern route between Luck and Centuria or St. Croix Falls offers a diverse, alternative to the flat and straight trail. The east and west loops between Danbury and Oakland skirt lakes, meander through a full canopy of tree crowns and generally take in a wide range of lakes and northwoods beauty. Expect rolling hills but not a lot of dramatic climbs and descents.

How To Get There

St. Croix Falls is about an hour from the Twin Cities. Take Interstate 35 north to Highway 8. Go east into Wisconsin. Turn south on Highway 35 toward Interstate Park, and stop at the Polk County Information Center just off the ramp. Trail begins at the information center. For mid-trail towns, stay on Highway 8 to Highway 35 north and pick up the trail at any one of the towns along the highway. Danbury, on the north end of the trail, can also be reached by taking Interstate 35 to Hinckley and heading east on Highway 48. Highway 48 becomes Highway 77 in Wisconsin.

Vital Trail Information:

Trail Distance: 47

Trail Surface: Limestone

Access Points: St. Croix Falls, Centuria, Milltown, Luck, Frederic, Lewis, Siren, Webster, Danbury

Fees and Passes: Wisconsin State Trail Pass; $4.00 daily fee or $15.00 for an annual pass. State Trail passes are good on all Wisconsin State Trails.

Trail Website:
www.polkcountytourism.com

St. Croix Falls to Luck: 15.4 miles

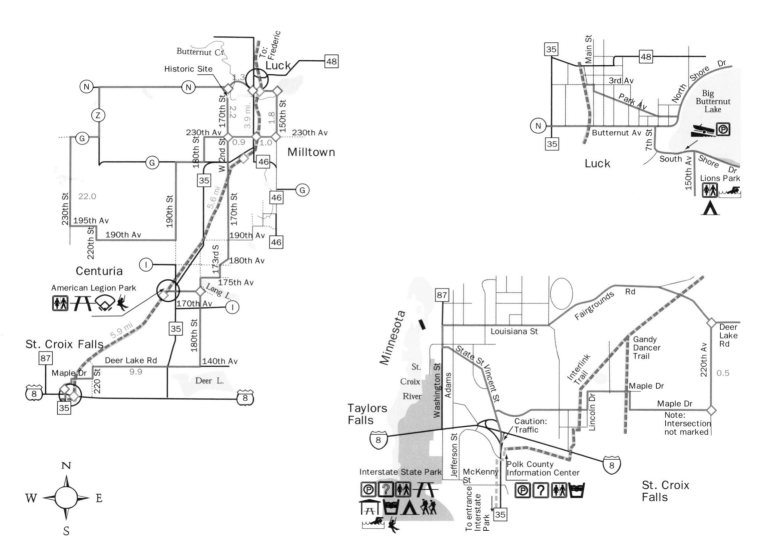

Luck
35 — Main St — 48
3rd Av
Park Av
Butternut Av — 7th St
North Shore Dr
Big Butternut Lake
South Shore Dr
150th Av
Lions Park
N
35

Butternut Ct
Historic Site
Luck
To: Frederic
48
N — N
Z
G — G
G
230th Av — 230th Av
Milltown
180th St
W 2nd St
170th St
150th St
35 — 46
46 — G
170th St
190th Av
46
230th St
22.0
195th Av
220th St
190th Av
190th St
Centuria
American Legion Park
173rd S
180th Av
175th Av
I — I
170th Av
Long L.
St. Croix Falls
87
Maple Dr
220 St
Deer Lake Rd
9.9
140th Av
Deer L.
8 — 35 — 8
35
180th St
5.9 mi
5.6 mi
3.9 mi
1.3
2.2
1.8
0.9
1.0

St. Croix Falls
87
Minnesota
St. Croix River
Taylors Falls
8
Interstate State Park
To entrance Interstate Park
35
Washington St
Adams
Jefferson St
McKenny St
State St
Vincent St
Louisiana St
Fairgrounds Rd
Caution: Traffic
Polk County Information Center
Interlink Trail
Lincoln Dr
Gandy Dancer Trail
Maple Dr
Maple Dr
220th Av
Deer Lake Rd
0.5
Note: Intersection not marked
8

N
W — E
S

Luck to Danbury: 32 miles

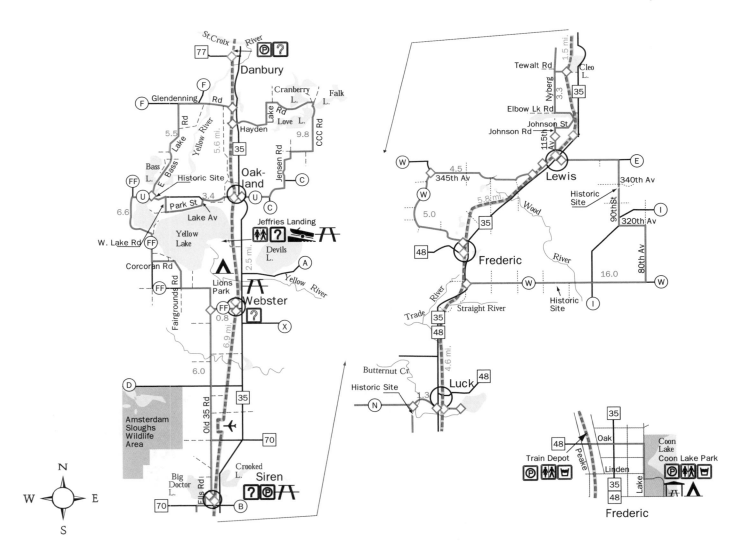

Tourist Information

Burnett County Tourism Dept.
Toll Free: (800) 788-3164
Phone: (715) 349-5999
Email: bctour@sirentel.net
Web: www.burnettcounty.com

Frederic Village Hall
Phone: (715) 327-4294
Email: fredericadmin@centurytel.net
Web: www.frederic-wi.com

Luck Wisconsin
Toll Free: (800) 222-7655
Phone: (715) 483-1410
Email: info@luckwisconsin.com
Web: www.luckwisconsin.com

Polk County Information, St. Croix Falls
Toll Free: (800) 222-7655
Phone: (715) 483-1410
Email: polkinfo@charterinternet.net
Web: www.polkcountytourism.com

Village of Centuria
Phone: (715) 646-2300
Email: info@centuria-wi.org
Web: www.centuria-wi.org
Webster Area Chamber of Commerce
Phone: (715) 866-4856
Email: websterfacts@websterwisconsin.com
Web: www.websterwisconsin.com

Lodging

Motels/Resorts

Luck
Luck Country Inn
Hwy 35 & 48
Toll Free: (800) 544-7396
Phone: (715) 472-2000
Email: info@luckcountryinn.com
Web: www.luckcountryinn.com

Siren
Best Western Northwoods Lodge
23986 State Rd 35 S
P.O. Box 49
Toll Free: (877) 349-7800
Phone: (715) 349-7800
Email: info@northwoodslodge.com
Web: www.northwoodslodge.com

The Lodge at Crooked Lake
24271 State Rd 35 N
P.O. Box 606
Toll Free: (877) 843-5634
Phone: (715) 349-2500
Email: mail@mylodge.com
Web: www.mylodge.com

St. Croix Falls
Holiday Inn Express Hotel & Suites
2190 US Hwy 8
Toll Free: (888) 465-4329
Phone: (715) 483-5775

Bed and Breakfast

Osceola
Pleasant Lake Bed & Breakfast
2238 60th Ave
Toll Free: (800) 294-2545
Phone: (715) 294-2545
Email: plakebb@centurytel.net
Web: www.pleasantlake.com

St. Croix Falls
Wissahickon Farms Country Inn
2263 Maple Dr
Phone: (715) 483-3986
Email: wissainn@yahoo.com
Web: www.wissainn.com

Taylors Falls
High Woods B&B
35930 Wild Mountain Rd
Phone: (651) 465-5307
Email: highwood@frontiernet.net
Web: www.highwoods.net

Lodging cont'd

Bed and Breakfast

Taylors Falls

The Cottage B&B
950 Fox Glen Dr
Phone: (651) 465-3595
Email: info@the-cottage.com
Web: www.the-cottage.com

The Old Jail B&B
349 Government St
P.O. Box 203
Phone: (651) 465-3112
Email: oldjail@frontiernet.net
Web: www.oldjail.com

Camping

St Croix Falls

Interstate State Park Campground
Hwy 35
P.O. Box 703
Phone: (715) 483-3747
Email: Maureen.Yunker@wisconsin.gov
Web: www.dnr.state.wi.us

Taylors Falls

Wildwood Campground
P.O. Box 235
Toll Free: (800) 447-4958
Phone: (651) 465-6315
Email: camp@wildmountain.com
Web: www.wildmountain.com

Webster

DuFour's Pine Tree Campground
29199 Hayden Lake Rd
Phone: (715) 656-4084

Bike Rental

St. Croix Falls

Wissahickon Farms Country Inn
2263 Maple Dr
Phone: (715) 483-3986
Email: wissainn@yahoo.com
Web: www.wissainn.com

Bike Repair

St. Croix Falls

Wissahickon Farms Country Inn
2263 Maple Dr
Phone: (715) 483-3986
Email: wissainn@yahoo.com
Web: www.wissainn.com

Festivals and Events

Centuria
July

Centuria Memory Days
Enjoy a parade, softball tournaments, a
craft fair, street dance, tractor pull and
classic car show. First Weekend.
Toll Free: (800) 222-7655
Phone: (715) 646-2300
Web: www.centuria-wi.org

Frederic
June

Frederic Lions Bike Race and Tour
Compete in a thirty-eight mile bike
race on the scenic back roads around
Frederic, then a 5K walk and run. Check
website for date.
Web: www.fredericlionsclassic.com

October

Mixed Sampler Guild Quilt Show
Over fifty quilters from multiple states show off their work at the high school. Second Weekend.
Toll Free: (800) 222-7665
Phone: (715) 483-1410
Web: www.frederic-wi.com

Luck
July

Lucky Days Celebration
Participate in the "In and Out of Luck" Run/Race/Walk, parade, midway, food and street dance. Third Weekend.
Toll Free: (800) 222-7655
Phone: (715) 483-1410
Web: www.polkcountytourism.com

Milltown
June

Fisherman's Party
Come for a parade, food, carnival, tractor show, softball tournament and fishing contests. Third Weekend.
Toll Free: (800) 222-7655
Phone: (715) 825-2222
Web: www.milltown-wi.com

Siren
July

Fourth of July Celebration
Celebrate your independence with a 5K run/walk, bed race, parade, boat parade and fireworks. First Weekend.
Toll Free: (800) 788-3164
Phone: (715) 349-5999
Web: www.sirenwis.com

August

Summer Fest
You will find a sidewalk sale, arts and crafts, a softball tournament, waterskiing show, kiddy parade, classic car and truck show and chicken BBQ. First Weekend.

Festivals and Events cont'd

Frederic
July

Gem & Mineral Show
Local artists show jewelry, raw rocks and polished rocks at the high school. Check website for dates.
Toll Free: (800) 222-7655
Phone: (715) 349-2241
Web: www.frederic-wi.com

Toll Free: (800) 788-3164
Phone: (715) 349-5999
Web: www.sirenwis.com

St. Croix Falls
July

Polk County Fair
The fair has horse shows, live entertainment, tractor and truck pulls, carnival rides and farm animals. Fourth Weekend.
Toll Free: (800) 222-7655
Phone: (715) 483-1410
Web: www.communityhotline.com/PolkCountyFair

Wannigan Days
Enjoy a parade, talent show, kids' activities, the queen coronation, an arts and crafts fair, music, a fiddle contest and flapjack breakfast. Check website for dates.
Toll Free: (800) 222-7655
Phone: (715) 483-3580
Web: www.scfwi.com
Webster

August

Gandy Dancer Days
Check out the street dance, queen pageant and sidewalk sales. Second Weekend.
Toll Free: (800) 788-3164
Phone: (715) 866-4856
Web: www.websterwisconsin.com

Alternate Activities

Balsam Lake
Polk County Museum
See Native American artifacts, lumbering era artifacts and armed forces displays.
Phone: (715) 483-3979
Web: www.co.polk.wi.us/museum

Alternate Activities cont'd

Grantsburg

Crex Meadows Wildlife Area

See sandhill cranes, bald and golden eagles, thousands of ducks and geese at this 2,400 acre refuge of prairie and wetlands. Navigate an extensive road system with well marked informational and directional signs.
Phone: (715) 463-2739
Web: www.crexmeadows.org

Osceola

Osceola & St. Croix Valley Railway

Experience rail travel as it was during the first half of the century. See the 1916 red brick depot, and take a train ride on weekends and holidays, April to October.
Phone: (715) 755-3570
Web: www.trainride.org

St. Croix Falls

St. Croix Festival Theater

Watch non-profit professional theater productions of classical, contemporary and forgotten works, May through December.
Phone: (715) 483-3387
Web: www.festivaltheatre.org

St.Croix National Scenic Riverway Visitor's Center

Trace the wild St. Croix and Name-kagon Rivers for more than 250 miles. Staff will help plan canoe trips.
Phone: (715) 483-3284
Web: www.nps.gov/sacn

Interstate Park

Try camping or hiking, visit the interpretive center and take in stunning views of the scenic St. Croix River from Wisconsin's oldest state park.

Phone: (715) 483-3747
Web: www.dnr.state.wi.us

Taylors Falls

Taylors Falls Scenic Boat Tours

Four trips wind daily down the St. Croix River. June through August.
Toll Free: (800) 447-4958
Phone: (651) 465-6315
Web: www.wildmountain.com

Wild Mountain

Spend a day on waterslides, alpine slides and Go-Karts.
Toll Free: (800) 447-4958
Phone: (651) 465-6315
Web: www.wildmountain.com

Webster

Forts Folle Avoine Historical Park

See the reconstructed 1802 fur trade post and enjoy eighty acres of hiking along the Yellow River.
Phone: (715) 866-8890
Web: www.theforts.org

Restaurants

Centuria
Al's Diner
Phone: (715) 646-2931

Frederic
Bean's Country Griddle
Phone: (715) 327-5513

Luck
Café Wren
Phone: (715) 472-4700
Web: www.cafewren.com

The Luck-E
Phone: (715) 472-2578

Oakwood Inn
Phone: (715) 472-8987

Main Dish Family Restaurants
Phone: (715) 472-2378

Milltown
Milltown Drive In
Phone: (715) 825-3389

Siren
Kris' Pheasant Inn & Sports Bar
Phone: (715) 349-5755
Web: www.wisconsinhunter.com/Ads/pheasinn.html

Main Street Café
Phone: (715) 349-2536

Little Mexico
Phone: (715) 349-5874

St. Croix Falls
Dam Bistro
Phone: (715) 483-5003

Coffee Time
Phone: (715) 483-1148

St. Croix Café
Phone: (715) 483-9079

Webster
Tracks Dining Car Café
Phone: (715) 866-7332

The World Famous Tap
Phone: (715) 866-9950

About The Trail

With a state park at either end, the undeveloped shores of the Chippewa River near the middle and a mix of hardwood forests and agriculture for its entire length, this trail offers a scenic look at an attractive part of western Wisconsin. The trail name comes from Old Abe, a bald eagle that became the mascot of Company C of the 8th Wisconsin Infantry during the Civil War.

Trail Highlights

The middle section, just north of Jim Falls, skirts the edge of Old Abe Lake, then passes through a forest of oak, birch, maple and cherry. Look upriver at the small bridge over the pond for a picturesque view of the Coban Bridge, a 1906 overhead truss bridge. The bridge was moved to this spot during the winters of 1916 and 1917 by horse and sled when the Wissota Dam was built. The 175 foot steel structure in Cornell is the only known pulpwood stacker in the world. The visitor center at the base describes the history and operation of the stacker. The trail extends to Brunet Island State Park near Cornell. Follow the trail to the Park, then ride the three mile park road as it circles the island.

About The Roads

This is flat to rolling land. Expect a low to moderate rollercoaster ride as you move toward or away from the river. The routes flatten out in the river floodplain and beyond the valley. Agricultural fields are small to midsized and intermingled with woodlots. Traffic is generally very low as long as you stay away from main connector routes like County Road S and the state highways. Highway 178 on the west side of the Chippewa River is very scenic, but traffic is high and fast, and the road is narrow, not recommended.

Road Highlights

The park road in Brunet Island State Park circles the island under a canopy of evergreens. Allow time for frequent stops at beaches and picnic grounds. This is a very peaceful road, where bikes generally travel as fast as automobiles. County Road K, north of the Coban Bridge, is closer to the river and offers a better view than the trail. For a unique experience, cross the one way Coban Bridge. The deck is wood and planks have been laid in two rows at the width of auto tires. A marker just south of the bridge highlights its history. Use caution when crossing Highway 178 to get to the marker.

How To Get There

From the Twin Cities, take Interstate 94 east to the Highway 29/40 exit east of Menomonie. Follow Highway 29 east to Seymour Cray Sr. Boulevard. Go north approximately 4.2 miles to County Road S and turn right. Go east 2.2 miles on County Road S to the intersection of County Roads S and O. The trailhead is on the left. Stay on County Road S to Jim Falls for a mid-trail start, or go through Jim Falls to Highway 27, then north on Highway 27 to Cornell to start at Brunet Island State Park.

Vital Trail Information:

Trail Distance: 22

Trail Surface: Asphalt

Access Points: Lake Wissota, Jim Falls, Cornell, Brunet Island State Park

Fees and Passes: Wisconsin State Trail Pass; $4.00 daily fee or $15.00 for an annual pass. State Trail passes are good on all Wisconsin State Trails.

Trail Website: www.chipppewa-wi.com

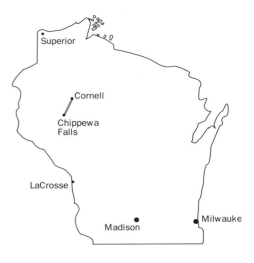

Chippewa Falls to Cornell: 22.2 miles

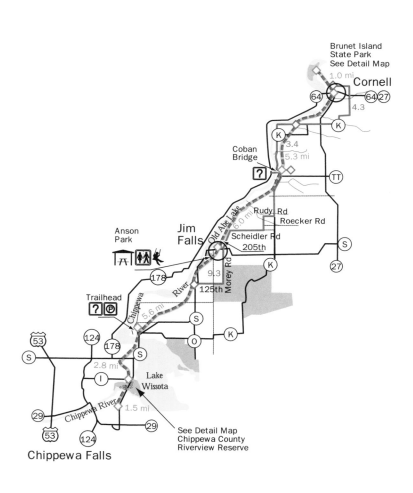

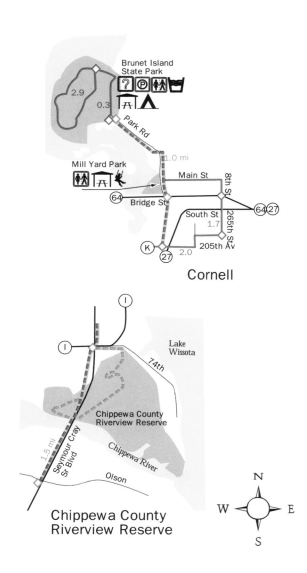

Lodging

Motels/Resorts

Chippewa Falls
HideAway Resort
    5967 167th St
    Phone: (715) 720-7367
    Email: hideaway@discover-net.net
    Web: www.discover-net.net/~hideaway/

Cornell
Edgewater Motel
    24250 State Hwy 178
    Phone: (715) 239-6295

Bed and Breakfast

Chippewa Falls
McGilvray's Victorian B&B
    312 W Columbia St
    Toll Free: (888) 324-1893
    Phone: (715) 720-1600
    Email: melanie@mcgilvraysbb.com
    Web: www.mcgilvraysbb.com

Pleasant View B&B
    16649 96th Ave
    Toll Free: (866) 947-7682
    Phone: (715) 382-4401
    Email: relax@pleasantviewbb.com
    Web: www.pleasantviewbb.com

Holcombe
Happy Horse B & B
    24469 Hwy 27
    Phone: (715) 239-0707
    Email: happyhorsebb@centurytel.net
    Web: www.merrimountmorgans.com

Camping

Chippewa Falls
Lake Wissota State Park
    18127 County Hwy O
    Phone: (715) 382-4574
    Email: allen.middendorp@wisconsin.gov
    Web: www.dnr.state.wi.us

Pine Harbor Campground
    7181 185th St
    Phone: (715) 723-9865

Cornell
Brunet Island State Park
    23125 255th St
    Phone: (715) 239-6888
    Email: Michael.Rivers@wisconsin.gov
    Web: www.dnr.state.wi.us

Bike Repair

Chippewa Falls
Spring Street Sports
    12 W Spring St
    Phone: (715) 723-6616
    Email: sss@charter.net
    Web: www.springstreetsports.com

Tourist Information

Chippewa Falls Chamber
    Toll Free: (866) 723-0340
    Phone: (715) 723-0331
    Email: info@chippewachamber.org
    Web: www.chippewachamber.org
    Cornell Development Association, Inc
    Toll Free: (866) 723-0331
    Phone: (715) 239-3710
    Web: www.cityofcornell.com

Festivals and Events

Chippewa Falls

May

Leinenkugel's Chippewa Valley Century Ride

The ride begins and ends in Irvine Park and has thirty-five, fifty, seventy-five and 100 mile stages. Stop by the Brat Feed at the end. Memorial Day Weekend. Check website for details.
Toll Free: (866) 723-0340
Phone: (715) 723-5557
Web: www.chippewavalleyride.us

July

Northern Wisconsin State Fair

Enjoy the midway, free grandstand show, livestock and crafts. Check website for dates.
Toll Free: (866) 723-0340
Phone: (715) 723-2861
Web: www.norwisstatefair.com

August

Pure Water Days

This four day event features the Heritage Fun Fest, a farmers market, quilt show, bowling and softball tournaments, music, beer, walk/run races, a skateboard contest and parade. Second Weekend.

Toll Free: (866) 723-0340
Phone: (715) 723-0331
Web: www.chippewachamber.org

September

Oktoberfest

It's family fun at the Northern Wisconsin Fair Grounds with German food, music on four stages and beer gardens. Check website for date.
Toll Free: (866) 723-0340
Phone: (715) 723-0331
Web: www.chippewachamber.org

Cornell

June

Cornell Community Fair

There is a parade, live music and the Lion's Club chicken BBQ at Mill Yard Park. Check website for dates.
Toll Free: (866) 723-0331
Phone: (715) 239-3710
Web: www.cityofcornell.com

July

July 3rd Fireworks

The Lion's Club hosts a chicken BBQ at Mill Yard Park on the night before the 4th.
Toll Free: (866) 723-0331
Phone: (715) 239-3710
Web: www.cityofcornell.com

September

Pork in the Park

Fill up on the roasted pork dinner and homemade pies. There are activities for children, a polka band and a dance contest at the Mill Yard Park. Check website for dates.
Toll Free: (866) 723-0331
Phone: (715) 239-3710
Web: www.cityofcornell.com

Alternate Activities

Chippewa Falls

Historic Walking Tour of Downtown Chippewa Falls

Thirty-six historic buildings and points of interest are listed on the National Register of Historic Places.
Toll Free: (866) 723-0340
Phone: (715) 723-0331
Web: www.chippewachamber.org

Heyde Center for the Arts

Check out the renovated high school, live theater, musical performances, art shows, dance and festivals.
Phone: (715) 726-9000
Web: www.cvca.net

Lake Wissota State Park

The park has hiking, biking, camping and swimming.
Phone: (715) 382-4574
Web: www.dnr.state.wi.us

Irvine Park and Zoo

Spend the day in 318 acres of natural wooded areas and a zoo. Try hiking, picnicking, playing at the playgrounds and touring the Sunny Valley School House Museum and Norwegian Log Home.
Toll Free: (866) 723-0340
Phone: (715) 723-0051
Web: www.chippewachamber.org

Alternate Activities cont'd

Chippewa Falls

Rose Garden/Lily Garden
This is a gardener's paradise: 500 roses, teas, floribunda, grandifloras, miniatures and climbers. Located at corner of Jefferson and Bridgewater Avenue.
Toll Free: (866) 723-0340
Phone: (715) 723-0331
Web: www.chippewachamber.org

Leinenkugel's Brewery Tours
Half hour tours run until 4:00pm Monday through Thursday and weekends, and until 8:00pm on Friday. Reservations recommended.
Toll Free: (888) 534-6437
Phone: (715) 723-5557
Web: www.leinie.com

Cook Rutledge Mansion
See fine examples of High Victorian Italianate architecture.
Phone: (715) 723-7181
Web: www.chippewachamber.org

Chippewa Falls Museum of Industry & Technology
Learn the history of local manufacturing and processing from 1840s to present including Cray Super Computer collection. $2.00 for adults, $1.00 children under 18.
Phone: (715) 720-9206
Web: www.cfmit.org

Cornell

Mill Yard Park
See the only known pulp wood stacker in the world. It's 175 feet high and was used from 1913 to 1972. Learn more in the visitor center.
Toll Free: (866) 723-0331
Phone: (715) 239-3710
Web: www.cityofcornell.com

Brunet Island State Park
Island Park in the Chippewa River has a scenic drive, camping, swimming and hiking.
Toll Free: (888) 947-2757
Phone: (715) 239-3710
Web: www.cityofcornell.com

Restaurants

Chippewa Falls

Bake & Brew Café
117 N Bridge St
Phone: (715) 720-2360

James Sheeley House Restaurants
236 W River St
Phone: (715) 726-0561
Web: www.jamessheeleyhouse.com

Olson's Ice Cream Parlor & Deli
611 N Bridge St
Phone: (715) 723-4331

The Fill Inn Station
104 W Columbia St
Phone: (715) 723-8282
Web: www.fillinnstation.com

Cornell

Sandi's Drive In
401 Bridge St
Phone: (715) 239-6555

Lake Wissota

High Shores Supper Club
17985 County Hwy X
Phone: (715) 723-9854
Web: www.highshores.com

About The Trail

This attractive trail has the feel of a Victorian era carriage road next to a canal. Downsville, at the midpoint, is an excellent starting or turn-around point for those who don't want to ride the entire trail. Near its southern tip the trail enters the Dunnville Wildlife Area, a wetland prairie in the Chippewa River floodplain. The southern end of the trail connects with the Chippewa State Trail after crossing the Chippewa River on an 860 foot railroad trestle.

Trail Highlights

Its hard to go wrong on this trail. From Menomonie to Downsville the trail and river run right next to each other. Watch for the historic site of the Downsville Cut Stone Company about two and a half miles south of Downsville. Go another mile south and enter a very remote and beautiful stretch of river. The prairie portion of the Dunnville Wildlife Area radiates a wonderful purple hue in late August. Closer to the river, the vegetation changes to erratic clumps of brush in an ever-shifting sandy shoreline. The trestle bridge offers great views of the river.

About The Roads

Expect a mix of woods and farmland and low to medium rollers. Traffic is low on the county roads and slightly higher on the short stretches of state highways, such as Highway 72 near Downsville. The steepest terrain is near the river.

Road Highlights

Hardscrabble Road, south of Downsville, is also hard climbing if traveling south to north. Hardscrabble is shady and lightly traveled and offers occassional views of the river valley to the west. If you are looking for a short diversion from the trail, this is the road to take. County Roads C and D offer a pair of steep climbs near the river, then rolling, rural panoramic views. Paradise Valley Road, a quiet road with low underbrush on both sides and occasional views of the river, parallels the trail north of Irvington from a vantage point slightly inland and higher.

How To Get There

Menomonie is about thirty miles west of Eau Claire on Interstate 94. Take the Highway 25 exit south off Interstate 94. Go south about 2.5 miles to Highway 29 west. Go west on Highway 29 about one half mile. The trailhead is on the left side of the road just after crossing the Red Cedar River. See the city map for details. Continue south on Highway 25 about six miles to Downsville.

Vital Trail Information:

Trail Distance: 14

Trail Surface: Limestone

Access Points: Menomonie, Irvington, Downsville

Fees and Passes: Wisconsin State Trail Pass; $4.00 daily fee or $15.00 for an annual pass. State Trail passes are good on all Wisconsin State Trails.

Trail Website:
www.dnr.state.wi.us/org/land/parks/trails

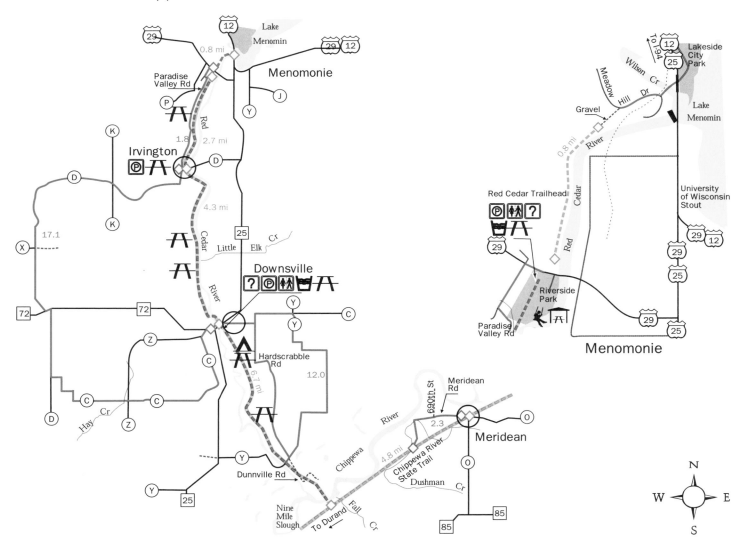

Menomonie to Chippewa River Trail: 14.5 miles

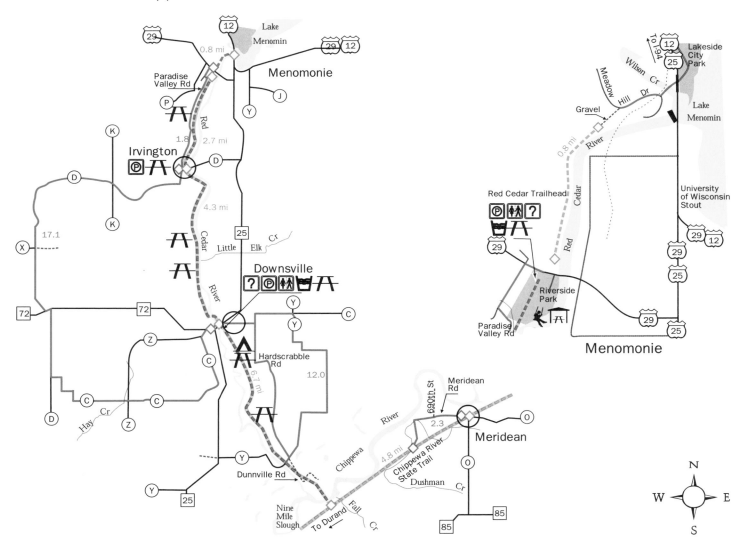

Tourist Information

**Greater Menomonie Chamber
of Commerce**
Toll Free: (800) 283-1862
Phone: (715) 235-9087
Email: info@menomoniechamber.org
Web: www.menomoniechamber.org
Main Street Menomonie
Phone: (714) 235-2666
Email: mainstreet342@wwt.net
Web: www.mainstreetmenomonie.org
Menomonie Park and Recreation
Phone: (715) 232-1664
Email: menorec@menomonierecreation.org
Web: www.menomonierecreation.org

Red Cedar State Trail, DNR, Menomonie
Phone: (715) 232-1242
Web: www.dnr.state.wi.us

Lodging

Motels/Resorts

Downsville
The Creamery Restaurants & Inn
P.O. Box 22
Phone: (715) 664-8354
Fax: (715) 664-8353
Email: visit@creameryRestaurants-inn.com
Web: www.creameryRestaurants-inn.com

Menomonie
AmericInn
1915 N Broadway
Toll Free: (800) 396-5007
Phone: (715) 235-4800
Fax: (715) 235-5090
Email: menomonie.wi@americinn.com
Web: www.americinn.com

Best Western/Holiday Manor
1815 N Broadway
Toll Free: (800) 622-0504
Phone: (715) 235-9651
Web: www.bestwesternmenomonie.com

Motel 6
2100 Stout St
Toll Free: (800) 466-8356
Phone: (715) 235-6901
Web: www.motel6.com

Bed and Breakfast

Menomonie
Hansen Heritage House
919 13th St
Phone: (715) 235-0119
Email: innkeeper@hansenheritagehouse.com
Web: www.hansenheritagehouse.com

Oaklawn Bed & Breakfast
423 Technology Dr E
Phone: (715) 235-6155
Email: info@oaklawnbnb.com
Web: www.oaklawnbnb.com

Bike Rental

Menomonie
Trail Head Sports
  Phone: (714) 233-1852

Bike Repair

Menomonie
Simple Sports
  326 Main St
  Phone: (715) 233-3493
  Email: simplesports@hotmail.com>
  Web: www.simplesports.us

Trail Head Sports
  Phone: (715) 233-1852

Festivals and Events

Downsville
August
  Discover Downsville Days
  This is a celebration of abundance at
  the Creamery Restaurants, featuring
  arts and crafts, local food processors
  and growers, a puppet show and other
  activities for kids. Fourth Weekend.
  Phone: (715) 664-8600
  Web: www.discoverdownsvillewi.com
  Menomonie

All Summer
  Outdoor Concerts
  Outdoor concerts by the Ludington
  Guard Band, the oldest community
  concert band in Wisconsin, take place
  at Wilson Park Band Shell at 8:00pm on
  Tuesday evenings.
  Toll Free: (800) 283-1862
  Phone: (715) 235-9087
  Web: www.menomoniechamber.org

June
  Drums along the Red Cedar
  Listen to the Drum and Bugle competi-
  tion at the Williams Center downtown.
  Check website for details.
  Phone: (715) 203-0018
  Web: www.darc.us

August
  Dunn County Fair
  The fair offers animal exhibits, rides,
  games and special events. Check web-
  site for dates.
  Toll Free: (800) 283-1862
  Phone: (715) 232-4005
  Web: www.menomoniechamber.org

  Fur Trade Rendezvous
  At the Russell J. Rassbach Heritage
  Museum, learn about life in a fur trader
  encampment. Experience horse-drawn
  wagon rides, stone cutting demonstra-
  tions and more. Check website for dates.
  Phone: (715) 232-8685
  Web: discover-net.net/~dchs

Alternate Activities

Downsville
Empire in Pine Lumber Museum
  Relive the logging camp era of Dunn
  County's early days. Displays depict
  operations of Knapp, Stout & Company,
  once the largest white pinery in the
  world, as well as a blacksmith shop.
  Open Friday, Saturday and Sunday,
  12:00pm-5:00pm.
  Phone: (715) 232-8685
  Web: www.discover-net.net/~dchs

Lodging cont'd

Camping

Menomonie
Twin Springs Campground
  Cedar Falls Rd
  N 6572 530th St
  Phone: (715) 235-9321

Alternate Activities cont'd

Menomonie
Farmers Market
You can buy fresh produce and arts and crafts every Saturday and Wednesday from May through October.
Toll Free: (800) 283-1862
Phone: (715) 235-9087
Web: www.menomoniechamber.org

Wakanda Waterpark
The outdoor swimming facility features a zero depth pool that increases to four feet, a 230 foot waterslide, interactive water play equipment and two lap lanes. The park also has sand volleyball courts, playground equipment, picnic shelters, a concessions stand and a deck with lounge chairs.
Phone: (715) 232-1664
Web: www.menomonierecreation.org

Russell J. Rassbach Heritage Museum
Exhibits chronicle the development of Dunn County through extensive collections of artifacts and photographs. They feature a timeline from prehistoric times to white settlement. Open Wednesday through Sunday, 10:00am-5:00pm.
Phone: (715) 232-8685
Web: discover-net.net/~dchs

Wilson Place Mansion Museum
This museum of local history includes furnishings of the lumber baron, William Wilson.
Toll Free: (800) 368-7384
Phone: (715) 235-2283

Roscoe's Red Cedar Outfitters
Explore the local adventure scene with canoe and tube rentals.
Phone: (715) 235-3866

Hoffman Hills State Recreation Area
This hilly, wooded recreation area features a sixty foot observation tower at the top of the hill, a self-guided nature trail and hiking trails.
Phone: (715) 232-1242
Web: www.dnr.state.wi.us

Bullfrog Fish Farm
Poles and bait are available. Take the hatchery tour and have your catch cleaned and iced.
Phone: (715) 664-8775
Web: www.eatmyfish.com

Mabel Tainter Theater
The lavishly furnished and restored 1889 theater has an exhibit gallery, hand-carved woodwork, bronze cast opera seats and a rare working Steere and Turner tracker pipe organ. See a variety of performances.
Toll Free: (800) 236-7675
Phone: (715) 235-0001
Web: www.mabeltainter.com

Restaurants

Downsville
The Creamery
Phone: (715) 664-8354
Web: www.creameryRestaurants-inn.com

Durand
Corral Bar & Riverside Grill
Phone: (715) 672-8874
Web: www.corralbarandriversidegrill.com

Menomonie
Kernel Restaurants
Phone: (715) 235-5154

Grazi's
Menu: Fine Dining
Phone: (715) 232-8878
Web: www.grazisRestaurants.com

Acoustic Café
Phone: (715) 235-1115

Ted's Pizza
Phone: (715) 235-0600
Web: www.tedspizzapie.com

About The Trail

This trail runs from the park-like setting of Eau Claire's city trail through the open farmland of Caryville, into Dunnville Wildlife Area west of Meridean and finishes in Durand. The Red Cedar Trail intersects the Chippewa between Durand and Meridean at an 860 foot railroad trestle across the Chippewa River.

Trail Highlights

Blend two trails for a unique look at the Dunnville Wildlife Area and the Chippewa River. Start in Meridean, ride west to the intersection with the Red Cedar Trail, cross the trestle and continue north along the Red Cedar Trail to Downsville. For an unforgettable sunset, end your day on the railroad trestle over the Chippewa River. The middle area of the trail passes through wide open farm fields and can get a bit tedious. Consider the road alternate.The eastern edge of the trail is interesting in a different way. Beginning at the Highway 85 rest area, the trail winds along the Chippewa River, then crosses near Highway 12 on a beautiful old railroad bridge and follows the North Shore past the University of Wisconsin, Eau Claire, into Owen Park. The ride through town is quite pleasant with historical markers and great views of the river.

About The Roads

Hilly, twisting and low traffic, the best road routes start from the Highway 85 rest area. If you like hills, these are ideal roads for loops of twelve to thirty-five miles.

Road Highlights

Highway 85 has traffic, but the shoulder is paved. Mitchell Road is relatively flat with a beautiful full canopy tree cover. County Road F has long, medium rollers, surrounded by a blend of forest and fields. County Road W is a narrow, snakelike road. It twists and turns, climbs and descends, creating scenic views and narrow, intimate trails through the woods. The southern end of County Road Z repeats the snake-like motions of County Road W, but passes through a more open landscape. Schuh and Town Hall Roads provide an interesting rolling alternate to the flatlands surrounding the trail between the Highway 85 rest area and Caryville.

How To Get There

Eau Claire is eighty-seven miles east of the Twin Cities on Interstate 94 and eighty-seven miles north of La Crosse on Highway 53. You can avoid going into Eau Claire by taking the Highways 37/85 exit off Interstate 94. Stay on Highway 85 to the rest area. Caryville, Meridean and Durand can be reached off Highway 85. If you are from Eau Claire, you can get on the state trail by following the Eau Claire city trail along the Chippewa River through town. See city and trail maps for details.

Vital Trail Information:

Trail Distance: 29

Trail Surface: Asphalt

Access Points: Eau Claire, Highway 85 Rest Stop, Caryville, Meridean, Durand

Fees and Passes: Wisconsin State Trail Pass; $4.00 daily fee or $15.00 for an annual pass. State Trail passes are good on all Wisconsin State Trails.

Trail Website: www.dnr.state.wi.us/org

Eau Claire to Durand: 29 miles

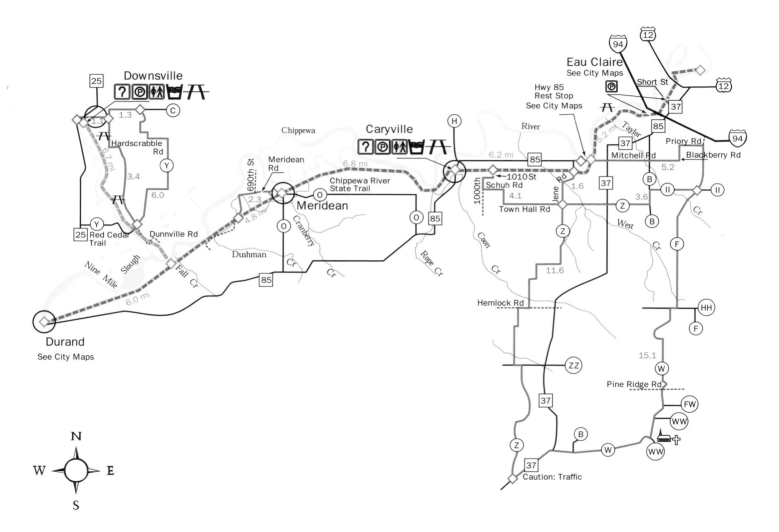

City Maps

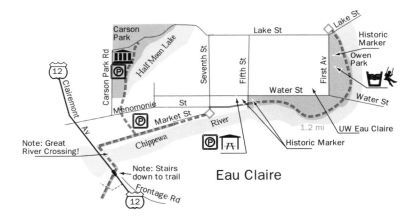

Eau Claire

Hwy 85 Rest Stop

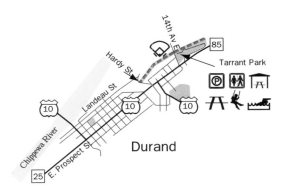

Durand

Tourist Information

Chippewa Valley Convention & Visitors Bureau
Toll Free: (888) 523-3866
Phone: (715) 831-2345
Email: info@chippewavalley.net
Web: www.chippewavalley.net

Lodging

Motels/Resorts

Augusta
Woodland Store, Motel & Campground
S5340 State Rd 27
Phone: (715) 286-2112
Email: owner@woodlandcountrystore.com
Web: www.woodlandcountrystore.com

Eau Claire
Holiday Inn Campus Area
2703 Craig Rd
Toll Free: (888) 465-4329
Phone: (715) 835-2211
Web: www.holiday-inn.com/
eau-campus

The Plaza Hotel & Suites
1202 W Clairemont Ave
Toll Free: (800) 482-7829
Phone: (715) 834-3181
Web: www.plazaeauclaire.com

Westgate Motel
1436 N Clairemont Ave
Phone: (715) 834-3580

Bed and Breakfast

Eau Claire
Fanny Hill Victorian Inn & Dinner Theatre
3919 Crescent Ave
Toll Free: (800) 292-8026
Phone: (715) 836-8184
Email: office@fannyhill.com
Web: www.fannyhill.com

The Atrium
5572 Prill Rd
Toll Free: (888) 773-0094
Phone: (715) 833-9045
Email: info@atriumbb.com
Web: www.atriumbb.com

Camping

Augusta
Woodland Store, Motel & Campground
S5340 State Rd 27
Phone: (715) 286-2112
Email: owner@woodlandcountrystore.com
Web: www.woodlandcountrystore.com

Bike Rental

Eau Claire
Riverside Bike & Skate
937 Water St
Phone: (715) 835-0088

Bike Repair

Eau Claire
Anybody's Bikeshop
411 Water St
Toll Free: (800) 870-7118
Phone: (715) 833-7100

Eau Claire Bike & Sport
403 Water St
Phone: (715) 832-6149
Email: terry@bikeandsport.com
Web: www.bikeandsport.com

Riverside Bike & Skate
937 Water St
Phone: (715) 835-0088

Festivals and Events

Eau Claire
July
    Country Jam, USA
This outdoor country music festival has more than thirty top national acts, side stage entertainment, food and camping at the Summer Festival Grounds. Check website for dates.
Toll Free: (800) 780-0526
Web: www.countryjam.com

Festivals and Events cont'd

Eau Claire
August

Festival in the Pines
Enjoy arts and crafts, food vendors, games, rides and family entertainment in Carson Park.
Toll Free: (800) 472-6654
Phone: (715) 552-5504
Web: www.festivalinthepines.com

Pioneer Days
Browse the flea market, steamer, games, food stand, tractor pull, crosscut saw competition and parade. Second Weekend.
Toll Free: (888) 523-3866
Phone: (715) 833-0444

Alternate Activities

Dunnville
Dunnville Wildlife Area
Right on the trail, the Wildlife Area is where the Chippewa and Red Cedar trails intersect.
Toll Free: (888) 523-3866
Phone: (715) 831-2345
Web: www.dnr.state.wi.us

Eau Claire
Hank Aaron Statue
See the bronze sculpture in Carson Park. Aaron began his playing days for the Eau Claire Bears in 1952.
Toll Free: (888) 523-3866
Phone: (715) 831-2345
Web: www.chippewavalley.net

Rude Trude Flyfishing Services
Learn to fly fish for brook, brown and rainbow trout with lessons or the guide service. Trout season is from May to September.
Phone: (715) 832-2377
Web: www.rudetrude.com

Riverside Bike & Skate
Offers canoeing, kayaking, paddle and pedal trips on the Eau Claire and Chippewa Rivers.
Phone: (715) 835-0088

Ski Sprites Waterski Show
Water ski performances on Half Moon Lake include barefooting, jumping, pyramids and more. Stop by Wednesday and Sunday evenings at 6:30pm, June through Labor Day.
Toll Free: (888) 523-3866
Phone: (715) 831-2345
Web: www.skisprites.com

Chippewa Valley Museum
Learn more about Ojibwa Indian culture and frontier heritage. The museum includes Anderson Log House and the one room Sunnyview School.
Phone: (715) 834-7871
Web: www.cvmuseum.com

Paul Bunyan Logging Camp
Walk through 1900s logging era buildings, including a bunkhouse, cook shanty, heavy equipment building, blacksmith shop, and barn in Carson Park.
Phone: (715) 835-6200
Web: www.paulbunyancamp.org

Fanny Hill Victoria Inn & Dinner Theater
Dine on good food and take in professional dinner theater performances.
Toll Free: (800) 292-8026
Phone: (715) 836-8184
Web: www.fannyhill.com

Restaurants

Durand
Durand House
Phone: (715) 672-5975

Shari's Chippewa Club
Phone: (715) 672-8785
Web: sharischippewaclub.com/

Corral Bar and Riverside Grill
Phone: (715) 672-8874
Web: www.corralbarandriversidegrill.com

Eau Claire
Mona Lisa's
Phone: (715) 839-8969

Racy D'Lene's Very Coffee Lounge
Phone: (715) 834-0000

Acoustic Café
Phone: (715) 832-9090
Web: www.theacoustic.com

O'Leary's Pub & Grill
Phone: (715) 834-6611

Mogie's Pub
Phone: (715) 836-9666

Houligans Steak & Seafood Pub
Phone: (715) 835-6621
Web: www.houligans.net

Grand Avenue Café
Phone: (715) 831-1100

About The Trail

Eighteen bridges, Mississippi River bottoms and open prairie mark the scenery along this trail. The dam in Onalaska backs up the Mississippi creating scenic Lake Onalaska. Plan your ride to be next to the lake for a stunning sunset. The trail crosses the many branches of the Black River. Sit quietly at the bridges for glimpses of shorebirds, beaver, muskrats, etc.This is a very quiet, remote trail with a lot of diversity. The town of Trempealeau is worth leaving the trail to see. Ask about the outdoor music schedule at the Trempealeau Hotel and stop for a meal. The food is very good.

Trail Highlights

The bridge at Lytles Landing passes over the main branch of the Black River and well into the lowlands surrounding the Mississippi River. It's long, low and inviting. For a unique experience spend some time in the Trempealeau National Wildlife Refuge. You may see turkeys on Wildlife Drive, egrets and Great Blue Herons in the marshes, plus pelicans and migratory waterfowl at the obseration deck. The surface isn't as solid for bike tires as the trail, but traffic is low and the combination of prairie, wetland and natural history signs makes it worth an extended visit. Pick up a brochure at the parking lot.

About The Roads

Choose your route according to your riding needs. The roads are flat south of Highways 35/54 and hilly north. The flat roads pass through corn fields and open farmland. The hilly roads offer a mix of woodlots, pasture and farmland, some of it from high, scenic vantage points. Most of the roads in this area are paved and low traffic as long as you stay off the major highways.

Road Highlights

The county roads north of Highways 35/54 pass through deep, dry valleys called coulees. This kind of riding is addictive. The road slowly rises and falls as long as you are following a creek or small river. Passing from one watershed to another, however, guarantees lots of large hills. For a flatter loop with occasional views of Lake Onalaska, a backwater of the Mississippi, try the roads around Brice Prairie. You can start near Midway and end at Lytles Landing by taking County Roads Z and ZB. Avoid County Road ZN, especially near Midway, because of traffic. The road route through Onalaska follows low traffic, back roads, but isn't especially interesting. It does lead to Rowe Park, a large, well appointed city park, and to the trailhead at the Chamber of Commerce building. A connector from the trailhead leads to the La Crosse River Trail.

How To Get There

Onalaska is just north of La Crosse in southwestern Wisconsin. Interstate 90 passes along the southern edge of Onalaska. Take Highway 35 north from Interstate 90 to get to the trailhead. See the city map. Continue north on Highway 35 to Midway or Trempealeau. From the northwest, cross the Mississippi River on Highway 54 in Winona. Highways 35 and 54 meet in Wisconsin. Continue along Highway 35 to Trempealeau or Perrot State Park.

Vital Trail Information:

Trail Distance: 22

Trail Surface: Limestone

Access Points: Perrot State Park, Trempealeau, Lytles Landing, Midway, Onalaska

Fees and Passes: Wisconsin State Trail Pass; $4.00 daily fee or $15.00 for an annual pass. State Trail passes are good on all Wisconsin State Trails.

Trail Website: www.dnr.state.wi.us

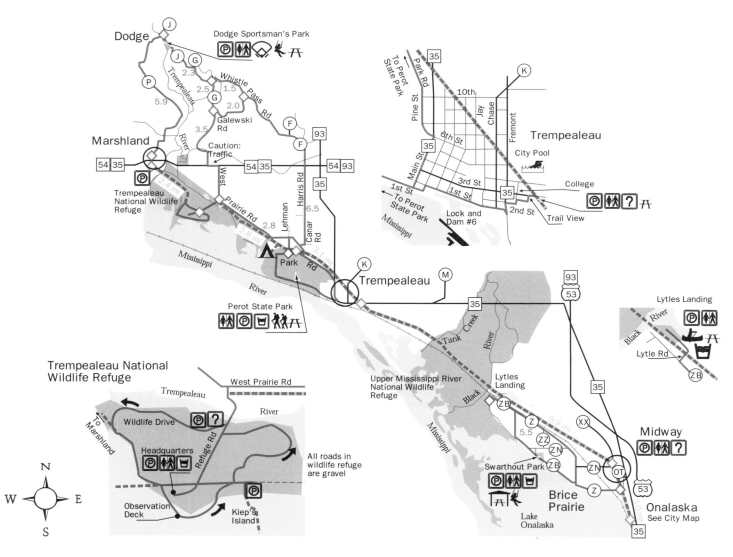

Onalaska to Marshland: 21 miles

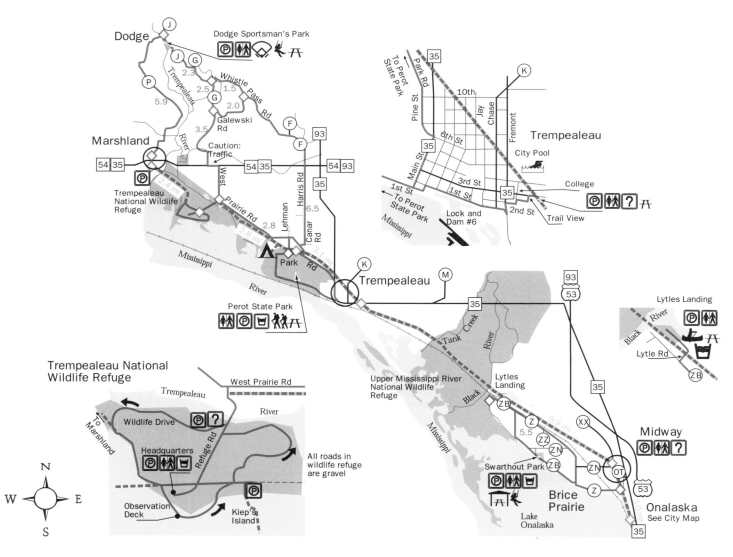

Dodge

Dodge Sportsman's Park

Whistle Pass Rd
2.3
2.5 1.5
2.0
Galewski Rd
3.5

Marshland

Caution: Traffic

54 35

Trempealeau National Wildlife Refuge

93
35
6.5

93
54 35
54 93
35

To Perot State Park
Park Rd
35
35
10th
Pine St
6th St
Jay Chase
Fremont
Trempealeau
City Pool
3rd St
1st St
1st St
2nd St
College
Trail View
To Perot State Park
Lock and Dam #6

Mississippi

West Prairie Rd
2.8
2.8 mi
Lehman
Harris Rd
Canar Rd
3.1 mi
Park Rd

Mississippi River

Perot State Park

K Trempealeau

M

35

Tank Creek

Black River

93
53

Lytles Landing

Black River

Lytle Rd

ZB

Upper Mississippi River National Wildlife Refuge

Lytles Landing

Black

ZB
9.9 mi
Z
5.5
ZZ
ZN
XX
ZB
ZN
Z
OT
Z
53
35

Midway

Trempealeau National Wildlife Refuge

Trempealeau
West Prairie Rd
River

Wildlife Drive

Headquarters

Refuge Rd

All roads in wildlife refuge are gravel

To Marshland

Observation Deck

Kiep's Island

Swarthout Park

Brice Prairie

Lake Onalaska

Onalaska
See City Map

35

N
W   E
S

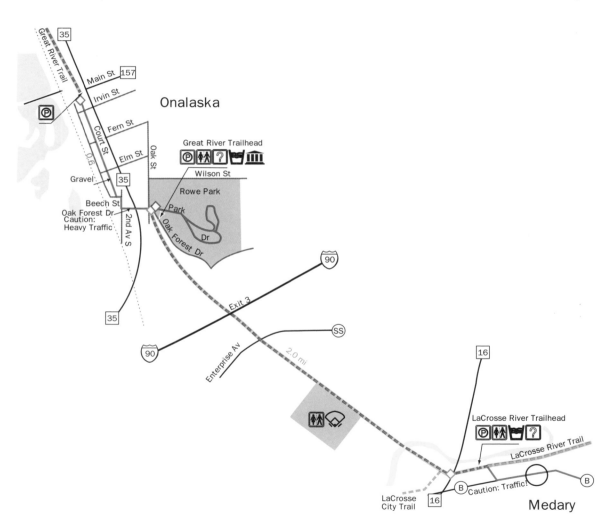

Great River Trail

35

Main St 157

Irvin St

Onalaska

P

Fern St

Court St

Elm St

0.6

Oak St

Great River Trailhead

P 🚻 ? 🗑 🏛

Wilson St

Gravel

35

Rowe Park

Beech St
Oak Forest Dr
Caution:
Heavy Traffic

2nd Av S

Park

Oak Forest Dr

Dr

35

90

Exit 3

90

SS

Enterprise Av

2.0 mi

🚻 ⛱

16

LaCrosse River Trailhead

P 🚻 🗑 ?

LaCrosse River Trail

LaCrosse
City Trail

16

B Caution: Traffic!

B

Medary

N
W • E
S

Tourist Information

Onalsaska Center for Commerce and Tourism
Toll Free: (800) 873-1901
Phone: (608) 781-9570
Email: info@discoveronalaska.com
Web: www.discoveronalaska.com

Perrot State Park and Great River Trail
Phone: (608) 534-6409
Web: www.dnr.state.wi.us

Trempealeau Chamber of Commerce
Phone: (608) 534-6780
Email: chamber@trempealeau.net
Web: www.trempealeau.net

Lodging

Motels/Resorts

Onalaska
Baymont Inns & Suites
3300 Kinney Coulee Rd N
Toll Free: (877) 229-6668
Phone: (608) 783-7191
Web: www.baymontinns.com

Comfort Inn
1223 Crossing Meadows Dr
Toll Free: (877) 424-6423
Phone: (608) 781-7500
Web: www.choicehotels.com

Lake Motel
926 2nd Ave N
Phone: (608) 783-3348

Onalaska Inn
651 2nd Ave S
Phone: (608) 783-2270

Shadow Run Lodge
710 2nd Ave N
Toll Free: (800) 657-4749
Phone: (608) 783-0020
Email: info@shadowrunlodge.com
Web: www.shadowrunlodge.com

Trempealeau
Inn on the River
11321 Main St
Phone: (608) 534-7784
Email: innontheriver@triwest.net
Web: www.innontheriverwisconsin.com

Lodging cont'd

Motels/Resorts

Trempealeau

Pleasant Knoll Motel
11451 Main St
Toll Free: (888) 210-8790
Phone: (608) 534-6615
Email: stay@pleasantknoll.com
Web: www.pleasantknoll.com

The Historic Trempealeau Hotel
150 Main St
Phone: (608) 534-6898
Web: www.trempealeauhotel.com

Bed and Breakfast

Onalaska

Rainbow Ridge Farms B & B
W 5732 Hauser Rd
Toll Free: (888) 347-2594
Phone: (608) 783-8181
Email: rrbnb1@yahoo.com
Web: www.rainbowridgefarms.com

The Lumber Baron Inn Bed & Breakfast
421 2nd Ave N
Phone: (608) 781-8938

Trempealeau

Lucas House Bed & Breakfast
24616 2nd St
Phone: (608) 534-6665
Email: lucasinntremplo@aol.com
Web: www.trempealeau.net/lucas

Camping

La Crosse

Bluebird Campground
N2833 Smith Valley Rd
Phone: (608) 781-2267

LaCrosse

Goose Island Campground
W6488 County Rd GI
Phone: (608) 788-7018

Trempealeau

Perrot State Park
Rt 1, Box 407
Toll Free: (888) 947-2757
Phone: (608) 534-6409
Web: www.dnr.state.wi.us

Bike Rental

La Crosse

Smith's Cycling & Fitness
125 N 7th St, Ste D
Phone: (608) 784-1175
Web: www.smithsbikes.com

Trempealeau

The Historic Trempealeau Hotel
11332 Main
Phone: (608) 534-6898
Web: www.trempealeauhotel.com

Bike Repair

La Crosse

Smith's Cycle & Fitness
125 N 7th St, Ste D
Phone: (608) 784-1175
Web: www.smithsbikes.com

Festivals and Events

LaCrosse

September
Oktoberfest
The LaCrosse Oktoberfest grounds feature a German Fall Festival with food, music entertainment, a carnival, crafts, sporting events and a torchlight parade. Check website for dates.
Phone: (608) 784-3378
Web: www.oktoberfestusa.com

Festivals and Events cont'd

Onalaska

May

Sunfish Days

Check out the kids' fishing derby, craft fair, volleyball and softball tourneys, carnival rides, petting zoo, parade, live music, beer garden and food stands at the Omni Center at Van Riper Park. Check website for details.
Toll Free: (800) 873-1901
Phone: (608) 781-9570
Web: www.onalaskasunfishdays.com

July

Salute to the Fourth

Celebrate America with kids' games, craft and food booths, a beer tent, and evening fireworks in conjunction with LaCrosse Symphony Orchestra. Always July 1st, regardless of day of the week.
Toll Free: (800) 873-1901
Phone: (608) 781-9570
Web: www.discoveronalaska.com

September

Fall 15 Great River Walk

Appreciate your natural surrounding on a four, nine, or fifteen mile fitness walk along the Great River Trail from Onalaska to Trempealeau. You'll find shuttles and snacks on the trail and dinner, prizes and entertainment in Trempealeau. Advance registration is required. Call for date.
Toll Free: (800) 873-1901
Phone: (608) 781-9570
Web: www.discoveronalaska.com

Trempealeau

All Summer

Stars under the Stars

An outdoor summer concert series features national acts at the historic Trempealeau Hotel concert grounds.
Phone: (608) 534-6898
Web: www.trempealeauhotel.com

May

Blues Bash

Nationally and internationally famous blues bands play from early afternoon through the evening at the Trempealeau Hotel concert grounds. Check website for date.
Phone: (608) 534-6898
Web: www.trempealeauhotel.com

Reggae Sunsplash

Enjoy Jamaican style music, food and crafts from early afternoon through the evening at Trempealeau Hotel concert grounds. Check website for details.
Phone: (608) 534-6898
Web: www.trempealeauhotel.com

Trempealeau Hipbreaker Bike Tour

Go on the ten, twenty-three or forty-three mile tour along the Mississippi River and Perrot State Park. Check website for details and date.
Phone: (608) 534-6780
Web: www.ridebctc.com

July

Catfish Days

There is a bike tour and race, an arts and crafts fair, flea market, fishing tournament, kids' games and parade, live music, dancing, a carnival, beer tent, parade on Sunday and fireworks in the evening. Call for date.
Phone: (608) 534-6780
Web: www.trempealeau.net

Alternate Activities

Onalaska

Upper Mississippi River National Wildlife Refuge

The refuge contains 240,000 acres of fish and wildlife habitat and extends 260 miles along the Mississippi River. Popular viewing spots along the Wisconsin portion include Lake Onalaska, Trempealeau National Wildlife Refuge and Lake Pepin near Stockholm.
Phone: (507) 452-4232
Web: www.fws.gov/midwest/UpperMississippiRiver

Bird Watching

Try bird watching along the Mississippi River during spring and fall migration at Highway 35 North overlooking Lake Onalaska. There are two observation points with interpretive signs.
Phone: (608) 783-8405
Web: www.wisconsinaudubon.org

Trempealeau

Trempealeau Hotel

Historic Trempealeau Hotel retains its classic 1888 charm while offering modern style. Located on the banks of the Mississippi, the hotel has bike and canoe rentals.
Phone: (608) 534-6898
Web: www.trempealeauhotel.com

Trempealeau National Wildlife Refuge

View a variety of animal and plant life in wetland, sand prairie and bottomland hardwood forest habitats. Roads are gravel but bikeable. Some go deep into the marshlands of the Mississippi River.
Phone: (608) 539-2311
Web: www.fws.gov/midwest/trempealeau

Long Lake Canoe Trail

Canoe through the Upper Mississippi River National Wildlife and Fish Refuge. Travel 4.5 miles in about two hours through slow moving water, sloughs and islands that are a haven for wildlife.
Phone: (608) 534-6780

Lock and Dam #6

Watch boats and barges go through the locks on the Mississippi River near Trempealeau.
Phone: (608) 534-6424
Web: www.recreation.gov

Perrot State Park

Explore 1,400 acres nestled among bluffs where the Trempealeau and Mississippi rivers meet. Scenic hikes to the top of the bluffs include Brady's Bluff Prairie, a goat prairie on the bluff rising 460 feet above the Mississippi River.
Phone: (608) 534-6409
Web: www.dnr.state.wi.us

Restaurants

Onalaska

Ciatti's Italian Restaurants
Phone: (608) 781-8686

Traditions Restaurants
Menu: Fine Dining
Phone: (608) 783-0200
Web: www.traditionsdining.com

Manny's Mexican Cocina
Phone: (608) 781-5601
Web: www.mannysmexican.com

Lakeview Restaurants & Lounge
Phone: (608) 781-0150

Seven Bridges Restaurants
Phone: (608) 783-6103
Web: www.7bridgesRestaurants.com

Trempealeau

Trempealeau Hotel
Phone: (608) 534-6898
Web: www.trempealeauhotel.com

Larry's Landing & Hungry Point
Phone: (608) 534-7771
Web: www.larrysathungrypoint.com

Ed Sullivan's
Phone: (608) 534-7775
Web: www.sullivanssupperclub.com

About The Trail

This trail has a rap for not being very scenic and there is some justification for it, but taken selectively, it has some real charms. The connecting road routes are very nice, so it is possible to tie together the better parts of the trail with scenic roads to create some very enjoyable rides. For long distance riders, the trail links the Great River Trail on the west with the Elroy-Sparta Trail to the east. It is possible to travel over 100 miles with only one minor break in the trail system.

Trail Highlights

Between Medary and West Salem the trail passes through the vast floodplain of the La Crosse River. Lots of marshland, wet prairie and backwaters offer good bird and wildife watching if you ride early morning or near sunset. Day time is good for viewing a wide variety of wetland grasses and flowers. Veteran's Memorial Park in West Salem is a unique memorial to local veterans who died in US wars. The Dutch Creek Swimming hole right off the trail in Bangor City Park offers a refreshing dip in a shaded creek. Great for cooling off on a hot summer day. The native prairie east of Rockland has some nice wildflowers but is a little disappointing as far as prairies go.

About The Roads

Take your pick. You get a little of everything from the nearly flat roads between Bangor and Sparta to the extremely long climb over Mindoro Pass. This is primarily dairy country where contour plowed fields of corn and alfalfa form a patchwork of zigzag fields mixed with pastures and woodlots. Monroe County has a cold weather theme between the county line and Sparta. Check out the road names as you ride them or cross them.

Road Highlights

The Mindoro loop climbs to high scenic vistas and rural panoramic views. The climbs are long and challenging. The descents are exciting. Mindoro is charming. The sidewalk rises six feet above the street to create a porch-like setting with roof, railings and rest benches. If the bank is open, stop in for a look at the collection of photos showing how Mindoro Pass was cut by hand near the turn of the century. While the Mindoro Loop spends its time on the ridge, the southern loop between Medary and Bangor follows the creeks and valleys. From west to east, the valley walls slowly close in until the road turns and begins a long, steep climb followed by a fast descent. East of Bangor, the road routes offer a diverse, nearly flat alternate to the trail. Take the trail one way and the roads on the way back. From Hammer Road to Sparta, take the trail because Iberia carries some traffic, including trucks.

How To Get There

Interstate 90 parallels the trail from La Crosse to Sparta. All trail towns are easily accessible from the interstate. To get to Medary, take the Highway 16 exit off Interstate 90, go south to County Road B and east on County Road B to the trailhead.

Vital Trail Information:

Trail Distance: 21

Trail Surface: Limestone

Access Points: Onalaska, Medary, West Salem, Bangor, Rockland, Sparta

Fees and Passes: Wisconsin State Trail Pass; $4.00 daily fee or $15.00 for an annual pass. State Trail passes are good on all Wisconsin State Trails.

Trail Website: www.lacrosserivertrail.org

LACROSSE RIVER TRAIL ◆ Southern Wisconsin

Medary to Sparta: 21 miles

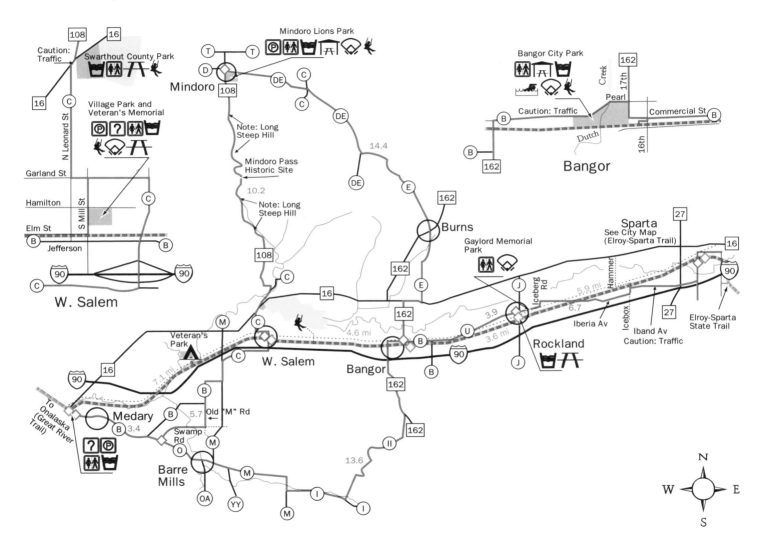

La Crosse River State Trail
Toll Free: (888) 540-8434
Phone: (608) 269-4123
Email: information@LaCrosseRiverStateTrail.org
Web: www.lacrosseriverstatetrail.org

Onalsaska Center for Commerce and Tourism
Toll Free: (800) 873-1901
Phone: (608) 781-9570
Email: info@discoveronalaska.com
Web: www.discoveronalaska.com

Sparta Chamber of Commerce
Toll Free: (888) 540-8434
Phone: (608) 269-4123
Email: spartachamber@centurytel.net

Sparta Convention and Visitors Bureau
Phone: (608) 269-4340
Web: www.spartawisconsin.org
Village of West Salem
Phone: (608) 786-1858
Email: info@westsalemwi.com
Web: www.westsalemwi.com

Wildcat Mountain State Park
Phone: (608) 337-4775
Email: Ronald.Campbell@wisconsin.gov
Web: www.dnr.state.wi.us

Toll Free: (888) 783-0035
Phone: (608) 786-1792
Email: neshonoc@diparks.com
Web: www.neshonoclakeside.com

Bed and Breakfast

La Crosse
Chateau La Crosse
410 Cass St
Toll Free: (800) 442-7969
Phone: (608) 796-1090
Fax: (608) 796-0700
Email: chateaulax@aol.com
Web: www.chateaulacrosse.com

Four Gables Inn
W5648 Hwy 14-61
Phone: (608) 788-7958

Camping

Stoddard
Goose Island Campground
W6488 County Rd GI
Phone: (608) 785-9581

Tourist Information

Greater La Crosse Area Chamber of Commerce
Toll Free: (800) 889-0539
Phone: (608) 784-4880
Email: lse_chamber@centurytel.net
Web: www.lacrossechamber.com

La Crosse Area Convention and Visitors Bureau
Toll Free: (800) 658-9424
Phone: (608) 782-2366
Email: info@explorelacrosse.com
Web: www.explorelacrosse.com

Lodging

Motels/Resorts

La Crosse
Guest House Motel
810 S 4th St
Toll Free: (800) 274-6873
Phone: (608) 784-8840
Email: robin@centuryinter.net
Web: www.guesthousemotel.com

West Salem
Neshonoc Lakeside Camp-Resort
N 5334 Neshonoc Rd

Lodging cont'd

Camping

West Salem
Neshonoc Lakeside Camp-Resort
 N 5334 Neshonoc Rd
 Toll Free: (888) 783-0035
 Phone: (608) 786-1792
 Email: neshonoc@diparks.com
 Web: www.neshonoclakeside.com

Veterans Memorial Campground
 N4668 County Rd VP
 Phone: (608) 786-4011

Bike Rental

La Crosse
Buzz's Bikes
 800 Rose St
 Phone: (608) 785-2737

Smith's Cycling & Fitness
 Phone: (608) 784-1175
 Web: www.smithsbikes.com

Sparta
See Elroy Sparta Trail

Bike Repair

La Crosse
Bikes Limited
 3337 Hanson Ct
 Phone: (608) 785-2326

Bike Repair cont'd

La Crosse
Buzz's Bikes
   800 Rose St
   Phone: (608) 785-2737

Smith's Cycling & Fitness
   Phone: (608) 784-1175
   Web: www.smithsbikes.com

Sparta
See Elroy-Sparta Trail

Bike Shuttle

Sparta
See Elroy-Sparta Trail

Festivals and Events

Onalaska
See Great River Trail

Sparta
See Elroy-Sparta Trail

West Salem
June
   Dairy Days Classique Bike Ride
   Peddle on an organized ride with the option of thirty-two or sixty-two miles, a sag wagon and rest stops. Registration is required. First Weekend.
   Phone: (608) 786-1858

   June Dairy Days
   The festivities include a kickoff breakfast, parade at noon on Saturday, a carnival, softball games, live music, clowns, magicians, food, dairy tents, bingo, a petting barn and stagecoach rides in Village Park: Check website for dates.
   Phone: (608) 786-1858
   Web: www.westsalemwi.com

July
   LaCrosse Interstate Fair
   See the rural fair with animals, 4-H projects, a carnival and food booths. Call for dates.
   Phone: (608) 786-1858

Alternate Activities

Bangor
Bangor City Park
   Cool off in the old-fashioned swimming hole in Dutch Creek. It is visible from the trail.
   Phone: (608) 486-4084

Onalaska
See Great River Trail

Ontario
Wildcat Mountain State Park
   The park offers scenic vistas and great hiking trails.
   Phone: (608) 337-4775
   Web: www.dnr.state.wi.us

Rockland
Restored Prairie
   Take in the view along the trail.
   Phone: (608) 486-4037

Sparta
See Elroy-Sparta Trail

West Salem
Historic West Salem
   This is the home of Hamlin Garland, Pulitzer Prize winning author. There are also two octagon homes and Thomas Leonard's colonial style home. Check out Veterans' Memorial Park.
   Phone: (608) 786-1858
   Web: www.westsalemwi.com

Wolfway Farm
   This is one of Wisconsin's Century Farms, where registered Holsteins are milked twice daily. Reservations are required.
   Phone: (608) 486-2686

Restaurants

Onalaska
See Great River Trail

Sparta
See Elroy-Sparta Trail

West Salem
Westview Inn
   Phone: (608) 786-1336

About The Trail

Developed in 1967, this is the grand-daddy of them all. It shows in the mature trees, full canopy and well maintained trail surface. Bicycling is the main tourism attraction here so you'll have plenty of companionship. The trail rises and drops very slowly as it passes through the hilly, scenic Driftless Area. Explore the three tunnels, spend an evening in one of the small trail towns and enjoy the camaraderie of riding with cyclists from around the nation. Three major bike trails converge at Elroy Commons in Elroy, creating a hub of bicycle activity. See city maps for details. Weekends and holidays are extremely busy.

Trail Highlights

The tunnels are unique and the lead up to the entrances rounds out the experience. The trail rises slowly and passes through deep road cuts near the tunnel entrances, creating a cool, damp micro environment. Bring flashlights for the tunnels and walk your bike. Water runs along both sides of the trail in the three-quarter mile long Tunnel #3, and falling water splashes loudly near the center. You'll get dripped on lightly in the tunnel. Note the cool breeze flowing out of the lower western end.

About The Roads

First timers come for the trail. Repeat visitors explore the roads. Expect grinding climbs, hair-raising descents, horse drawn Amish buggies, virtually no traffic, and pastoral views that belong in picture books. The roads will give you the best sense of this hilly, scenic country. Traffic is minimal and the surfaces range from smooth to pebbly.

Road Highlights

The town roads between Kendall and Norwalk offer the most challenging climbs and descents near the trail. On one descent from east to west we hit fifty-two miles per hour. County Road T, south of Norwalk, follows a creek bed and stays flat. County Road F branches off and remains relatively flat for several miles, then climb long and hard to become rolling ridge top. Check out the church and convent in St. Mary's, then return to Norwalk via County Road U. Payback comes as County Road U nears Norwalk. 16th Avenue, near Tunnel #3 passes over the tunnel and appears to run right along the top at one point. There are no markings along here,so you will have to imagine the folks walking in the dark beneath you.

How To Get There

Sparta is approximately twenty-five miles east of La Crosse on Interstate 94. Take the Highway 27 exit. Go north to Avon Road and follow the city map to the La Crosse River Trailhead. To go directly to the Elroy-Sparta Trailhead or to the trail towns, take the Highway 16 exit off Interstate 94. Go west on Highway 16 (toward Sparta) and turn south on Highway 71. To get to Elroy, take Interstates 90/94 to Exit 61 for New Lisbon. Take Highway 80 south thirteen miles to Elroy.

Vital Trail Information:

Trail Distance: 33

Trail Surface: Limestone

Access Points: Sparta, Norwalk, Wilton, Kendall, Elroy

Fees and Passes: Wisconsin State Trail Pass; $4.00 daily fee or $15.00 for an annual pass. State Trail passes are good on all Wisconsin State Trails.

Trail Website: www.elroy-sparta-trail.org

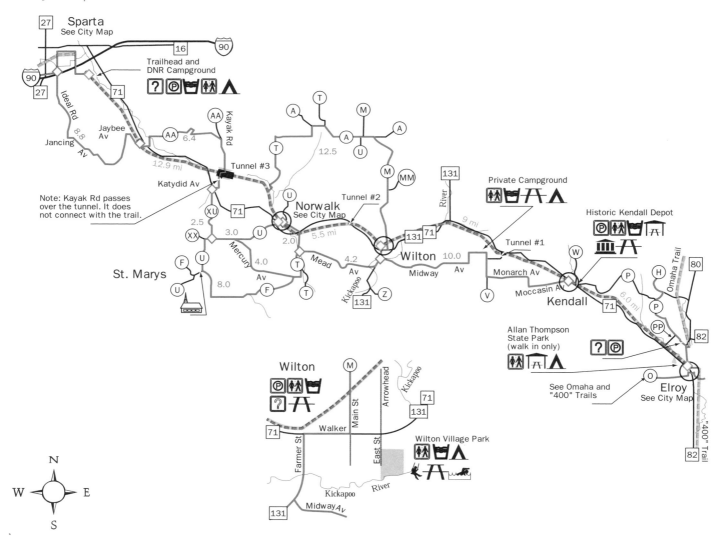
Elroy to Sparta: 33.4 miles

Sparta
See City Map

Trailhead and
DNR Campground

Ideal Rd

Jaybee Av

Jancing Av

Kayak Rd

AA

AA 6.4

8.8

12.9 mi

Tunnel #3

Katydid Av

Note: Kayak Rd passes
over the tunnel. It does
not connect with the trail.

XU

71

2.5

XX

3.0

St. Marys

Mercury Av

4.0

F

U

8.0

U

U

F

T

T

Mead Av

2.0

5.5 mi

Norwalk
See City Map

Tunnel #2

U

A

T

A

12.5

M

A

U

M

MM

4.2

Kickapoo

Z

131

Wilton

Midway Av

131 71

10.0

River

131

9 mi

Private Campground

Monarch Av

V

W

Tunnel #1

Moccasin Av

Kendall

71

6.0 mi

Historic Kendall Depot

P

H

P

PP

82

Omaha Trail

80

Allan Thompson
State Park
(walk in only)

See Omaha and
"400" Trails

O

Elroy
See City Map

"400" Trail

82

Wilton

M

Arrowhead

Kickapoo

71

131

Walker

Main St

East St

Farmer St

71

Wilton Village Park

Kickapoo

River

131

Midway Av

N
W   E
S

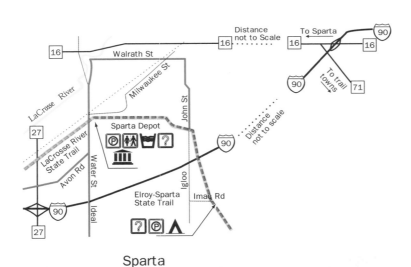

Sparta

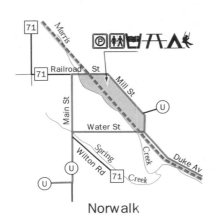

Norwalk

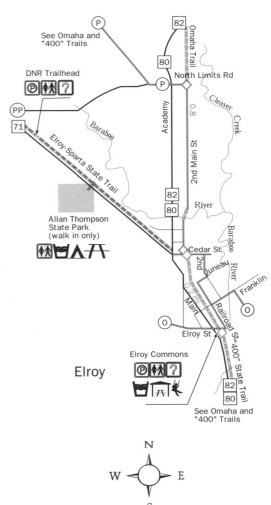

Elroy

Tourist Information

Elroy Commons Information Center
Toll Free: (888) 606-2453
Phone: (608) 462-2410
Email: elroy@comantenna.com
Web: www.elroywi.com

Kendall Depot
Phone: (608) 463-7109
Email: kdepot@centurytel.net
Web: www.elroy-sparta-trail.com

Sparta Area Chamber of Commerce
Toll Free: (888) 540-8434
Phone: (608) 269-4123
Web: www.spartachamber.org

Village of Norwalk
Phone: (608) 823-7760
Village of Ontario
Phone: (608) 337-4381

Village of Wilton
Phone: (608) 435-6666
Email: villageofwilton@centurytel.net

Lodging

Motels/Resorts

Kendall
Country Livin' Motel
Hwy 71
Phone: (608) 463-7135
Email: bellasedona86004@aol.com
Web: fp1.centurytel.net/CountryLivin/

Sparta
Best Nights Inn
303 W Wisconsin St
Toll Free: (800) 201-0234
Phone: (608) 269-3066
Email: info@bestnightsinn.com
Web: www.bestnightsinn.com

Country Inn By Carlson
737 Avon Rd
Toll Free: (888) 201-1746
Phone: (608) 269-3110
Web: www.countryinns.com

Justin Trails Resort
7452 Kathyrn Ave
Toll Free: (800) 488-4521
Phone: (608) 269-4522
Email: info@justintrails.com
Web: www.justintrails.com

Spartan Motel
1900 W Wisconsin St
Phone: (608) 269-2770

Super 8 Motel
716 Avon Rd
Toll Free: (800) 800-8000
Phone: (608) 269-8489
Email: McTagEri@wynhg.com
Web: www.super8.com

Wilton
Mid-Trail Motel
P.O. Box 296
Hwy 71
Phone: (608) 435-6685
Web: www.mid-trail-motel.com

Bed and Breakfast

Elroy
Eastview
33620 Cty P
Phone: (608) 463-7564
Email: eastview@centurytel.net
Web: www.eastviewbedandbreakfast.com

Waarvik's Century Farm
N4621 County Rd H
Phone: (608) 462-8595
Email: waarvik@hotmail.com
Web: www.waarvikcenturyfarm.com

Lodging cont'd

Bed and Breakfast

Kendall

Cabin at Trails End
23009 Knollwood Rd
Phone: (608) 427-3877

Sparta

Franklin Victorian Bed and Breakfast
220 E Franklin St
Toll Free: (888) 594-3822
Phone: (608) 366-1427
Email: innkeeper@franklinvictorianbb.com
Web: www.franklinvictorianbb.com

Justin Trails Resort
7452 Kathyrn Ave
Toll Free: (800) 488-4521
Phone: (608) 269-4522
Email: info@justintrails.com
Web: www.justintrails.com

The Strawberry Lace Inn
603 N Water St
Phone: (608) 269-7878
Email: innkeeper@strawberrylaceinn.com
Web: www.strawberrylaceinn.com

Wilton

Dorset Ridge Guest House
22259 King Rd
Phone: (608) 463-7375

Camping

Elroy

Primitive DNR Campground
Phone: (608) 337-4775

Schultz Park

City Park in Elroy
Toll Free: (888) 606-2453
Phone: (608) 462-2410
Email: elroy@comantenna.com
Web: www.elroywi.com

LaFarge

Kickapoo Valley Reserve
S3661 State Hwy 131
Phone: (608) 625-2960
Email: kickapoo.reserve@krm.state.wi.us
Web: kvr.state.wi.us

Norwalk

Village Park
102 Mill St
Phone: (608) 823-7760

Ontario

Brush Creek Campground
S 190 Opal Rd
Off Hwy 33
Phone: (608) 337-4344

Wildcat Mountain State Park
E13660 State Hwy 33
P.O. Box 99
Phone: (608) 337-4775
Email: Ronald.Campbell@wisconsin.gov
Web: www.dnr.state.wi.us

Sparta

Leon Valley Campground
9050 Jancing Ave
Phone: (608) 269-6400
Email: leonvalley@centurytel.net
Web: www.campleonvalley.net

Primitive DNR
Trailhead
Phone: (608) 337-4775

Wilton

Tunnel Trail Campground
26983 State Hwy 71
Phone: (608) 435-6829
Email: info@tunneltrail.com
Web: www.tunneltrail.com

Wilton Village Campground
400 East St
Phone: (608) 435-6666

Bike Rental

Elroy

Elroy Commons Trailshop
Railroad St
Toll Free: (888) 606-2453
Phone: (608) 462-2410
Email: elroy@comantenna.com
Web: www.elroy-sparta-trail.com

The Bike Hut
W9187 County Hwy O
Phone: (608) 462-5001

Bike Rental cont'd

Kendall
Kendall Depot - Elroy-Sparta Trail Headquarters
113 White
Phone: (608) 463-7109
Email: kdepot@centurytel.net
Web: www.elroy-sparta-trail.com

Sparta
Speed's Bicycle
1126 John St
Phone: (608) 269-2315
Email: speeds@centurytel.net
Web: www.speedsbike.com

Wilton
Tunnel Trail Campground
Rt 1
Phone: (608) 435-6829
Email: info@tunneltrail.com
Web: www.tunneltrail.com

Bike Repair

Elroy
The Bike Hut
W9187 County Hwy O
Phone: (608) 462-5001

Sparta
Speed's Bicycle
1126 John St
Phone: (608) 269-2315
Email: speeds@centurytel.net
Web: www.speedsbike.com

Bike Shuttle

Kendall
Kendall Depot - Elroy-Sparta Trail Headquarters
Phone: (608) 463-7109
Email: kdepot@centurytel.net
Web: www.elroy-sparta-trail.com

Festivals and Events

Elroy
June
Elroy Fair
Enjoy the carnival, horse pull, livestock judging, tractor pull, demolition derby, 4-H exhibits, music and food. Last Weekend.
Toll Free: (888) 606-2453
Phone: (608) 462-2410
Web: www.elroywi.com

Kendall
September
Labor Day Celebration
Take a day off work for volleyball, a parade, tractor pull, chicken BBQ and pancake breakfast.
Phone: (608) 463-7109

Norwalk
August
Black Squirrel Fest & Tractor Pull & Garden Club
Check out the BBQ chicken, softball, tractor pull and pie and ice-cream tent. There is a DJ on Saturday night and a pancake breakfast on Sunday. Second Weekend.
Phone: (608) 823-7760

Sparta
June
Butterfest
See the carnival, live entertainment, magic shows, arts and crafts exhibits, music, food booths, quilt show and parade. Second Weekend.
Toll Free: (888) 540-8434
Phone: (608) 269-4123
Web: www.spartachamber.org

August
Coulee Region Tour
This is a fully supported six day, five night tour of Wisconsin's Coulee Region. You'll travel thirty-five to sixty miles daily. Check website for dates.
Toll Free: (888) 540-8434
Phone: (414) 671-4560
Web: www.wisconsinbicycletours.com

Wilton
All Summer
Pancake Breakfast
This tasty event is sponsored by the Lions Club each Sunday at the Wilton Village Park, Memorial Day through Labor Day.
Phone: (608) 435-6666

Festivals and Events cont'd

Wilton

August

Wilton Wood Turtle Days
Join the town in celebration with fireworks, softball, volleyball, a parade and an arts and crafts show. First Sunday.
Phone: (608) 435-6666

Alternate Activities

Ontario

Drifty's Canoe Rental
Rent a canoe and paddle the Kickapoo River.
Phone: (608) 337-4288

Wildcat Mountain State Park
The park offers beautiful scenery, nature trails and camping.
Phone: (608) 337-4775
Web: www.dnr.state.wi.us

Kickapoo Paddle Inn
Rent a canoe and take a trip on the Kickapoo River.
Toll Free: (800) 947-3603
Phone: (608) 337-4726

Sparta

Paul and Matilda Wegner Grotto
Locally known as 'The Glass Church', this is an example of grassroots art. For more information contact the Local History Room at 200 West Main Street, Sparta.
Phone: (608) 269-8680
Web: www.monroecountyhistory.org

Down A Country Road
Take a tour of the Amish community and get a glimpse of this unique way of life, then browse the Amish gift shop. Highway 33 off Highway 27.
Phone: (608) 654-5318
Web: www.downacountryroadamish.com

Deke Slayton Memorial Space & Bicycle Museum
Deke Slayton, one of America's original astronauts, was born in the Sparta area and raised in Monroe County. Explore exhibits from the Mercury, Gemini, Apollo and Space Shuttle missions. Also learn about the history of bicycles.
Toll Free: (888) 200-5302
Phone: (608) 269-0033
Web: www.dekeslayton.com

Monroe County Local History Museum & Research Room
Learn about the story of Monroe County and its pioneer history through photographs, memorabilia and genealogical source materials including census records, church, cemetery and school records.
Phone: (608) 269-8680
Web: www.monroecountyhistory.org

M&M Ranch
You'll find old-fashioned fun for the whole family in this Western town and ranch with a blacksmith shop and auction barn. Enjoy horse trail rides, canoe rentals, a petting farm, covered garden, blackberry picking, a corn maze and pumpkin patch.
Phone: (608) 486-2722
Web: mandmranch.tripod.com

Cabin on the Rock
The cabin is located on a 365 acre, four generation working dairy farm. There are Holstein cows and calves and horseback riding atop Redrock Ridge. The cabin overlooks the farm and 200 acres of woodlands with plenty of hiking trails. It is just five miles from the Elroy-Sparta bike trail.
Phone: (608) 823-7865

Wilton

Circle "S" Trail Rides
Mosey along on horseback rides.
Phone: (608) 435-6975

Restaurants

Kendall
Zirks Bar & Grill
Phone: (608) 463-7115

Norwalk
Lil's Korner Bar
Phone: (608) 823-7708

Sparta
Sparta Grill
Menu: Home Style Cooking
Phone: (608) 269-0611
Web: www.spartagrill.com

Dorine's Family Inn
Phone: (608) 269-8258

Slice of Chicago
Phone: (608) 269-2181

Wilton
Gina's Pies Are Square
Phone: (608) 435-6541

Dorset Valley Restaurants & Bakery
Menu: Old Fashioned Amish Cooking
Phone: (608) 435-6525
Web: www.dorsetvalleyRestaurants.com

About The Trail

The Omaha Trail, a paved county trail from Camp Douglas to Elroy, is good for a quick break when traveling the interstate between the Twin Cities and Milwaukee or Chicago. The "400" Trail more or less follows the Baraboo River and passes through numerous wetlands. Early morning hours are best for wildlife viewing. Lift your eyes away from the trail during the day and take in the bluffs and mounds in the distance. Small towns with scenic parks dot the trail. Both trails meet at the Elroy-Sparta Trail in Elroy creating a lot of opportunities for the repeat or long term visitor.

Trail Highlights

The southern end of the Omaha Trail passes through some steep-walled valleys as it climbs to the tunnel south of Hustler. Pass through the 875 foot tunnel, then take a break at the rest stop with modern bathrooms and a hand pump for water. The trail follows another small valley before the land levels out near Hustler. Hemlock Park is a pretty little park across a small lake from the 400 Trail. Take McKinney Road to the park sign and drop down a steep hill to the water's edge. The pocket park bordering the Baraboo River on the north side of LaValle provides a shaded, restful stopping point. The first two miles from the Reedsburg Depot parallel an active rail line. The trail gets better after the active line branches off. Legion Park offers a pleasant break half a mile from the trail in Wonewoc. The ball diamond in Legion Park is the most romantic and impractical playing field I've ever seen.

About The Roads

The roads in this area go through the heart of the Driftless Area. If you don't mind lots of hills, these roads are a delight because of their low traffic and rural panoramas. Asphalt surfaces vary from smooth to patchy or pebbly.

Road Highlights

County Road H from Camp Douglas to the tunnel on the Omaha Trail is reasonably flat. It offers a good return route after going one way on the trail. The southern end of Tunnel Road is scenic, rolling and offers some great views of the trail. The east and west routes between Elroy and Wonewoc are prime roads if you don't mind hills. Stop at Wonewoc Park and refill your water bottle at the artesian well. Dutch Hollow Road has some traffic on weekends and holidays because of the lake cabins around Dutch Hollow Lake. Same story with County Road V between the trail and Reedsburg: it's worth riding if you are comfortable with some traffic.

How To Get There

Camp Douglas is on Interstates 90/94 about ten miles south of the intersection of the two highways near Tomah. To get to Elroy, stay on the interstate to Mauston, then take Highway 82 west. To get to Reedsburg, take Interstate 90/94 to Lake Delton, then Highway 23 south to Reedsburg. The Omaha and "400" Trails meet in Elroy, the eastern terminus of the Elroy-Sparta Trail. For more information about getting to the Elroy-Sparta Trail, see the previous chapter.

Vital Trail Information:

Trail Distance: 34

Trail Surface: Limestone

Access Points: Omaha: Camp Douglas, Hustler, Elroy, "400": Elroy, Union Center, Wonewoc, La Valle, Reedsburg

Fees and Passes: "400" Trail: Wisconsin State Trail Pass; $4.00 daily fee or $15.00 for an annual pass. State Trail passes are good on all Wisconsin State Trails. Omaha Trail: Daily pass $1.00.

Trail Website: www.400statetrail.org

Camp Douglas to Elroy: 12 miles

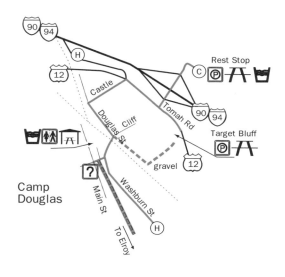

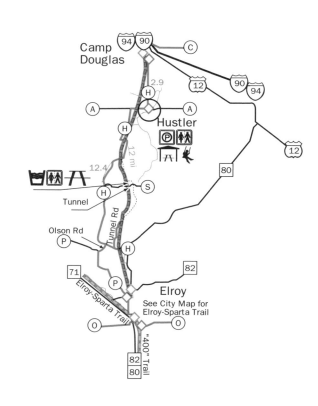

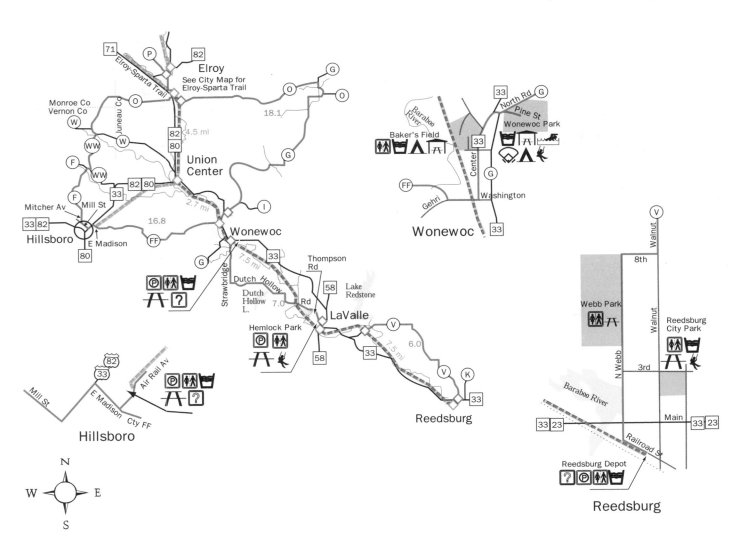

Tourist Information

"400" Trail Headquarters
Toll Free: (800) 844-3507
Phone: (608) 524-2850
Email: reedsbrg@rucls.net
Web: www.400statetrail.org

Elroy Commons
Toll Free: (888) 606-2453
Phone: (608) 462-2410
Email: elroy@comantenna.com
Web: www.elroywi.com

Hillsboro City
Phone: (608) 489-2521
Email: clerk.ss@mwt.net
Web: www.hillsborowi.com

Reedsburg Chamber of Commerce
Toll Free: (800) 844-3507
Email: reedsbrg@rucls.net
Web: www.reedsburg.org

Lodging

Motels/Resorts

Camp Douglas
K&K Motel
219 US Hwy 12
Phone: (608) 427-3100

Reedsburg
Comfort Inn
2115 E Main St

Phone: (608) 524-8535
Web: www.choicehotels.com

Copper Springs Motel
E7278 Hwy 23/33
Phone: (608) 524-4312
Email: chanson@jvlnet.com
Web: www.copperspringsmotel.com

Motel Reedsburg
1133 E Main St
Phone: (608) 524-2306

Parkview B&B
211 N Park St
Phone: (608) 524-4333
Email: info@parkviewbb.com
Web: www.parkviewbb.com

Lodging cont'd

Motels/Resorts

Reedsburg
Super 8
 1470 E Main St
 Toll Free: (800) 800-8000
 Phone: (608) 524-2888
 Web: www.super8.com

Voyageur Inn
 200 Viking Dr (Hwy H)
 Toll Free: (800) 444-4493
 Phone: (608) 524-6431
 Email: info@voyageurinn.com
 Web: www.voyageurinn.com

Union Center
Garden City Motel
 Hwy 80-82-33
 Phone: (608) 462-8253

Wonewoc
Chapparal Campground & Resort
 S320 Hwy 33
 Toll Free: (888) 283-0755
 Phone: (608) 464-3200
 Email: chapparal@chapparal.com
 Web: www.chapparal.com

Bed and Breakfast

Hillsboro
Debello Guest House
 Phone: (608) 489-3728

Inn Serendipity Woods Cabin
 S 3580 St. Patricks Rd
 Phone: (608) 329-7056
 Email: info@innserendipity.com
 Web: www.innserendipity.com

La Valle
Demaskie Den Guest House
 102 N East St
 Phone: (608) 985-7426

Mill House on Main
 203 E Main St
 Phone: (608) 985-7900

Reedsburg
Lavina Inn
 325 3rd St
 Phone: (608) 524-6706

Camping

Hillsboro
Hillsboro City Park
 Phone: (608) 489-2521

Reedsburg
Lighthouse Rock Campground
 S2330 County Hwy V
 Toll Free: (866) 629-7803
 Phone: (608) 524-4203
 Email: litehaus@dwave.net
 Web: www.dwave.net/~litehaus/local.htm

Wonewoc
Baker's Field Park
 Phone: (608) 464-3114

Chapparal Campground & Resort
 S320 Hwy 33
 Toll Free: (888) 283-0755
 Phone: (608) 464-3200
 Email: chapparal@chapparal.com
 Web: www.chapparal.com

Wonewoc Legion Park
 Pine St
 Phone: (608) 464-3114

Bike Rental

La Valle
Trail Break
 309 Trail
 Phone: (608) 985-8464

Bike Rental cont'd

Reedsburg
Chamber of Commerce
    240 Railroad St
    Toll Free: (800) 844-3507
    Email: reedsbrg@rucls.net
    Web: www.reedsburg.org

Bike Repair

Reedsburg
Baraboo River Bike Shop
    209 Grand Ave
    Phone: (608) 524-0798

Festivals and Events

Hustler
August
    Hustler Fest
    Don't let the name fool you. Spend a relaxing day at the parade and tractor pull, watching (or playing) three-on-three basketball, riding carnival rides, playing games, listening to music and dancing. Fourth Weekend.
    Phone: (608) 847-9389

Reedsburg
June
    Butter Festival
    Come for the parade, carnival rides, tractor and truck pulls, arts and crafts, Butter Run, music and food at Nishan Park on Father's Day Weekend. The big challenge is to find real butter at the festival.
    Toll Free: (800) 844-3507
    Web: www.reedsburg.org

October
    Harvest Fest
    Downtown on Main Street you'll find arts and crafts, contests, music, auto displays and food. First Saturday.
    Toll Free: (800) 844-3507
    Web: www.reedsburg.org

Alternate Activities

Camp Douglas
Mill Bluff State Park
    Check out the park's primitive camping, picnic shelters, swimming beach, hiking trails and beautiful rock formations. Open Memorial Day through Labor Day.
    Phone: (608) 427-6692
    Web: www.dnr.state.wi.us

Wisconsin National Guard Library and Museum
    Located at historic Volk Field, the museum is housed in an 1896 log lodge that has been restored to its original appearance. See exhibits, dioramas, video and slide programs inside, and view the aircraft, artillery and tanks on static display outdoors.
    Phone: (608) 427-1280
    Web: www.volkfield.ang.af.mil

Alternate Activities cont'd

La Valle

Carr Valley Cheese Company
Taste the products of 100 years of family cheese making: fresh curds daily. Take a self-guided tour Monday through Saturday.
Toll Free: (800) 462-7258
Phone: (608) 986-2781
Web: www.carrvalleycheese.com

LaValle

E-Z Roll Riding Stable
Go on a guided trail ride April 1 through November 1 or call for reservations for weekend rides anytime.
Phone: (608) 985-7722

Reedsburg

Park Lane Model Railroad Museum
Watch 3,000 models of trains, farm tractors, fire trucks and cars on operating layouts in 'N', 'Z' and 'HO' scales. Open mid-May through mid-September.
Phone: (608) 254-8050

Reedsburg Area Historical Society
The Pioneer Log Village has 1890s log homes, a church, blacksmith shop and school in the settlement. Open weekend afternoons Memorial Day through September.
Toll Free: (800) 844-3507

Exhibit of Norman Rockwell Art
Browse a large collection of Norman Rockwell Art located at the Voyager Inn.
Toll Free: (800) 444-4493
Phone: (608) 524-6431
Web: www.voyageurinn.com

Restaurants

Camp Douglas

Target Bluff Restaurants & Cheese Haus
Menu: German
Phone: (608) 427-6542
Web: www.german-haus.com

Elroy

See Elroy-Sparta Trail

Hustler

Suzy's Hustle Inn
Phone: (608) 427-3424

La Valle

Trail Break
Phone: (608) 985-8464

Reedsburg

Culver's Frozen Custard
Phone: (608) 524-2122
Web: www.culvers.com

Marty's Steakhouse
Toll Free: (800) 444-4493
Phone: (608) 524-6431
Web: www.voyageurinn.com/martys.htm

Longley's Restaurants
Phone: (608) 524-6497

Wonewoc

Summit House
Menu: Home Cooking
Phone: (608) 985-7211
Web: www.thesummithouseRestaurants.com

Mayer's Office
Phone: (608) 464-7463

Country Gals Café
Phone: (608) 464-7277

Club Chapparal
Menu: American Style
Toll Free: (888) 283-0755
Phone: (608) 464-3944
Web: www.chapparal.com

About The Trail

Formerly a Chicago and North Western Railway, the trail follows the top of Military Ridge, the divide between the watersheds of the Wisconsin River to the north, and the Pecatonica and Rock Rivers to the south. It comes off the ridge just east of Mount Horeb and drops nearly 400 feet into the Sugar River Valley. The drop is very gentle, 2% to 5%, and the changing terrain makes the eastern part of the trail quite interesting. Agriculture, woodlands, wetlands and prairies border the trail.

Trail Highlights

The most interesting part of the trail runs between Mount Horeb and the trailhead near Verona. The trail climbs slowly from east to west, often along the sides of hills, and passes through a mix of woodlots and agricultural lands. The trail runs near Highway 151/18 for most of the distance from Mount Horeb to Ridgeway where the noise and barrenness of the highway take away much of the pleasure of riding. The scenery imrpoves again halfway between Ridgeway and Dodgeville as the trail veers from the highway and offers some great scenic vistas to the north. Blue Mound State Park offers swimming and scenic overlooks. Governor Dodge State Park has a full range of recreation facilities. The sixty year-old Depot in Ridgeway has been restored.

About The Roads

This is the Driftless Area of Wisconsin, ideal for dairy farms, paved, lightly traveled roads and big hills. The opportunities for exploring are endless. For more information on bicycle friendly roads and bike trails, pick up a copy of the Madison and Dane County Bike Map by Bikeverywhere.

Road Highlights

The loop near Dodgeville offers everything the trail misses: hills and valleys, scenic vistas, constantly changing terrain and quiet roads. The hills are long; they occasionally climb a mile or more. For a short, flat out-and-back on a quiet road, take the Klevinville-Riley Road to County Road P. It nestles in among wetland trees and small creeks. The southern loop starts low along the Sugar River Valley, then climbs and rolls mightily as it loops back to the trail.

How To Get There

Verona is southwest of Madison on U.S. Highway 151/18. Take the County Road PB exit and turn right at the end of the ramp. You will be on the west side of the highway and going north on Nesbitt Road. There isn't a sign for Nesbitt Road, so make sure you are NOT going south on County Road PB towards Paoli. The trailhead is 1.1 miles north. By bike, the trail is accessible via the Capitol City Bike Trail. All trail towns can be readily accessed via Highway 151/18. Trail access in Dodgeville is at the intersection of County Road YZ and Johns Street. Take County Rd YZ 0.2 miles east of Highway 23. See the trail map.

Vital Trail Information:

Trail Distance: 37

Trail Surface: Limestone

Access Points: Dodgeville, Ridgeway, Barneveld, Blue Mounds, Mount Horeb, Verona

Fees and Passes: Wisconsin State Trail Pass; $4.00 daily fee or $15.00 for an annual pass. State Trail passes are good on all Wisconsin State Trails.

Trail Website:
www.dnr.state.wi.us/org/land/parks

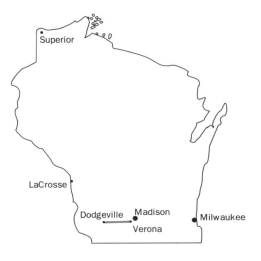

MILITARY RIDGE TRAIL 🚩 **Southern** Wisconsin

Dodgeville to Blue Mound State Park: 18.5 miles

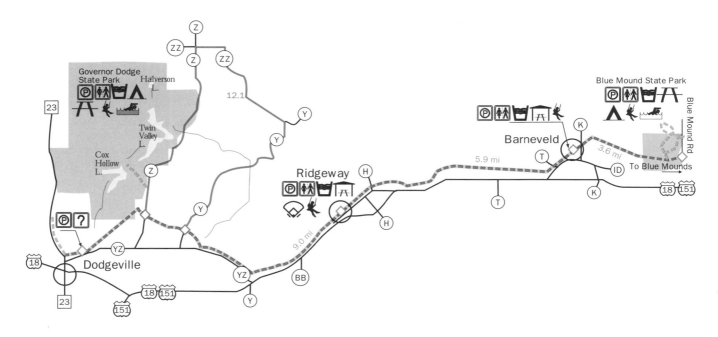

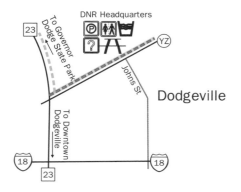

Blue Mound State Park to Verona: 18.8 miles

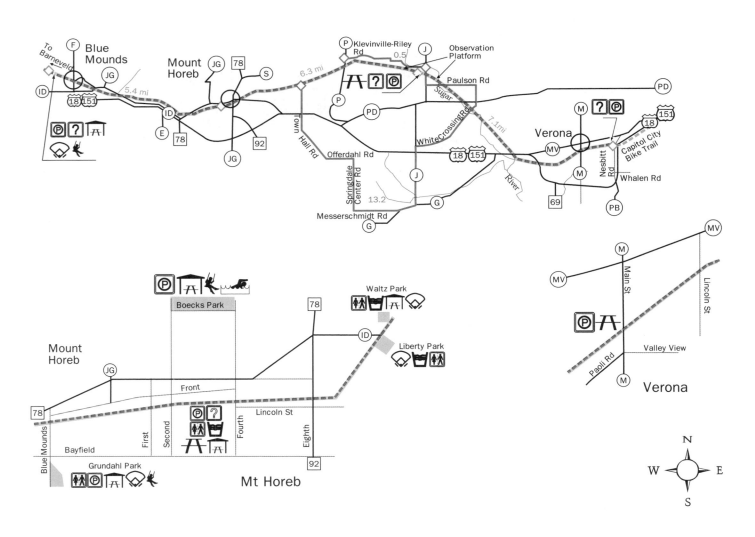

Tourist Information

Dodgeville Chamber of Commerce
Toll Free: (877) 863-6343
Phone: (608) 935-9200
Email: info@dodgeville.com
Web: www.dodgeville.com

Military Ridge State Trail
Phone: (608) 437-7393
Email: Cindy.Delkamp@wisconsin.gov
Web: www.dnr.state.wi.us

Mount Horeb Area Chamber of Commerce
Toll Free: (888) 765-5929
Phone: (608) 437-5914
Email: info@trollway.com
Web: www.trollway.com

Verona Chamber of Commerce
Phone: (608) 845-5777
Email: info@VeronaWI.com
Web: www.veronawi.com

Lodging

Motels/Resorts

Dodgeville
Pine Ridge Motel
405 County Rd YZ
Toll Free: (866) 935-6510
Phone: (608) 935-3386
Web: www.pineridgemotel.net

Super 8 Motel
1308 Johns St
Toll Free: (800) 800-8000
Phone: (608) 935-3888
Web: www.super8.com

Mount Horeb
Karakahl Country Inn
1405 Business 18-151 E
Toll Free: (888) 621-1884
Phone: (608) 437-5545
Email: karakahl@karakahl.com
Web: www.karakahl.com

Village Inn Motel
701 Springdale St
Phone: (608) 437-3350
Web: www.littlebedder.com

Lodging cont'd

Bed and Breakfast

Dodgeville

Grand View B & B
4717 Miess Rd
Phone: (608) 935-3261
Email: innkeeper@grandviewbb.com
Web: www.grandviewbb.com

Mount Horeb

Arbor Rose B&B
200 N 2nd St
Phone: (608) 437-1108
Email: ArborRoseBandB@aol.com
Web: arborrosebandb.com

Gonstead Guest Cottage
602 S 2nd St
Phone: (608) 437-4374
Email: gonstead@mthoreb.com
Web: www.mthoreb.com/gonstead

Othala Valley Inn
3192 JG N
Phone: (608) 437-1073
Email: info@othalavalley.com
Web: www.othalavalley.com

Camping

Blue Mounds

Blue Mound State Park
4350 Mounds Park Rd
P.O. Box 98
Phone: (608) 437-5711
Email: Karl.Heil@wisconsin.gov
Web: www.dnr.state.wi.us

Dodgeville

Blackhawk Lake Camping
2025 County Hwy BH
Phone: (608) 623-2707
Email: bhlake@mhtc.net
Web: www.blackhawklake.com

Governor Dodge State Park
4175 State Rd 23 N
Phone: (608) 935-2315
Email: gruenka@wisconsin.gov
Web: www.dnr.state.wi.us

Bike Repair

Verona

Atkins Verona Bicycle Shoppe
517 Half Mile Rd
Phone: (608) 845-6644

Festivals and Events

Blue Mounds
June
Horribly Hilly Hundreds
Pedal in a long, challenging and very hilly bike ride. It's the worst, or best, in the Midwest. Check website for dates.
Toll Free: (888) 765-5929
Phone: (608) 437-4878
Web: www.horriblyhilly.com

Dodgeville
July

Dodgeville Blues Festival
Spend a day listening to great Blues and Zydeco music. See website for date.
Phone: (608) 935-9200
Web: www.dodgevillebluesfest.com

Mount Horeb
July
Art Fair
The fair, held in conjunction with the Sons of Norway Kaffe Stue, features hundreds of artists on "The Trollway" plus food and entertainment.
Third Weekend.
Toll Free: (888) 765-5929
Phone: (608) 437-5914
Web: www.trollway.com

August
National Mustard Day
Compete in the Mustard Games, then taste the mustard, visit celebrities and enjoy refreshments. First Weekend.
Toll Free: (888) 765-5929
Phone: (608) 437-5914
Web: www.trollway.com

Festivals and Events cont'd

Mt. Horeb

September

Thirsty Troll Brew Fest
Beer sampling features thirty-five craft brewers serving over 100 different beers. Check out the music, food and events. See website for dates.
Toll Free: (888) 765-5929
Phone: (608) 437-5914
Web: www.trollway.com

Verona

May

City-Wide Garage Sale
Mother's Day Weekend.
Phone: (608) 845-5777
Web: www.veronawi.com

June

Hometown USA Days
Have some good ol' American fun with carnival rides, a parade, games, nightly concerts, food, refreshments and a craft show. Check website for dates.
Phone: (608) 845-5777
Web: www.veronawi.com

Alternate Activities

Blue Mounds

Little Norway
The 1856 Norwegian Farmstead and 'Stavkirke' is a unique outdoor museum that features the largest privately-owned collection of Norwegian antiques in the country.
Phone: (608) 437-8211
Web: www.littlenorway.com

Cave of the Mounds
The cave includes a limestone cavern that connects to other rooms and galleries containing mineral deposits. Discovered in 1939, it is a registered National Natural Landmark.
Phone: (608) 437-3038
Web: www.caveofthemounds.com

Blue Mound State Park
The park offers camping, observation towers, a swimming pool and nature trails.
Phone: (608) 437-5711
Web: www.dnr.state.us

Alternate Activities cont'd

Dodgeville

Dolby Stables

Enjoy one and two hour guided rides in Governor Dodge State Park and a forty-five minute ride on the ranch. Reservations are not required, but are helpful. Open May 1 to November 1.
Phone: (608) 935-5205

Museum of Minerals and Crystals

See dazzling displays of rocks, minerals, crystals and flourescents from around the world.
Toll Free: (877) 863-6343
Phone: (608) 935-9200
Web: www.dodgeville.com

Governor Dodge State Park

Wisconsin's second largest park attracts visitors to its swimming, camping, boating and hiking opportunities.
Phone: (608) 935-2315
Web: www.dnr.state.wi.us

Mount Horeb

The Grumpy Troll Brew Pub

This microbrewery is located in an historic creamery and has hand-crafted beers. Tours are available.
Phone: (608) 437-2739
Web: www.thegrumpytroll.com

Mustard Museum

See the world's largest collection of mustard: more than 4,600 varieties. Bratwurst not included.
Toll Free: (800) 438-6878
Phone: (608) 437-3986
Web: www.mustardmuseum.com

Restaurants

Dodgeville

Jimmy's Restaurants & Lounge
Phone: (608) 935-3663

Thym's Supper Club
Phone: (608) 935-3344

Quality Bakery
Phone: (608) 935-3812

The Cook's Room
Phone: (608) 935-5282

Mt. Horeb

Main Street Pub & Grill
Phone: (608) 437-5733

The Grumpy Troll Brew Pub & Restaurants
Phone: (608) 437-2739
Web: www.thegrumpytroll.com

Verona

Avanti Italian
Phone: (608) 848-3315

Monte's Grill & Pub
Phone: (608) 845-9669

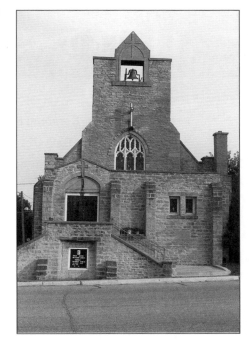

LEGEND

▭▭▭▭	State or Regional Bike Trail	◇▭▭▭◇ 11.5 mi	Mileage Between Markers * (state or regional trails only)
------	City Bike Trail	◇———◇ 6.4	Mileage Between Markers * (road routes)
———	Bike Route on Road		
———	Major Highway		* Cyclometer readings will differ depending on tire pressure, riding style and computer settings. Your mileage may differ slightly from the stated distances.
———	Paved Road		
———	Town Road (gravel or unknown surface)		

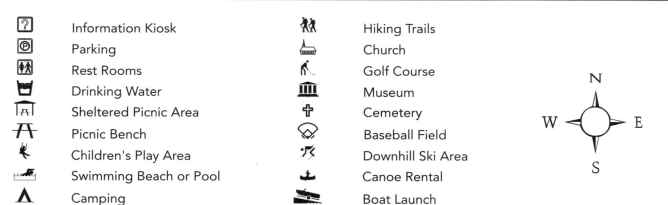

⁇	Information Kiosk	🚶🚶	Hiking Trails
Ⓟ	Parking	⛪	Church
🚹🚺	Rest Rooms	🏌	Golf Course
🚰	Drinking Water	🏛	Museum
⛱	Sheltered Picnic Area	✝	Cemetery
⛩	Picnic Bench	⬦	Baseball Field
🤸	Children's Play Area	⛷	Downhill Ski Area
🏊	Swimming Beach or Pool	🚣	Canoe Rental
⛺	Camping	🚤	Boat Launch

N

W — E

S

Revisions:
Did you find a mistake? Did the trail change? We'd like to hear about it. Contact us through
our website: www.bikeverywhere.com

DOUG SHIDELL

has been riding bicycles and writing about bicycling since 1970. He has written six books and numerous magazine and newspaper articles on the sport. Doug is the photographer for Bicycle Vacation Guide.

bikeverywhere